FIGHT CLUB

FIGHT CLUB

Live in Freedom by Breaking the Chains of Porn and Sexual Addiction Through Grace, Truth, and Transformation

Jared Paul Wilson

RESOURCE *Publications* • Eugene, Oregon

FIGHT CLUB
Live in Freedom by Breaking the Chains of Porn and Sexual Addiction Through Grace, Truth, and Transformation

Resource Publications
An Imprint of Wipf and Stock Publishers
199 W. 8th Ave., Suite 3
Eugene, OR 97401

www.wipfandstock.com

PAPERBACK ISBN: 979-8-3852-7282-2
HARDCOVER ISBN: 979-8-3852-7283-9
EBOOK ISBN: 979-8-3852-7284-6

DEDICATION

To my wife, Erin, whose love is the quiet strength beneath every page. Your grace fills the spaces between my words and the life we share. Your faith, kindness, and fierce support reflect his heart every day. And your sweet love for Lily, Bella, and Leo fills our home with incredible joy and peace. This book is as much yours as it is mine.

To my brother, Michael Broadway. Your faithfulness, courage, and loyalty have been a Jonathan-to-my-David presence in my life. You have stood shoulder to shoulder with me, fighting battles, celebrating victories, and reminding me who God is when I forget.

CONTENTS

INTRODUCTION

WELCOME TO *FIGHT CLUB: Live in Freedom*, the next chapter in your story. We are all familiar with the first rule of Fight Club. But that is not this Fight Club. Here, we talk about the fight against sexual addiction.

Our aim at *Fight Club: Live in Freedom* is nothing less than a transformative journey to provide a path where men and women can finally break free from pornography, fantasy, and sexual addiction through a powerful blend of biblical truth and clinically grounded insight. This discipleship pathway goes beyond overcoming destructive behaviors. *Fight Club: Live in Freedom* is not simply a set of quick fix tools or a self-help book. We are about discovering the abundant, shame-free life God created us to live and our hope is that through the journey, we discover a new way of life that is sustaining as we pursue freedom in and through Jesus.

Fight Club: Live in Freedom is a serious commitment, and we want to say that up-front. But every worthwhile pursuit demands sacrifice. Over the next three months, you will engage in twelve weekly combat challenges—intentional, stretching, and deeply personal practices designed to help us encounter God in the very places where addiction has held us captive. These challenges will require courage. They will ask us to face the pain we have avoided and to trust that God meets us right in the middle of it. As we engage in these weekly combat challenges, we will connect with God as we grow in our identity found in him and hear his voice louder than shame, fear, or addiction.

For those of you reading *Fight Club: Live in Freedom* within a community group, you will have the opportunity to experience connection as you are fully loved and fully known. There is something incredibly powerful that unfolds as groups begin sharing real stories, personal struggles, and difficult questions. As we open up in our groups, opportunity is created for the Holy Spirit to move.

God reveals truth.

Hearts soften.

Walls fall.

So, prepare for the fight of your life and remember, you are not alone, and you are not beyond hope. Your story is still being written. Fight Club is in your corner!

WEEK 1—XXX MARKS THE SPOT: WHERE SOCIETY GOT LOST

WEEKLY MEMORY VERSE

For our struggle is not against flesh and blood, but against the rulers, against the authorities, against the powers of this dark world and against the spiritual forces of evil in the heavenly realms.

—Ephesians 6:12

WEEKLY COMBAT CHALLENGE

Spend time reading the Bible daily.

NO TRUE NORTH

NAVIGATING A TWISTED MORAL LANDSCAPE

Ed was fifteen when he first discovered pornography and was ill prepared for what would become a lifelong fight. While Ed was raised in a Christian home, he did not receive the parental guidance needed to shield him from the addictive chains of pornography. His father had been cautious about spyware and malware when the internet first entered their home; however, there was little concern about the dangers of pornography. Additionally, Ed's parents had never really had "the talk" with him, limiting his sex education to a brief chapter in health class and the crude chatter of classmates. Though Ed was raised in church and understood that porn was wrong, he was not equipped to recognize the many forms it could take or the grip it would eventually have on him.

When Ed found porn for the first time, he did not even realize what he was viewing. It was an online fetish writer magazine that shared short stories, most of which were relatively tame in nature, but enough to make him crave more. Like a tide on the shore, the lure of pornography crept in quietly—subtle, steady—until he was drowning. Erotic literature led to more graphic forms of pornographic material that included images, chat rooms, and videos. To complicate matters, as Ed ventured deeper into unwanted addictive behavior, same sex attraction began to manifest.

Pornography had become the background noise of Ed's life, impossible to tune out. Temptation was prevalent everywhere, woven into the very fabric of his identity, showing up in the margins of almost everything in his life.

Ed began to doubt his salvation and questioned if God loved him. As his pornography addiction deepened, so did his shame and depression until suicidal thoughts began to manifest. Ed felt powerless against uncontrollable urges and trapped in a cycle that left him feeling broken and confused. His struggle with same-sex attraction and porn had become deeply woven into his story, leaving his longing for freedom a fading hope.

Ed's life was set on repeat: click, consume, collapse.

When he turned to the church for answers, it was a negative experience, leaving him feeling like a bad Christian. His pastor then broke confidentiality, making sacred trust public knowledge. Ed's private struggle with addiction quickly became church gossip.

Already isolated by his battle, Ed felt exposed and abandoned as he left his church in shame, feeling lonelier than ever. His community of church friends had been cut off. He had yet to experience a healthy dating relationship. He was a prisoner to his thoughts and fantasies. And everywhere he looked, he was overwhelmed by the enormity of it all. Ed felt he was losing a war in his own body and mind and he just wanted the nightmare to end.

Even in the midst of all the suffering and pain, Ed felt a call to ministry. He enrolled at a prestigious seminary, hoping for once that his willingness to obey would yield some relief in his battle. While the classwork encouraged him to grow spiritually, he still found himself isolated and struggling with temptation.

In a desperate attempt for freedom, Ed joined a Fight Club group to see what it was about. Ed encountered transforming grace. He was equipped with the tools to walk in freedom and step into the life God designed for him. As he immersed himself in the Bible, he began to recognize and break free from the lies that had once kept him bound.

Much like Ed's story, addiction takes us to a place of deep desperation, where we feel powerless against pornography and sexually compulsive behavior. It is possible your starting point this week echoes his emotions. We believe God has led us to this place of raw vulnerability and honest surrender—because it is there, in our brokenness, that we finally grow weary of the addiction cycle and long for real change. God specializes in bringing dead things back to life, and our prayer as we begin this journey is to experience that kind of restoration.

Week 1 is overwhelming, depressing, and—in many ways—just feels hopeless.

For our struggle is not against flesh and blood, but against the rulers, against the authorities, against the powers of this dark world and against the spiritual forces of evil in the heavenly realms.

—Ephesians 6:12

Paul reminds us that our real fight is going to be overwhelming. It is against unseen spiritual forces of evil. But God does not want us to be overcome by that evil. Trouble and hardship are a part of life—Jesus himself said we would face them—but he also urged us in John 16:33 to "take heart," because he has overcome the world. The week 1 combat challenge is to spend time reading the Bible daily because when we are in Scripture, we give the Holy Spirit margin to work in our lives. The Bible is powerful, alive, and an objective truth. Hebrews 4:12 says it is a "double edged sword that cuts between the soul and the spirit."

Let's get ready for the fight of our life. Hell's coming hard, but heaven hits harder. This is more than a battle—it's your breakthrough. Let's fight.

DAY 1

CALM BEFORE COLLAPSE: A PORNDEMIC

On September 8, 1900, Galveston, Texas was a booming port city known as the "Wall Street of the Southwest." Though experts had warned a major hurricane could ravage the island, the community largely ignored the cautionary concerns, dismissing the inconvenience of unforeseen danger. Their negligence in readiness left Galveston unprepared when an estimated category 4 storm made landfall, leaving the island overwhelmed by the storm surge and fierce winds. The hurricane became the deadliest natural disaster in US history, leveling the city and leaving destruction and death in its wake.

Pornography, much like the 1900 Galveston hurricane, is leaving destruction in its path as it indiscriminately cripples a generation that has either ignored or not prepared for its devastating impact.

To fully understand how pornography is sweeping across the globe with devastating force, we must first define what it is—a challenge in itself, as the definition continues to be highly subjective. Every culture and religion identifies pornography by a different set of standards. Fight Club adopts the definition of the word as it originated in the Greek.

The word pornography is derived from a combination of two Greek words. *Porne*, meaning "prostitute," and *graphos*, meaning "writing." Essentially, the two-word tandem means writing about prostitutes or drawing about prostitutes. By that standard, anything including graphic sexual depictions or vividly portraying the emotional and physical sensations of sex may be considered pornographic. While pornography most commonly appears as images or videos of nude or partially clothed individuals engaging in sexual acts, it has adopted many other forms as well. Erotic stories, digital images, video games, social media, mobile apps, adult phone conversations, music, and other media can contain or is pornographic content.

Pornography use is widespread in the developed world, with some US studies showing that 70 percent of men and 40 percent of women have viewed pornography within the past year.[1] Another survey noted that one out of three Americans seek out porn monthly.[2] To further put it in perspective, approximately 40 million US adults visit porn websites weekly.[3]

1. Grubbs et al., "Self-Reported Addiction."
2. Barna Group, "Porn Phenomenon," 32–33.
3. Logue, "Pornography Statistics," para. 2.

Porn is not merely a Western dilemma. Globally, statistics reveal that nearly 30 percent of all internet traffic is linked to pornography, and the industry itself is valued at an estimated $97 billion worldwide.[4] The widespread—and potentially harmful—surge in pornography consumption has led to what many refer to as a "porndemic." While several factors have fueled the steady rise in porn consumption, a few key aspects have contributed in creating the perfect storm.

High speed internet is a significant factor in the porndemic surge. In 2012, there were an estimated 25 million pornographic websites, roughly 12 percent of all websites at the time.[5] By 2022, the volume of online pornographic content had grown to over 10,000 terabytes.[6] As of 2025, PornHub ranks ninth among the ten most-visited websites with 4.14 billion monthly views, following giants like Google, Facebook, and YouTube.[7] Uniquely, only PornHub and Google share a bounce rate as low as 26 percent, indicating that the vast majority of visitors stay to explore multiple pages.[8] The average bounce rate for the other top ten websites is nearly double, at 45 percent. In one month alone, PornHub recorded 2.14 billion visits, surpassing the combined traffic of Netflix, TikTok, Pinterest, and Instagram.[9] It is no surprise that roughly 35 percent of everything downloaded on the internet is pornographic content.[10]

The prevalence of the smartphone has been influential in the porndemic. While 98 percent of pornographic content is accessed online, 69 percent of that viewing is on smartphones.[11] The surge in smartphone use globally has gone hand in hand with the rise in pornography consumption because of a cultural shift in growing acceptance, easier access, and a wide-range in varying content and taboos. Dr. Patrick Carnes, a leading expert in sexual addiction, notes that digital media—especially smartphone-accessible pornography—has dramatically expanded both the availability

4. Birches Health, "Porn Addiction," para. 13.
5. Rosen, "Pornography and the Erotic Phantasmagoria."
6. Jahnen et al., "Pornography in the Sex Life."
7. Semrush, "Most Visited Websites," fig. 1.
8. HostingAdvice, "33 Most Visited Websites," fig. 1.
9. Semrush, "Top 100," fig. 1.
10. Omega Recovery, "Increase in Porn Addiction," para. 9.
11. Regnerus et al., "Documenting Pornography."

and variety of unwanted addictive behaviors, affecting individuals at every stage of life.[12]

Anonymity offers a sense of privacy and secrecy that other addictive substances simply cannot match. While Num 32:23 warns us that sin will inevitably be revealed, we continue our destructive path under the false pretense that anonymity makes us immune to the devastating consequences. To further complicate our ease of access to viewing porn, much of it is free. Though it is challenging to pinpoint the exact percentage of online pornography that is free, the vast majority of online porn is accessible for free. With just a few clicks, we can privately access an endless array of explicit content without cost, judgment, or accountability.

The violent Galveston storm of 1900 served as a difficult lesson on the consequences of ignoring potential dangers. In response, the city built a seventeen-foot seawall in a massive engineering effort to prevent future devastation, and it has served their community well time and again. Likewise, we at Fight Club choose to face the destructive surge of pornography and sexual addiction by offering hope as we become better equipped to shelter against the chaos this storm brings.

DAILY FIGHT PLAN

1. In what ways do you see the world unprepared for the global impact of pornography like the 1900 hurricane?
2. Which statistic(s) did you find most alarming in "Calm Before Collapse: A Porndemic"? Why?
3. How does the following verse apply to the danger of uncontrolled sexual sin?

   But each person is tempted when they are dragged away by their own evil desire and enticed. Then, after desire has conceived, it gives birth to sin; and sin, when it is full-grown, gives birth to death.
   —JAMES 1:14–15
4. How have you witnessed the destructive turmoil porn can cause in someone's life?

12. Smith, "Recovery and Treatment."

DAY 2

FROM FANTASY TO FALLOUT

Jim and Pam had been married for eighteen years. They had two kids, were active in their church, and well-regarded in their community. From the outside, their marriage looked solid. But behind closed doors, Jim carried a secret porn addiction he never confessed.

To Jim, it seemed harmless. Just a way to blow off steam when work was chaotic or home life felt overwhelming. He convinced himself it wasn't really cheating—just a private escape. Jim's justification for addictive behavior allowed him to sidestep responsibility for his actions and delay the long-term implications for his choices.

As Jim's addiction progressed over the years, so, too, was his willingness to engage in more risky behavior. Porn turned into browsing hookup apps. Fantasies turned into opportunities. Eventually, Jim began a physical affair.

The lies unraveled one evening when Pam stumbled across text messages Jim forgot to delete. In an instant, the years of secrecy came crashing down. The truth he thought he could bury surfaced and the weight of his choices landed hard on the marriage he thought he could protect while still feeding his addiction.

Deception and denial are like buying pornography consumption on credit—the relational marriage debt is merely delayed, not avoided, with interest accruing daily. While it may feel hidden for a time, Luke 8:17 warns us what's done in secret will one day be brought to light. If false pleasure poisons the sanctity of marriage, where is the cure?

Fortunately, God has an opinion on sex and marriage because it was his idea.

May you rejoice in the wife of your youth. A loving doe, a graceful deer—may her breasts satisfy you always, may you ever be intoxicated with her love.

—Proverbs 5:18–19

Marriage should be honored by all, and the marriage bed kept pure, for God will judge the adulterer and all the sexually immoral.

—Hebrews 13:4

God designed us as sexual beings. So, it is no surprise that Scripture speaks extensively about sex. While the Bible affirms sex as a good and sacred gift within marriage, it offers more warnings about its misuse than it does instructions for its proper expression. The Bible provides numerous verses about what is not permissible in sex because it views sexual intimacy as a sacred act intended for the covenant of marriage, and therefore, it sets boundaries around sexual expression to protect individuals and relationships.

The counterfeit intimacy of porn cheapens marital sex and strikes at the core of a healthy marriage. The problem is, we are consuming more porn today than ever in history. A study published by *Cureus* found that since the year 2000, porn consumption and solo masturbation have increased by more than 91 percent.[13] The research suggests that society is becoming increasingly reliant on porn for sexual satisfaction—leading to a noticeable decline in sexual intimacy between partners. There is a belief that marriage will resolve one's porn problem. The truth is, marriage can't fix a porn problem, but a porn problem can tear apart both your marriage and your intimacy.

If porn is the prelude, adultery is the encore.

Research from Steven Stack at Wayne State University found that people who consume porn are more than 300 percent more likely to have an affair on their spouse.[14] Unsurprisingly, another study showed a strong link between watching internet porn and being more sexually permissive overall.[15] Likewise, watching porn as a couple doesn't strengthen relationships—it actually makes them over 317 percent more likely to cheat.[16]

Marriage is tough enough without inviting a screen between the sheets.

The rate of first marriages ending in divorce is 42–45 percent, while second marriage divorce rates are 60 percent, and third marriage divorce

13. Irizarry et al., "Problematic Pornography Consumption."
14. Stack et al., "Adult Social Bonds."
15. Lo and Wei, "Exposure to Internet Pornography."
16. Douthat, "Is Pornography Adultery?"

rates are 73 percent.[17] In light of how prevalent divorce rates already are, we should be alarmed that pornography is cited as a factor in 56 percent of divorces.[18] That means if nearly half of marriages fail and more than half of those failed marriages cite porn as a significant reason why, we are not practicing for a healthier sex life in marriage by using porn, we are practicing for divorce.

Porn does not only impact men in marriage—online sexual activity has a serious effect on women, too. Statistics reveal significantly different outcomes when women engage with pornographic content. Women who engage in online sexual activity have roughly 40 percent more offline sexual partners than women who do not consume porn.[19] While divorce rates double when men view pornography online, the statistic triples for women.[20]

A marriage rooted in Scripture grows in strength and grace—because love flourishes when it's fed by truth—so make time today for our weekly combat challenge.

DAILY FIGHT PLAN

1. The Bible speaks positively about sex within marriage. How do you understand God's heart behind setting boundaries around sex outside of marriage?
2. What factors do you think might explain why pornography use appears to correlate with higher infidelity or divorce rates in women than in men?
3. How has porn shaped your views of intimacy and connection in your relationships? If married, how has this shown up in your relationship with your spouse?
4. In your own words, write a prayer asking God to help you desire and steward relationships, including marriage, in a way that honors him.

17. McKinley, "32 Shocking Divorce Statistics," para. 2–3.
18. Wilkinson and Finkbeiner, "Divorce Statistics," no. 69.
19. Daneback et al., "Internet Study of Cybersex."
20. Perry and Schleifer, "Till Porn Do Us Part?"

DAY 3

WIRED FOR LUST: A PORN HIJACKED GENERATION

Oscar was a dedicated family man that strived for an authentic Christ-centered home. He guided his family as best he could and they were active in their local church. When it was discovered that Oscar's young child was hiding a secret pornography addiction, it came as a complete shock. Oscar had been careful in his parenting and yet, porn found its way into the sanctity of their home.

What Oscar failed to realize was just how prolific and accessible porn is. An innocent birthday gift—a Paperwhite Kindle—became the very tool through which his daughter was exposed to porn. An accidental exposure led to addictive behavior fueled by curiosity. Though the images went against her morals and values, she returned day after day, until her behavior changed and Oscar raised questions. Although Oscar was initially shocked, what unsettled him more was the realization that pornography had found its way into his home—a place he believed was securely protected.

Frequent online activity and social media use by children and adolescents highlight one of the darker sides of technological advancement—a constant risk for exposure to porn. Easy access paired with a growing reliance on digital media for connection and intimacy are major drivers in the rise of porn consumption across generations.[21]

As production of porn shifts from studios to smartphones, anyone is a potential creator.

Today, pornography shows up, whether welcomed or not, on nearly every screen connected to the internet. In fact, a significant amount of it now originates from everyday homes with nothing more than a Wi-Fi signal. Among young women ages thirteen to twenty-four who consume porn, roughly 40 percent report having shared a nude image through text, email, or an app.[22] What they fail to realize is the content lives on, feeding into a vicious cycle where their trauma is relived over and over, simultaneously becoming the indulger's trauma, too. Sexting is a growing issue for adolescents:[23]

21. Andamon et al., "Regain Consciousness."

22. Barna Group, "Porn Phenomenon," 23.

23. Thorn, "Youth Perspectives," 16; Barna Group, "Porn in the Digital Age," 16.

- One in seven adolescents report having sent a nude image or video of themselves to someone else, and of that 13 percent, one in three reports sharing the content with an adult.
- Twenty-five percent of minors believe sharing nude images of themselves is normal.
- Approximately one in eight minors know a friend who has received money or gifts in exchange for sharing images.

Attitudes about porn have shifted, too.

Just 11 percent of young people aged thirteen to twenty-four identify a fully nude and sexually provocative image as pornography, meaning nearly half of today's youth no longer define a Playboy centerfold as pornographic in nature.[24] Thirty-six percent of young men aged thirteen to twenty-four admit to occasionally discussing pornography with their friends, and 90 percent describe those conversations as encouraging, accepting, or hold a casual indifference towards it.[25] What we are observing is a collective increased pro-porn attitude that both normalizes the material and diminishes desire to quit.[26]

Youths' attitude towards pornography is less shocking when we consider the average age of first exposure to porn is twelve, with 15 percent of children seeing porn by the age of ten.[27] Recent studies reveal that younger generations—94 percent of men and 87 percent of women—have viewed more pornography and at a higher frequency than older generations, largely due to the accessibility provided by smartphones.[28] Youth today can view more pornography in a twenty-four-hour binge than their grandparent saw in a lifetime.

Because exposure to porn begins at a young age, it plays a significant role in shaping arousal patterns and scripting sexual behavior. When early and repeated exposure pairs with habitual masturbation, it influences sexual behavior, a process known as perceptual learning—a learned behavior that in time feels natural or innate. The danger of early exposure to porn is that some individuals develop an addiction before they've even had real-life romantic experiences. Their grasp of sexuality forms entirely

24. Barna Group, "Porn in the Digital Age," fig. 3.
25. Barna Group, "Porn Phenomenon," 14.
26. Mengzhen et al., "Decline in Intentions to Stop."
27. Common Sense Media, "Teens and Pornography," 5.
28. Ley, "Accessibility and Anonymity," para. 10.

within a fantasy world. They have never held hands, never kissed, never dated—none of it. Instead, they are isolated in front of a screen with no genuine human connection, conditioning their brains through unhealthy sexual experiences.

A recent study reveals just how devious the content our youth is exposed to truly is as it conditions their perception of sexuality:[29]

- 83 percent of boys and 57 percent of girls have viewed group sex online.
- 69 percent of boys and 55 percent of girls have viewed same-sex intercourse online.
- 39 percent of boys and 23 percent of girls have viewed sexual bondage online.
- 32 percent of boys and 18 percent of girls have viewed bestiality online.
- 18 percent of boys and 10 percent of girls have viewed rape or sexual violence online.
- 15 percent of boys and 9 percent of girls have viewed child pornography.

Do not be afraid or discouraged because of this vast army. For the battle is not yours, but God's.

—2 Chronicles 20:15

As a parent, Oscar was discouraged because he had been vigilant, and yet porn entered the sanctity of his home. He turned to Fight Club to better equip himself and learned that while vigilance matters, God is our greatest defense. When we invite him into all areas of our household, we are not merely protecting our children—we are shepherding them with his guidance. Powerless on our own, wisdom and strength come from God, so continue to be diligent in practicing Fight Club's week 1 challenge to spend time reading the Bible daily.

29. Enough Is Enough, "Stats," para. 29.

DAILY FIGHT PLAN

1. What age were you first exposed to pornography? Can you recall/describe the emotions experienced?
2. In what ways, if any, have you seen pornography negatively influence your home or family?
3. What statistics related to widespread pornography exposure was most concerning to you and why?
4. How does the following verse encourage the war on your youth?

   The Lord will fight for you; you need only be still.
   —Exodus 14:14

DAY 4

PIXELATED PRIDE

We all dislike being told what we can or cannot believe or say. Understandably, many in the LGBTQIA+ community carry deep pain for their choices—whether from real or perceived injustice. At Fight Club, we are committed to speaking truth in love, with an understanding that we are all broken. With that said, we do not affirm LGBTQIA+ ideology, recognizing it as one of many expressions of sexual brokenness.

Biblically, there are no good guys and bad guys—everybody is both.

Compared to heterosexual adolescents, LGBTQIA+ youth statistically initiate porn use earlier and engage with it more frequently.[30] Pornography normalizes behavior, desensitizing and minimizing shock, as we invite through a pixelated screen that which we would never allow in through the front door. This raises the classic chicken-or-egg question: Does early porn consumption influence the development of the LGBTQIA+ identity, or does it stem from a deeper desire for identity exploration and emotional connection? To answer this question with grace, we must turn to God's word.

Therefore God gave them over in the sinful desires of their hearts to sexual impurity for the degrading of their bodies with one another. They exchanged the truth about God for a lie, and worshiped and served created things rather than the Creator—who is forever praised. Amen. Because of this, God gave them over to shameful lusts. Even their women exchanged natural sexual relations for unnatural ones. In the same way the men also abandoned natural relations with women and were inflamed with lust for one another. Men committed shameful acts with other men, and received in themselves the due penalty for their error. Furthermore, just as they did not think it worthwhile to retain the knowledge of God, so God gave them over to a depraved mind, so that they do what ought not to be done.

—Romans 1:24–28

Paul offers three exchanges in Romans: absolute truth for relative truth, worship of God for sexual exploration, and natural heterosexuality

30. Bőthe et al., "Problematic and Non-Problematic Pornography."

for unnatural homosexuality. We firmly believe that truth determines what is ethical. The LGBTQIA+ community, on the other hand, believes that which is ethical—according to its own standards—determines what is true. Their terminology sounds welcoming and affirming, but the LGBTQIA+ community is merely offering the same empty exchange Paul warns of. Likewise, Isaiah offered a similar exchange.

Woe to those who call evil good and good evil, who put darkness for light and light for darkness, who put bitter for sweet and sweet for bitter.

—Isaiah 5:20

Isaiah's condemnation towards the people of Judah warns of normalizing sin. The LGBTQIA+ community is actively doing this as they victimize their movement and villainize opposing beliefs. The sad irony is the LGBTQIA+ individuals are truly victims of their own behavior. Rates of anxiety and depression are significantly higher among LGBTQIA+ populations, with substance use nearly double that of heterosexual individuals.[31] There is no joy in their sexual revolution. It's an empty exchange. Sin deceives with small steps but carries us far. Sin holds us gently but binds us tightly. Sin promises safety but robs us of more than we ever imagined.

A large cross-sectional survey of more than six thousand students offers us our first insight into the link between pornography and identifying within the LGBTQIA+ movement. The study highlights significant trends in escalating extreme pornography consumption, with 46 percent of participants reporting a shift to new or unfamiliar genres, 61 percent viewing content misaligned with their sexual orientation, and 32 percent developing a preference for increasingly extreme or violent material.[32] An article published by the *New York Post* further supports the fact that frequency in porn viewership directly correlates with consumers identifying as LGBTQIA+.[33]

- 13 percent of those viewing porn weekly identify as bisexual.
- 20 percent of those viewing porn a few times a week identify as bisexual.

31. Substance Abuse and Mental Health Services Administration, "2020 National Survey on Drug Use."

32. Dwulit and Rzymski, "Prevalence, Patterns, and Self-Perceived."

33. Kaplan, "More Porn You Watch," para. 1–5.

- 27 percent of those viewing porn daily identify as bisexual.

While the LGBTQIA+ movement promotes and celebrates sexual fluidity, it is a masquerade. They dismiss the idea that gender identity is defined by biological characteristics, such as chromosomes or hormones, assigned at birth. Instead, they argue a person's internal sense of gender is their identity, regardless of if it aligns with the sex assigned at birth. This great exchange by the LGBTQIA+ leads to negative outcomes, as 40 percent of transgender individuals report having attempted suicide.[34] Simply visit a local department store and look at their furniture. Though their products may claim mahogany, oak, or walnut finish, it is all veneer. We cannot change the elemental composition of particle boards despite our best efforts. Likewise, the veneer of the transgender community masks a deeper need for God and our identity in him.

When we question our sexuality, we question our identity. When we question our identity, we lose sight of God's fingerprint on us. The Bible's stance is abundantly clear on LGBTQIA+. We are made as man and woman in the image of God, and Gen 1:27–28 defines the *what* and the *why* we are the way we are. Continue to seek absolute truth this week as you spend time reading the Bible daily.

Everything else is veneer.

DAILY FIGHT PLAN

1. In what ways have you observed your own consumption of porn content become more devious over the years?
2. What great exchange(s) can you identify in your addiction story?
3. How does the following verse conflict with the LGBTQIA+ concept of an ally?

   Acquitting the guilty and condemning the innocent—the Lord detests them both.

   —Proverbs 17:15

34. Austin et al., "Suicidality Among Transgender Youth," NP2696–NP2718.

DAY 5

DIGITAL DESIRE, REAL-WORLD RUIN

On November 13, 2022, Bryan Kohberger, a former criminology PhD student at Washington State University, entered an off-campus home in Moscow, Idaho, where he brutally stabbed four University of Idaho students to death as they slept. Armed with a large knife and wearing gloves and a mask, he carried out his military-style knife attack in the early morning hours before fleeing the scene. Investigators later linked him to the murders through surveillance footage, cellphone data, and DNA found on a knife sheath left at the scene. At sentencing, Kohberger accepted a plea deal that spared him the death penalty. He received four consecutive life sentences and a ten-year burglary term for his heinous crimes, with no possibility of appeal.

While Kohberger's motive remains the biggest mystery in the case, his online activity would suggest otherwise. Kohberger's digital history revealed disturbing content—referred to as "weird porn fetishes"—including searches for "drunk passed out girls" and "gagging girls."[35]

Even occasional pornography use can shape the way we think and what we believe. Teenage boys exposed to violent pornography are two to three times more likely to use violence against sexual partners than boys who have not seen it, and girls exposed are 1.5 times more likely to engage in threatening relational behavior.[36]

A survey of 1,500 young adult men revealed that 56 percent of those regularly consuming porn reported their preferences become "increasingly extreme or deviant."[37] The lure for more disturbing and morally unacceptable content leads consumers into darker waters. The term *teen* is one of the three most searched pornographic keywords worldwide.[38] We can draw two unsettling conclusions from the fact that underage girls—a concept that is not even legally permissible—is one of the three most sought after forms of pornography on the internet. The first is that people across the globe are constantly searching for and consuming porn involving or depicting teens. The second is that high demand for pornographic content

35. Rutt, "Bryan Kohberger Motive," para. 1–6.
36. Rostad et al., "Association Between Exposure."
37. Fight the New Drug, "Teen," para. 9.
38. Vincos, "Sex and the Searches," para. 4.

featuring teens shapes consumer attitudes, making sex with teens appear more normalized or thrilling.

One of the dangers with porn is that the goal post simply moves for the ever-growing extreme content available online. In 2019, there were 17 million reported cases of sexual abuse against children reported worldwide, which is 17 times the number of documented cases in 2010.[39] The FBI estimates there are roughly 40,000 public chat rooms where predators seek to abuse children.[40] FBI statistics point out that arrests for child pornography have rapidly surged 2,500 percent since 1996, largely due to online availability.[41] The only thing worse than an insatiable appetite for porn is having a smorgasbord of increasingly more deviant content to feed one's appetite.

Pornography addiction has created a market where lust meets greed, while both the victim and consumer pay the price.

Porn and sex trafficking are inseparably connected. Though the true incidents of adolescents lured into sex trade is difficult to identify, recent reports speculate that roughly 326,000 Americans under the age of eighteen are at risk for commercial sexual exploitation every year in the United States.[42] While much of the threat for trafficked children in the US historically came from runaways, more than half of all sex trafficking victims since 2000—55 percent—have been lured online, primarily through social media, dating apps, and other digital platforms.[43] As of 2023, the top three platforms utilized for recruiting victims of sex trafficking were Snapchat, Facebook, and Instagram.[44]

When we consume porn, we assume the lie that it is all consensual. At Fight Club, we emphasize that while some content may be consensual, much of it is not—and it is nearly impossible to distinguish between the two with certainty. The organization Rescue:Freedom, now known as Atlas Free, surveyed women rescued from sex trafficking in nine countries and 49 percent said their traffickers made pornographic videos.[45] The adult entertainment industry is built on broken souls and thriving where silence lives.

39. European Commission, "Communication from the Commission," para. 4.
40. Culina, "Socio-Economic Portrait," 155.
41. Prison Legal News, "FBI Claims," para. 1.
42. Kruger et al., "Facilitating a School-Based Prevention."
43. Feehs and Currier, "2020 Federal Human Trafficking Report," 17–26.
44. Human Trafficking Institute, "Federal Human Trafficking Report."
45. Fight the New Drug, "Why Do Some People Fight," para. 15.

No temptation has overtaken you except what is common to mankind. And God is faithful; he will not let you be tempted beyond what you can bear. But when you are tempted, he will also provide a way out so that you can endure it.

—1 Corinthians 10:15

It is time to be a part of the solution. It is time to choose freedom—not only for yourself but for the victims your addiction keeps in slavery. The most sought after help for addiction online across the US is porn, averaging more than thirty thousand searches a month, which is three times the number of people searching freedom from alcohol addiction.[46] What that says is you are a part of a growing number of people that are sick and tired of being sick and tired. That is what this twelve-week Fight Club journey is about!

You are not alone. And you are not beyond hope. Your story is still being written. Fight Club is in your corner.

DAILY FIGHT PLAN

1. What was the most alarming statistic you encountered in this day's reading and why?
2. Why do you think pornography consumption often escalates or intensifies over time?
3. Do you feel like you have any true hope for freedom from porn and/or sexual addiction? Please explain your reasoning.
4. How have you observed the week 1 combat challenge to spend time in the Bible daily impact your week?

46. Castillo, "Porn Addiction Tops List," para. 1.

WEEK 2—GUARDRAILS

WEEKLY MEMORY VERSE

And the peace of God, which transcends all understanding, will guard your hearts and your minds in Christ Jesus. Finally, brothers, whatever is true, whatever is noble, whatever is right, whatever is pure, whatever is lovely, whatever is admirable—if anything is excellent and praiseworthy—think about such things.

—PHILIPPIANS 4:7–8

WEEKLY COMBAT CHALLENGE

Set up guardrails in your life.

LIVING COUNTERCULTURALLY

FROM URGE TO ACTION

Stanley was a bright high school student with his whole life ahead of him. He came from an affluent family and had every advantage—academic opportunity, a stable home, and a strong spiritual foundation. He was raised to love the Lord, knew Scripture inside and out, and had been protected from many of life's harsh realities. After returning from his first church camp, he appeared to be on fire for God.

But then things began to shift.

A sharp conflict between Stanley's father and leaders at their church led the family to leave. They tried visiting a few other congregations, but none felt quite right. Eventually, they stopped attending altogether. What began as a temporary transition became a long-term spiritual drift. Without the routine of worship and the support of community, Stanley began to lose his footing.

He gradually pulled away from his church friends and grew closer to his teammates on the varsity sports team. They invited him to parties during his senior year and he began to embrace a new crowd and lifestyle. At one of those parties, he met an attractive and more experienced girl. They started dating and within weeks they were sleeping together.

Around the same time, his friends began sharing explicit content and conversations about sex. Out of curiosity, Stanley began exploring online. What he found intrigued him. Soon, that curiosity became a daily habit. And that habit quickly manifested into an addiction to pornography.

Stanley's relationship did not survive when he left for college—but his addiction did. With more freedom and less accountability, he began having casual sex and feeding his craving for instant gratification. Through these casual hookups, Stanley began to connect with a new group of friends, people who shared and encouraged his lifestyle. They didn't challenge his choices—they normalized them. Meanwhile, Stanley was thriving in his computer science program. By his junior year, he had developed strong technical skills and a growing reputation for his talent.

It wasn't long before some of his friends introduced him to another opportunity: making easy money through the dark web. It sounded low-risk—nothing too dangerous—just small hacking jobs, stealing data, accessing personal records like social security numbers. It was illegal, but it paid well and seemed far removed from real consequences.

Then one day, while doing a job for cash, Stanley was approached by a mysterious contact offering a much larger payout. But there was a catch—they needed proof he wasn't law enforcement. As an exchange, they sent him a video containing child pornography and he was expected to send a similar pornographic video of children to them in return. This digital handshake was something neither the FBI nor police could or would do. The payout was too enticing for Stanley to ignore, so he made the fateful choice to accept the job by sending the video. Stanley spiraled further into the dark world of cybercrime and child pornography.

The end was inevitable. In his senior year of college, Stanley's world came crashing down. At 3:00 a.m., FBI agents kicked down his door. They pulled him from his bed, slammed him to the floor, handcuffed him, and seized every computer and device he owned. The truth he had hidden for so long was finally exposed.

By morning, his name was in the newspaper headlines. The local paper labeled him as a child predator. After a swift trial, Stanley was sentenced to many years in federal prison. His future, once so full of promise, was snuffed out in an instant.

Stanley never imagined his life would end up this way. But it did not happen all at once. It was a slow fade, one small compromise at a time. Gradually, he gave in to the culture around him, letting darkness creep in through doors he never should have opened.

This week, our combat challenge is to set up guardrails in our lives. We will learn strategic and effective ways to put them in place. If we want to walk in freedom, it begins with courage to stand against a culture that numbs the conscience and celebrates compromise. Easier said than done. But absolutely necessary.

DAY 1

CHAOS: WHERE THE WILD THINGS ARE

According to a recent Barna study, 78 percent of unchurched men and 75 percent of Christian men view pornography to some degree. The same study found that 44 percent of all women view pornography, which is a 5 percent increase over the past eight years.[1] While culture has embraced the convenience of pornography access, we must start at the beginning if we are to fully grasp the depths in which this cultural battle was born.

Now the earth was formless and empty, darkness was over the surface of the deep, and the Spirit of God was hovering over the waters.

—Genesis 1:2

In Gen 1:2, the original Hebrew text describes the state of the earth prior to God's creative work as *tohu wa-bohu*, a phrase meaning "formless and void," yet the phrase carries a deeper meaning of disorder, emptiness, and unformed reality. The original Greek translation describes the earth as being *Χάος*, the root for the English word *chaos*. So, before there was order, there was chaos.

God took chaos and created something that he deemed *good*.

But could God ever have created something that was not good? Is it even within his wheelhouse of skills? The answer, of course, is *no*. As addicts, it is easy to become angry and blame the world, God included, for the chaotic and sexualized culture we navigate—a world where freedom from addiction seems unattainable.

But you must not eat from the tree of the knowledge of good and evil, for when you eat of it you will surely die.

—Genesis 2:17

Enter free will. The opportunity to either obey God or to pretend you are god, living by your own rules. One is selfless while the other is selfish. Culture argues free will is evidence of a cruel and unfair God, one setting us up for failure. What we will discover in our Fight Club journey is that God did not create addiction, we did.

1. Barna Group, "Beyond the Porn Phenomenon," 6–23.

God warned Adam and Eve that they would die if they chose their wants over his. There is something uniquely profound about the Hebrew word for *death* God uses in Gen 2:17 because it has a dual form. One of life's certainties is that we will all die a physical death, but we also have a spiritual death. Prior to Adam and Eve's disobedience in the garden of Eden, they only knew consequences abstractly. How could they fully grasp the magnitude of unfaithfulness? They had never truly experienced punishment. They could not know the overwhelming shame and destruction of disobedience that ultimately led to a legacy of sin.

Adam and Eve sinned and sin was born.

The meaning for the Greek word *sin* is an archery term to describe "missing the mark." Essentially, sin represents our failure to achieve God's best. We are not perfect, so we miss the mark a lot. We fail individually, relationally, politically, and so on. Specific to Fight Club, sin is evident in our sexual brokenness. With sin comes chaos.

I looked at the earth, and it was formless and empty; and the heavens, and their light was gone.

—Jeremiah 4:23

The only other time in the entire Hebrew Bible that the words *tohu* and *bohu* are used to describe a state of chaos is in Jer 4:23 after sin entered. This verse portrays a scene of utter devastation—a reversal of creation itself. The earth is reduced to chaos, formless and void, while the heavens are stripped of their light. It is a striking picture of the catastrophic consequences of sin. God created order from chaos and then our sin created chaos from order.

It's like dismantling a symphony that was composed by God himself. Each life, each gift, each command was written to play in harmony with his design. But we ignored his direction and played our own tune, the result isn't freedom—it's dissonance. What was once order became chaos, not because God stopped conducting but because we stopped obeying and following him.

But how can we obey God in a culture promoting high speed sexual entertainment anytime and anywhere? According to the Pew Research Center, smartphone ownership in the US has surged from 35 percent in 2011 to 91 percent today.[2] Likewise, recent studies show that 95 percent

2. Pew Research Center, "Mobile Fact Sheet," para. 2.

of teens carry a smartphone.[3] With pornography present on 12 percent of all websites, we've reached a point where watching porn is easier than reheating leftovers because even the microwave makes you wait thirty seconds.[4] The Parents Television Council reports that major streaming services offer roughly 268 percent more adult-focused content on streaming platforms than content suitable for families.[5]

Unless we are willing to live counterculturally, opposing the subpar standard for a hypersexualized society, freedom will be beyond our reach. To be countercultural, we must live counterculturally, prepared to make the difficult choices so that God brings order back into our chaotic life.

DAILY FIGHT PLAN

1. Where do you feel that a sexualized culture has influenced the choices and/or trajectory of your life most?
2. In what ways have you seen "chaos" sexually in your life?
3. How can you find hope in living counterculturally, moving further away from chaos and closer to order?
4. Write a prayer asking God to reveal the ways cultural influences have fueled your addiction and to realign your heart with his truth.

3. Drah, "Cell Phone Addiction Statistics," para. 15.
4. Ahmed et al., "Internet Is for Porn."
5. Parents Television and Media Council, "Families Need Not Subscribe," para. 4.

DAY 2

FLIP THE SCRIPT: COUNTERCULTURAL HAPPINESS

Following Jesus is radically countercultural. It's not a slight variation of the norms set by a sexualized world—it stands in bold contrast. Our lives should reflect that difference. We're called to live differently, think differently, and act differently. Jesus does not simply set the standard, he is the standard for how we live within a sexualized culture.

In Matt 5–7, Jesus shared an extremely countercultural Sermon on the Mount. His message was filled with statements like, "You have heard it said, but I say to you . . .," or, "You believed and lived like this, but now I am telling you how it really should be done." Jesus was acknowledging the world's perspective while doubling down on absolute truth.

Truth is absolute. Truth is concrete and leaves no room for compromise.

Blessed are the poor in spirit, for theirs is the kingdom of heaven. Blessed are those who mourn, for they will be comforted. Blessed are the meek, for they will inherit the earth. Blessed are those who hunger and thirst for righteousness for they will be filled. Blessed are the merciful, for they will be shown mercy. Blessed are the pure in heart, for they will see God. Blessed are the peacemakers, for they will be called sons of God. Blessed are those who are persecuted because of righteousness, for theirs is the kingdom of heaven.

—MATTHEW 5:3–10

Jesus' sermon, known as the Beatitudes, comes from the Latin word *beatus*, meaning blessed or happy. The first thing we notice is that Jesus desires for us to be *blessed*—a word that goes far beyond mere happiness, which ebbs and flows with circumstances. In this context, *blessed* speaks to a deep, lasting well-being and a unique spiritual joy that only comes from being united with him.

Blessed are the poor in spirit, for theirs is the kingdom of heaven.

Imagine an island paradise with crystal-clear water that lacks nothing and offers a deep sense of contentment. The ancient Greeks had such an island, Makarios. Jesus began his famous sermon on the mount with *Makarios*, a full and abundant life unlike culture offers. We have a word for that today: *blessed*. Culture interprets blessed as those who are fortunate, privileged, and without need. This is where Jesus flips the script because he did not identify the confident, strong, and esteemed as blessed. The poor in spirit are the ones that recognize without God, they have nothing, and that God's blessing begins when he alone satisfies our needs. Culture says we must fix our addiction, shame, and brokenness before we come to Jesus. Jesus simply says, "Come."

Blessed are those who mourn, for they will be comforted.

Jesus is expressing a mourning over our personal sin and our broken culture. This is unlike the shame addicts often experience, leading to negative behavior and isolation. The grief he describes is sincere and heartfelt, driving us towards God. It is in biblical mourning we discover God as our Comforter and see the destructiveness of addiction. This is a healthy brokenness because, in it, we find comfort only God can provide.

Blessed are the meek, for they will inherit the earth.

Culture views meekness as weakness, an inability to take control and fix our addictive behaviors. Jesus again flips the script because meekness is not weakness; it is power under control. When we live countercultural lives and submit our addictive behavior to God, living under his authority, we experience the fullness of God and live in freedom.

Blessed are those who hunger and thirst for righteousness, for they will be filled.

Our physical needs mirror our spiritual needs. Our souls are starving and our hearts are parched. There's a deep, unshakable need inside us all and culture suggests the grass is greener elsewhere. Here's the tragedy: that very ache is meant to draw us to God, yet we keep turning to the quick fix of porn and short-term pleasures that leave us emptier than before. Could it be that the grass looks greener everywhere else because we are chasing everything but righteousness? Think about how consistently and persistently we pursue food and drink. What if we craved righteousness with that same intensity?

Blessed are the merciful, for they will be shown mercy.

Forgiveness is difficult and comes at a cost; however, holding onto unforgiveness costs even more. While culture believes unforgiveness is power, it only poisons hearts and breeds bitterness, not freedom. It robs us of peace, joy, and being fully present. That's not the life God wants for us. We should be eternally grateful for God's mercy, because without it, our sins would have crushed us. Likewise, we will learn in our Fight Club journey that we must be merciful and forgive, releasing the hold it has on our hearts.

Blessed are the pure in heart, for they will see God.

While culture tells us to follow our heart, Jer 17:9 warns us that the heart is deceitful above all things. In the Sermon on the Mount, Jesus acknowledges our need for a pure heart. The Greek word for heart, *kardia*, refers to the core of who we are and the place where our emotions, desires, and decisions flow from. Jesus wants us to desire things pleasing to him, free from the corruption and contamination of sexual sin, because our behavior is an overflow of the heart.

Blessed are the peacemakers, for they will be called sons of God.

Addicts often go to great lengths to gaslight or justify their actions. When we begin to see peacemaking the way God does, both cultivating and maintaining restoration, it shifts everything. We don't have to be right. We don't have to excuse our actions. Being a peacemaker is not easy, but even addicts have the potential to bring peace because we are children of God.

Blessed are those who are persecuted because of righteousness, for theirs is the kingdom of heaven.

Jesus yet again flips the script when he identifies our persecutions as a result of pursuing him. Culture will mock you for pursuing freedom from pornography and sexual addiction. They view it as a healthy outlet for stress, not addiction. They believe it enhances their sex life and prevents infidelity. They assume porn doesn't harm anyone. They also believe the "religious" are the only ones with a "sex problem."

DAILY FIGHT PLAN

1. Jesus lived counterculturally and called each of us to do as he did. Which Beatitude do you sense will be the most difficult for you to put into practice—and why?
2. If those who mourn are blessed, what would it look like to bring grief to God instead of hiding it?
3. Jesus says, "Blessed are the pure in heart." What does purity of the heart mean beyond just stopping a behavior?
4. How has culture pushed back whenever you have tried to live in freedom from sexual sin?

DAY 3

GUARDRAILS: STAY IN YOUR LANE

Roy desperately wanted freedom from pornography. He had grown up in a Christian family, and those on the outside would have assumed his life was picture perfect. He had a budding career, a newly engaged fiancée, and was active within his local church. But the side of Roy that remained hidden behind closed doors was plagued with shameful recognition of an addiction he could not overcome.

Roy's best efforts to find freedom were followed by uncontrolled bingeing. When Roy turned to the church for help, he was met with more shame that pushed him further into hiding because it left him feeling that he simply lacked faith, willpower, and self-control. Roy accepted the lie that he was on a collision course with destruction.

Early one morning after another all-night binge, looking disheveled and defeated, Roy met with his accountability partner. What happened next changed the trajectory of Roy's battle with addiction.

Let your eyes look straight ahead, fix your gaze directly before you. Make level paths for your feet and take only ways that are firm. Do not swerve to the right or the left; keep your foot from evil.

—Proverbs 4:25–27

These verses in Proverbs encourage us to remain focused and intentional in our approach to life, emphasizing that the wise stay on the right path, avoiding distractions that veer us off course. In the literal roads of life, guardrails serve as a safety barrier, protecting us from straying into various roadside hazards. Likewise, we must set up guardrails in our lives to maintain control and avoid the repeated crash and burn that addicts often endure from the temptations and dangers looming just off the path.

As a dog return returns to its vomit, so fools repeat their folly.

—Proverbs 26:11

Healthy guardrails in life do not just protect us from danger; they also guide us toward wise living. Guardrails for the sexually broken not only protect us from temptation, but they redirect us to a life of wise living. If we want to effectively find freedom from sexual addiction and pornography, we must establish healthy guardrails early in our Fight Club journey.

So, where do we set up guardrails in our lives?

Guardrails are meant to serve as a cautionary warning, minimize risk, and allow us time to act wisely. Highway guardrails are placed within the safety of the clear zone. A guardrail at the bottom of a cliff is ineffective in maintaining a driver's safety. Likewise, guardrails we set up in our lives must be placed within the safety of the clear zone, allowing us time to recover and regain control.

> *Therefore, since we are surrounded by such a great cloud of witnesses, let us throw off everything that hinders and the sin that so easily entangles, and let us run with perseverance the race marked out for us. Let us fix our eyes on Jesus, the author and perfecter of our faith, who for the joy set before him endured the cross, scorning its shame, and sat down at the right hand of the throne of God.*
>
> —Hebrews 12:1–2

Roy realized that pursuing freedom required guardrails that minimized his risk for destructive behavior. He identified his smartphone as an ongoing source of temptation, but he needed it for work. He downloaded an app that locked the "smart" services of his phone at a specific time each night, rendering it safe until the phone was unlocked each morning. While this guardrail did not eliminate Roy's temptation, it did minimize the risk of relapse. Roy found he was able to live in freedom and build healthy habits without the fear of veering off course with late-night binges.

While guardrails look different for everyone, our journey will be greatly decided by how we navigate the challenge of being countercultural and setting up guardrails.

Here are a few examples of guardrails:

- Parent your phone; put it to bed before you and make it sleep in.
- Go full 2003—get a flip phone and embrace your inner grandparent.
- Put a spiritual seat belt on your computer—filters save lives (and testimonies).
- Relocate your desktop to the land of judgmental glances. It's good for the soul.

- Eliminate novels, music, or movies with graphic adult content.
- Abstain from social media for a season. It's not like your thumb needs the workout.
- Designate a charging station for electronics to rest, recharge, and mind their own business in a shared space, away from bedrooms and bathrooms.

Our natural instinct as we begin to identify guardrails is to immediately make excuses for all the reasons they are not realistic. This natural pushback is fueled by an unwillingness of the heart to resist change. We will look at the dangers of compromise tomorrow. Today, we challenge you to begin identifying areas within your life that addiction continually causes failure and what guardrails in those areas might look like.

DAILY FIGHT PLAN

1. In what ways do you find yourself veering off course in life?
2. Thinking back on your most recent relapse, how could guardrails have helped you stay safe in your lane?
3. Identify areas of your life that you believe need guardrails. (Hint: think of the locations, patterns, and devices that facilitate your ongoing struggle.)
4. Ask God for a willing heart to do whatever is necessary to set up guardrails in your life.

DAY 4

SPIRITUAL DRIFTING

Robert had a porn problem and desperately wanted to find freedom from addiction. He was open with his friends about his struggle, and they challenged him to set up guardrails to avoid slipups. Week after week, Robert found he could not make it more than a couple of days before falling into porn on his PlayStation. His friends continued to encourage him to set up guardrails and relocate his PlayStation out of his bedroom. No matter how many reasons they gave to relocate his easy access, Robert had an excuse for why it should stay. Robert was *almost* willing to do anything to find freedom.

Spiritual death happens one small compromise at a time.

Several months later, Robert's compromise had left him apathetic in his freedom journey. He had made many life changes, yet he could not find freedom from addiction. His friends continued to warn him of his compromise and he eventually agreed to relocate his gaming platform to a public location in the house, no longer safe in the privacy of his bedroom. What happened next was incredible. Robert went a week . . . and then two weeks . . . and then a month . . . and then a year without viewing porn.

> *Blessed are those who obey his laws and search for him with all their hearts. They do not compromise with evil, and they walk only in his paths.*
>
> —Psalms 119:1–2

We make excuses to avoid the burden of guardrails in our lives. Excuses lead to compromise and compromise leads to spiritual drifting. Drifting is dangerous for the sexual addict because it is subtle and takes place through a series of small compromises. Like a rowboat with a small leak, you can dismiss it as no big deal. But that leak won't fix itself, and eventually, you're sinking.

What feels like a minor compromise today can become a major setback tomorrow. A 1 percent shift in the wrong direction is nothing at first, but over one thousand miles, it's catastrophic. The effects often go unnoticed until we have drifted from the freedom we were pursuing.

As we identify the areas of our lives where guardrails are necessary, be on the lookout for the inevitable excuses that follow. Just know, every compromise has a solution.

"I can't give up my phone, it's my alarm clock." Here's a novel idea, buy an alarm clock.

"I'd give up my smartphone, but I need it for work." Get a work phone and leave it there.

"Social media is how I keep up with family." Reach out and call someone.

"I need my cable sports package." Cable companies can remove problem stations.

Culture will look upon your guardrails as radical, unnecessary, and proof that you are too weak to do it alone. Culture argues that guardrails are restrictive and prevent us from living in freedom, but the addict must recognize freedom only comes in living apart from unwanted compulsive behavior.

> *You have heard that it was said, "Do not commit adultery." But I tell you that anyone who looks at a woman lustfully has already committed adultery with her in his heart. If your right eye causes you to sin, gouge it out and throw it away. It is better for you to lose one part of your body than for your whole body to be thrown into hell. And if your right hand causes you to sin, cut it off and throw it away. It is better for you to lose one part of your body than for your whole body to go into hell.*
>
> —MATTHEW 5:27–30

During the same countercultural message that Jesus discussed the Beatitudes, he also spoke on the concept of guardrails and freedom that comes from radically amputating areas of our lives that lead to compromise and spiritual drifting. Jesus is calling us to deal radically with temptation because it is only reasonable to destroy the things in our lives that seek to destroy us.

Radical amputation opens the door for transformation.

> *Do not conform any longer to the pattern of this world,*
> *but be transformed by the renewing of your mind.*
>
> —ROMANS 12:2

Paul said, "Don't be conformed . . . be transformed." The key difference is that conforming is passive, happening when we let culture shape us. Transformation is active and requires intention. Last week, we were challenged to spend time reading the Bible daily, inviting the Holy Spirit to rewire our thinking, and allowing his truth to reshape our identity. If you did not take up last week's challenge, understand you are being shaped either way.

If we pour hot Jello into a mold, the Jello will take its form as it cools. It doesn't matter how unique or colorful the liquid; once it hits the mold, it conforms. Culture wants to shape our values, our identity, our sense of worth, our beliefs about sex, success, and happiness. And if we're not paying attention, we'll start to solidify into something God never intended.

You're going to take a shape either way. The question is—which mold?

DAILY FIGHT PLAN

1. Why is it easy to begin spiritually drifting in life and not recognize it until you are already off course?
2. How will guardrails help you identify the moment you begin drifting?
3. What would transformation—not just self-control—look like for you and how can you be more intentional about the process?

Do not conform any longer to the pattern of this world, but be transformed by the renewing of your mind. —ROMANS 12:2

DAY 5

PURITY PRECEDES POWER

As the old joke goes, "Quitting is easy, I've done it hundreds of times." If you have ever asked yourself how long it takes to quit porn, you are really asking about recovery—not quitting. Recovery is not a one-time event; it's a lifelong journey. There is no quick fix, but as we become further equipped in our Fight Club journey, we find victory in our recovery. Guardrails are a key aspect to recovery, and today we will look at why.

Guardrails keep us on the path of purity, and purity precedes power.

Many of those who believed now came and openly confessed their evil deeds. A number who had practiced sorcery brought their scrolls together and burned them publicly. When they calculated the value of the scrolls, the total came to fifty thousand drachmas. In this way the word of the Lord spread widely and grew in power.

—Acts 19:18–20

This story in Acts is a powerful moment of repentance in Ephesus. New believers, once involved in sorcery, publicly confessed their sins and burned their costly books of magic, an act of radical amputation, as they moved away from their wayward drifting in full devotion to Jesus. The value of all the assets burned would be worth approximately five million dollars today. These new believers realized they could not follow Jesus and hold onto their wickedness—though they had five million reasons to compromise. Instead, Acts 19 illustrates how the call of Jesus challenges cultural norms and leads to a rejection of practices contrary to God's will.

Purity is modeled by the actions of the believers who confessed and renounced their evil practices, demonstrating a desire for unwavering obedience to God by setting up firm guardrails that left no room for compromise. In their radical obedience, growth and influence of God's kingdom spread with power. The Greek word *power* used in Acts 19 means *to be able* and signifies an inherent strength or ability to perform something. We may want to quit porn, but God is inviting us to experience so much more. When we put guardrails in place, oftentimes requiring radical amputation, we experience the power of freedom in him.

Our idea of freedom is upside down from God's design. We assume we need power first—to protect ourselves, to feel strong—and then we can pursue purity. And why wouldn't we believe that? Culture tells us we must be strong, capable, and independent enough to do it ourselves. But Scripture flips that order: choose purity first, and power will follow. When we get the order wrong, the consequences can be extreme.

In Josh 7, Israel was fresh off a major battle by overthrowing the well-fortified city of Jericho through miraculous means. God gave clear commands for the army of Israel in that battle, one of which described in verse 17 was to not take any of the devoted things from the city of Jericho when it fell. While a clear command, temptation can make us do some dangerously foolish things.

But the Israelites acted unfaithfully in regard to the devoted things; Achan son of Carmi, the son of Zimri, the son of Zerah, of the tribe of Judah, took some of them. So the Lord's anger burned against Israel.

—JOSHUA 7:1

In the midst of one of Israel's greatest victories, where God's power was on full display, Achan's temptation blinded him and he drifted off course, compromising his integrity and character for a moment of selfish indulgence. He coveted that which was not his and buried the treasures under his tent. Achan did not realize the dangers of lacking guardrails and how it impacts others.

Chapter 7 goes on to describe how Israel went into their next battle against Ai feeling extremely confident, but the ramifications of Achan's sin carried into that battle and Israel was routed, leaving the Jews downhearted and Joshua greatly distressed.

The Lord said to Joshua, "Stand up! What are you doing down on your face? Israel has sinned; they have violated my covenant, which I commanded them to keep. They have taken some of the devoted things; they have stolen, they have lied, they have put them with their own possessions. That is why the Israelites cannot stand against their enemies; they turn their backs and run because they have been made liable to destruction. I will not be with you anymore unless you destroy whatever among you is devoted to destruction."

—JOSHUA 7:10–12

Joshua, with the Lord's help, identified Achan as the one that disobeyed. Though Achan confessed, his choices had grim consequences. Achan, his sons and daughters, his livestock, tent, belongings, and the stolen treasure were stoned and burned.

Then the Lord said to Joshua, "Do not be afraid; do not be discouraged. Take the whole army with you, and go up and attack Ai. For I have delivered into your hands the king of Ai, his people, his city and his land."

—JOSHUA 8:1

Purity precedes power and it all starts with guardrails. When we cut off access to the source of temptation and turn to Jesus, he provides the power to resist and overcome. Establish guardrails by radically amputating the areas of our lives that habitually lead to unwanted sexual behavior. Decide today that compromise is not an option because it will lead to drifting.

DAILY FIGHT PLAN

1. How do you see radical amputation demonstrated in both Acts 19 and Josh 7?
2. Achan believed his sin was hidden, yet it shaped his entire family's legacy. How has your addictive behavior influenced relationships, trust, or spiritual direction around you?
3. Write a prayer asking God to form in you a nonnegotiable commitment to set and uphold guardrails in your life.

WEEK 3—WHICH EMOJI ARE YOU . . . REALLY?

WEEKLY MEMORY VERSE

Search me, God, and know my heart; test me and know my anxious thoughts. See if there is any offensive way in me, and lead me in the way everlasting.

—PSALM 139:23

WEEKLY COMBAT CHALLENGE

Identify your B.L.A.S.T.E.D. emotions.

NUMB NOW, PAY LATER

HIDING FROM EMOTIONS, NOT JUST GOD

Kevin was intelligent, outspoken, and effortlessly talented as a teenager, acing tests without trying and turning in projects that often made teachers do double takes. He grew up in a Christian home and had a strong sense of right and wrong. Life came easy for Kevin until, like many curious teens, he stumbled across pornography. At first, it was just a quiet habit—one he kept hidden behind good grades and polite smiles. But then, the bottom fell out of his world. At just fifteen, Kevin lost a parent. And in that cavern of emotional grief, porn became more than curiosity—it became comfort.

While porn did not knock Kevin off his academic track, it quietly rewired him. He still graduated top of his class, but behind the awards and accolades was a teenager silently drowning in emotional grief he was unequipped to manage.

Stuff it, numb it, repeat—an emotional routine that kept Kevin in bondage to porn.

Kevin's home life deteriorated and when tensions boiled over, he moved out, no longer feeling welcome in his home. He left for college and bounced between relatives during breaks. Outwardly, Kevin was building a future. Inwardly, he was escaping emotional pain the only way he knew how, by numbing it. Porn became his medication.

After graduation, degree in hand, Kevin hit the job market and it hit back. The economy had tanked. Nobody was hiring in his field. Bills had to be paid. Kevin took a job outside of his educational field, feeling the disapproval of his family. They expressed frustration and disappointment that led Kevin to medicate further still.

Years passed and jobs changed, but Kevin never quite lived up to what others expected of him—never quite lived up to what he expected of himself. Kevin learned to tune out the comments, and initially, he was content; but year by year, his friends slowly married and moved on. Eventually, Kevin found himself single, unemployed, and still avoiding the emotions that spurred his destructive behavior with an addiction to porn.

Kevin moved back to his hometown. He had no plan. No direction. No peace. But for the first time in years, Kevin was quiet enough to listen and hear what God had to say. And God was ready to speak. One afternoon, Kevin was out for a walk, hoping to clear the fog in his mind. By chance, he came across an old friend that casually invited him to visit his local church. Kevin hesitated—church wasn't exactly on his to-do list—but something inside nudged him to say yes.

Step by step, Sunday by Sunday, Kevin began to listen. The words he heard stirred something deep he hadn't felt in years. Slowly, he started spending time with Christian friends after service, people who welcomed him without judgment. Some even mentioned job leads, opening doors he hadn't dared knock on before.

One day, Kevin overheard a group talking openly about their battles with porn addiction. Their honesty caught him off guard. It was the spark he needed to face his own struggle. Taking a bold next step, he signed up for Fight Club, a place where he could learn to overcome the chains of pornography and sexual addiction. It was within Fight Club that Kevin began to understand the complexity of addiction and identify the emotions he had always hid from in the past.

As Kevin grew in the freedom only God offers, he also grew emotionally healthier. As he healed, opportunities that previously seemed impossible to reach began to unfold in his life. A friend introduced him to a remarkable woman. Before long, they were married. Not long after, they welcomed their first child.

In just three years, Kevin's life flipped: from jobless to employed in a new career, from isolation to belonging, from addiction and emotionally illiterate to living in freedom, and from single to husband and father.

While Kevin's redemption story is powerful, it poses a real question: Why did it take Kevin thirty-seven years—three decades and more—to truly begin living?

The answer: Kevin had been at war all along. A battle raging in his mind, unseen and unrecognized. A battle he was losing. This week, we are going to dive deeper into the battlefield of the mind. We will discuss why many people feel stuck, just like Kevin. Our weekly combat challenge is to start identifying our B.L.A.S.T.E.D. emotions, a tool we will learn more of in day 1. Identifying emotions is hard to do because addiction—especially to porn—is often about avoiding pain. We don't feel our emotions because we have trained ourselves to escape them, and over time, our emotional radar goes offline.

This week, there is no more numbing; we are facing and fighting. This battle will challenge us in ways we have avoided for years, sometimes decades. Continue to practice our last two combat challenges by staying in the word and maintaining healthy guardrails because they will keep us grounded as we look inward and identify painful emotions we have destructively navigated away from over the years.

It's time to name the pain and break the chain. Keep on fighting!

DAY 1

EMOTIONAL AWARENESS: FEEL TO HEAL

Have you ever noticed how easy it is to name the emotions you feel *after* you use porn—shame, regret, guilt—but how hard it is to identify the ones that push you *toward* it? That's no accident.

Porn doesn't solve the problem; it silences the pain. It numbs the negative emotions we do not want to feel, offering a temporary escape instead of a true solution. But it's a false fix. So often, we are torn between thoughts of faith and thoughts of fear. Faith tells us we can bring our painful emotions and feelings to him and face it together. Fear tells us we are better off avoiding unwanted emotions through self-medication and compulsive behavior.

The mind becomes the battlefield, and most of life's battles are won or lost right there.

God invites us into healing, but healing requires honesty. We cannot receive freedom from what we refuse to face. We must have faith that God is bigger than our emotions and learn to identify them. Being emotionally aware is not weakness; it is the starting point of spiritual restoration. In Fight Club, we practice the ABC's of emotional awareness—acknowledge, break down, cast your cares—because emotions demand to be felt. God designed them that way.

The wisdom of the prudent is to give thought to their ways,
but the folly of fools is deception.

—Proverbs 14:8

Acknowledging our emotions is important for the porn and sex addict because it is the first step in processing them instead of being controlled by them. Fight Club utilizes the acronym B.L.A.S.T.E.D. Our weekly combat challenge is to use this tool as we learn to identify our emotions, especially the ones preceding temptation.

B—*Boredom* can feel unbearable, and addicts tend to run from anything that feels like pain. We crave stimulation, something to fill the silence. When boredom sets in, it often becomes a trigger, making us more vulnerable to the pull of porn or other sexual escapes.

L—*Lonely* is a fitting emotion for sex addicts because instead of bonding with others, we seek out false intimacy—temporary escapes that only deepen the isolation we are trying to escape.

A—*Anxiety* and *anger* both can serve as powerful emotions that lead to porn use and unwanted sexual behavior.

S—*Stress* and *sadness* are emotions that can become overwhelming, leading to sexual behavior as a way to escape or numb the pain. Instead of processing what's really going on, we seek relief in a moment of false comfort.

T—*Tired* is an emotion fueled by an empty gas tank where we no longer have capacity. Exhaustion is dangerous for the addict because our brains need rest.

E—*Empty* is the name we give to an emotion we cannot identify, a spiritual or physiological feeling we default to when we know something is wrong—but we can't quite put it into words. We seek wholeness in places that can never truly deliver, a pursuit that always overpromises and underdelivers.

D—*Disconnected* and *depressed* are emotions that often work in tandem. We must recognize there are different forms of disconnection: relational, emotional, and spiritual. Disconnection can lead to depression, which leads to greater disconnection and greater depression.

Let us examine our ways and test them, and let us return to the Lord.

—Lamentations 3:40

Breaking down the source of our B.L.A.S.T.E.D. emotions is what we do once they are acknowledged because they may point to something deeper beneath the surface, rooted in unresolved shame, insecurity, past trauma, and spiritual brokenness. The word *examine* in Lam 3:40 comes from the Hebrew word *chaphas*, suggesting a serious and careful examination of our ways. We must move beyond the superficial acknowledgement of painful emotions and break down the motives behind them. Our B.L.A.S.T.E.D. emotions may bring forth pain as we determine and confront the cause instead of covering up the symptoms through self-medication.

When we break down the source, we will not miss the opportunity for true healing that comes from returning to the Lord. We must avoid relying on our own coping mechanisms and place our trust in God—the only One who can heal us at the root.

Fight Club: Live in Freedom

Cast your cares on the Lord and he will sustain you;
he will never let the righteous be shaken.

—Psalms 55:22

Casting your cares is not passive. The literal translation in Hebrew implies the forceful and physical action of releasing something. Emotions are not meant to be ignored or buried. But while emotions are a gift, not every emotion is meant to stay. Some emotions need to be acknowledged, processed, and then cast off so they no longer take up permanent roots. If we intend to live differently, we must examine our hearts and uncover the emotions that influence our decisions. Practice your ABCs and identify those B.L.A.S.T.E.D. emotions this week.

DAILY FIGHT PLAN

1. Why do you think it is so difficult to identify your emotions prior to temptation, yet so easy to recognize after giving in to sin?
2. Are there any B.L.A.S.T.E.D. emotions you can already identify as common to you and what are they?
3. Are you worried about what you might reveal as you unpack your emotions and identify the root of them?
4. What do you believe casting out negative emotions will look like in your life?

DAY 2

WHEN OUR MINDS DON'T MIND

No one sets out to derail their life. No one plans to become an addict. No one dreams of making foolish, selfish, or destructive choices that inescapably sets one up for a less than desirable trajectory in life. But the truth is, few people make the intentional decision to prepare themselves *not* to. For the next three weeks, we will take a closer look at key battlegrounds—mind, body, and soul—upon which our war of addiction is waged.

Gabe could not understand why he continued to actively engage in viewing porn despite how much he hated the way it made him feel. He would tell himself that this time would be the last time, only to find his addiction pulling him back time and time again. Gabe was determined to avoid porn, yet he found that even in the midst of prayer, reading his Bible, or distracting himself with an extensive list of other activities, he could transition to viewing porn in an instant.

Gabe was experiencing a battlefield of the mind he was not prepared to confront. When it comes to porn, the real fight is not just against the content—it's against the way our brains are wired to cope. If we continue using porn despite the damage it causes, we have to ask, what immediate need or emotional relief is it meeting? Until we understand that, we cannot begin to break the cycle.

Addiction rarely happens by accident. While porn and toxic sexual behavior are addictive, there are usually deeper roots at play. Unresolved emotional pain, past trauma, or mental health struggles often fuel the compulsive cycle. In other words, addiction is like a vehicle—the body supplies the horsepower, but the mind steers the direction—and we cannot move forward if our minds are stuck in reverse.

If our battles are first won or lost in the mind, we must explore what that looks like.

We demolish arguments and every pretension that sets itself up against the knowledge of God, and we take captive every thought to make it obedient to Christ.

—2 Corinthians 10:5

Porn stands as a direct argument against God and his authority—especially his authority over our lives—because it invites us to reject his design, reducing others to objects for personal consumption. It distorts the meaning of sexuality, twisting something sacred into something selfish. The word *captive* comes from the Greek *aichmalōtizō*, meaning to control, to conquer, or to bring into submission. This is not passive. We take action. We take thoughts captive. We make them submit.

Taking our thoughts captive means choosing to invite God into the very places where we struggle the most. It is not about avoiding our battles—it's about facing them with him. God isn't distant from our sexual struggles; he wants us to draw near to him in the midst of them. That is where the healing begins in the battleground of the mind, but it does not end there.

Every thought. Every time. Make them obedient to Christ.

The word *obedient* in 2 Cor 10:5 comes from the Greek word *hupakoē*, which means to bring under control or into alignment. Just like a car, everything may look fine on the outside—the paint is shiny and the engine runs—but if the wheels are out of alignment, that car will drift off course despite the driver's best intentions. A bad alignment means a constant and tiresome fight to keep control, and over time, that misalignment causes real damage—to the tires, the steering, even the frame. At its core, porn promotes a version of humanity that is completely out of alignment with God's vision for dignity, relationship, and wholeness. This is the call: We don't let our thoughts run wild—we make them obedient under Christ's rule.

But how do we make thoughts obedient when our minds don't mind? We want to obey, but our minds rebel. We want to focus, but our minds drift. We want to pray, but our minds wander. Our minds seem to have a mind of their own.

For I do not do the good I want to do, but the evil I do not want to do—this I keep on doing.

—Romans 7:19

It appears Paul's mind did not mind either. He is describing the same battle that Gabe and everyone else faces. Here's the truth: If we want lasting transformation, it has to start here. We must learn how to take every thought captive. It starts with recognizing our need to invite God into areas we avoid with porn. When thoughts and emotions come, do not hide—bring them straight into God's presence.

Don't run. Don't shrink back in shame.

Instead, be honest. Identify the temptation and acknowledge the emotions you are feeling. Tell Jesus exactly where you are struggling. He's not far off—he's your present help in the midst of it. Ask him for his perspective. Ask him to show you what is beneath the surface of the temptation.

DAILY FIGHT PLAN

1. Can you relate with Gabe's story and why or why not?
2. In what ways have you seen your addiction as a battle of the mind?
3. Which do you find more challenging, taking thoughts captive or making them obedient to Christ?
4. *For I do not do the good I want to do, but the evil I do not want to do—this I keep on doing.* —ROMANS 7:19

   Where have you experienced the inner conflict Paul describes—doing what you don't want to do—and how has that shown up in your life?

DAY 3

REWIRED AND BOUND

It's been said that the mind is the devil's playground—and for good reason. It's where battles are waged, lies are planted, and temptations take root. While we cannot ignore the spiritual aspect of addiction, we must recognize that the body's response to porn is orchestrated by its most intricate organ, the brain. Whether through fantasy, sexual activity, explicit content, or masturbation, the brain floods the system with a powerful mix of chemicals designed to produce excitement, pleasure, and short-lived satisfaction.

God wired us to experience pleasure, and dopamine plays a central role in that.

Within our brains is a place reliant on dopamine receptors, known as the *reward pathway*. If the body is hungry, the brain recalls—often in vivid detail—where food was found before. Dopamine, a powerful chemical known as the brain's *reward signal*, is released when we take risks, do new things, or experience excitement. It creates a sense of achievement and pleasure, reinforcing the behavior and urging us to repeat it.

In a healthy, well-functioning brain, these receptors receive and process dopamine at a normal, balanced rate. Unfortunately, what God created for good has been abused with porn, leading many to refer to porn as the new drug.[1] Over time, the brain begins to crave neither intimacy or connection as pornography hijacks our neurological system, flooding the brain with unnaturally high and prolonged dopamine surges that exceed even natural sexual experiences.

To put this in perspective, eating raises dopamine to about 150 percent of baseline, nicotine to 200 percent, and sexual activity to roughly 250 percent.[2] Pornography surpasses even that threshold, driving dopamine well beyond 250 percent and sustaining those levels for hours through endless novelty and stimulation. Another study reveals that drugs like cocaine and amphetamines may create sharper spikes, but they fade more quickly, revealing two alarming truths.[3]

First, three man-made substances—meth, cocaine, and porn—are estimated to trigger higher dopamine releases than sex. Second, and even more concerning, is that porn produces a more prolonged dopamine

1. Fight the New Drug, "'Fight the New Drug' Billboards," para. 5–9.
2. Buchwald, "Hidden Cost of Pornography," para. 14–16.
3. Freedom Fight, "Porn Addiction Research and Data," fig. 1.

release than any of the other natural or artificial stimulants. Not even sex, as God designed it, can match the dopamine surge generated by the endless buffet of pornographic content. With limitless access and variety, it's as simple as choosing your "flavor" of the day—and just like that, you're off again, chasing the next high.

Porn is not exclusive—it cuts across every age, background, and demographic—and the riskier the behavior, the more dopamine the brain produces. This is why sex addicts often escalate to more dangerous or taboo forms of sexual expression. This addictive behavior has a profound effect on the brain's prefrontal cortex—the area responsible for willpower, self-control, and making wise moral decisions. Under normal conditions, the prefrontal cortex steps in with executive control, helping us think clearly and act wisely.[4] The prefrontal cortex is essentially our *mom brain*, contributing to our capacity for morality, willpower, long-term planning, and impulse control.

When our *mom brain* is silenced, we do not make good decisions.

With repeated exposure to porn, dopamine receptors begin to deteriorate, and the prefrontal cortex weakens.[5] As this critical region loses strength, willpower fades. The brain's ability to regulate cravings diminishes, and what once felt like a desire now feels like an overpowering need.

MRI scans now reveal the physical changes in a brain addicted to porn compared to a healthy one. Remarkably, the brain of a porn addict closely resembles that of a heroin addict.[6] Why? Because the brain does not differentiate between sources of pleasure—it processes them the same way. In the case of sexual addiction, the brain becomes addicted to its own chemical highs, repeatedly flooding itself with dopamine until it loses the ability to regulate impulses, eroding the prefrontal cortex.

Do not conform to the pattern of this world, but be transformed by the renewing of your mind. Then you will be able to test and approve what God's will is—his good, pleasing and perfect will.

—Romans 12:2

There is hope. God has provided within the addicted mind the ability for neuroplasticity, the rewiring of our brains to reshape and reorganize

4. Gilkerson, "Your Brain on Porn," 7.
5. Gilkerson, "Your Brain on Porn," 7–8.
6. Blakeman, "Your Brain on Porn," fig. 1.

neural pathways as we become more Christlike.[7] As we recover from porn addiction, the brain may remain highly sensitive to triggers associated with past porn use, possibly even permanently.

At first, choosing a healthier alternative to porn may feel like a battle of willpower. But the more we intentionally shift, being transformed, the easier it becomes. Each conscious decision helps rewire our brains. With every repetition, the new neural pathway grows stronger, while the old, automatic response to cravings weakens. This is how real change takes root—one decision, one redirection at a time.

DAILY FIGHT PLAN

1. How does knowing the strong chemical component of porn addiction change the way you view your own behavior or recovery?
2. In what ways have you experienced your judgment, self-control, or focus being compromised when addiction diminishes your prefrontal cortex?
3. *Do not conform to the pattern of this world, but be transformed by the renewing of your mind. Then you will be able to test and approve what God's will is—his good, pleasing and perfect will.* —Romans 12:2

   In what ways does Rom 12:2 offer hope?

7. Your Brain On Porn, "Unwiring and Rewiring Your Brain," para. 1–4.

DAY 4

LOVING THE ILLUSION: THE OXYTOCIN EFFECT

Mose discovered porn during middle school while spending the night at a friend's home. As they stayed up late into the night, Mose and his friend came across a satellite channel that showed softcore pornography. From that moment on, Mose was hooked on the way porn made him feel. He longed for it from the moment he woke every morning, consuming his thoughts throughout the day. He constantly gave time and attention to porn, holding a strong desire and curiosity to know it more. Throughout Mose's teenage years, he prioritized and cherished his addiction, all the while deceiving others in an effort to protect and preserve his love for pornography.

Dopamine may be the reward signal in the brain that keeps us coming back for more in our addiction cycle, but oxytocin seals us to real people through touch, trust, and intimacy. God designed oxytocin with a purpose, often referred to as the *love hormone*, allowing us to bond when it is released.[8] When porn enters the picture, that glue sticks us to pixels instead of people, forming attachments and bonds where there are no real relationships. It is released during childbirth, breastfeeding, and skin-to-skin contact, creating a sense of calm, love, and deep connection between a parent and their child.[9] Likewise, researchers have found that couples in the early stages of romantic attachment have significantly higher levels of oxytocin and that it is also released during sexual activity, intensifying orgasms and strengthening emotional bonds through physical intimacy.[10]

Oxytocin does not distinguish between real people and artificial sources of stimulation.

When we repeatedly use porn, especially during sexual arousal and orgasm, oxytocin is still released. Our brains interpret porn as a relational experience, even though it is not. Over time, the brain begins to associate feelings of comfort, satisfaction, and emotional closeness not with a person, but with porn and sexual fantasy.

This is how we become bonded to pixels instead of people. The same chemical that God designed to deepen connection with a spouse creates false intimacy with images. The bond intensifies through repetition, making

8. Sekulić, "Neuroendocrinology of Romantic Love," 7.
9. Scatliffe et al., "Oxytocin and Early Parent-Infant," 445–53.
10. Santos-Longhurst, "Why Is Oxytocin Known," para. 1–2.

it more challenging to connect emotionally and sexually with a real partner, because the brain has already formed a chemical attachment elsewhere.

Since 1890, the US Census has tracked the age of marriage. Men and women today are waiting longer to get married. In 2024, the average age for a first marriage was 30.2 for men and 28.6 for women.[11] Today, men aged 25 to 34 are more than six times as likely to have never been married compared to 1970.[12] The increased ease in which we can access porn is a contributing factor underlying the rapidly growing decline in the desire to marry.[13] Research also shows that millennials and Gen Z are having less sex than previous generations, with the decline most pronounced among younger individuals—many of whom report never having had partnered sex.[14] Porn, though an imperfect substitute for intimacy, serves a purpose without relational effort.

Freedom from addiction requires us to reconcile our love of porn.

Jesus replied: "'Love the Lord your God with all your heart and with all your soul and with all your mind.' This is the first and greatest commandment. And the second is like it: 'Love your neighbor as yourself.'"

—Matthew 22:37

To love God without loving others is a dead faith. To love others without loving God is no faith.

We must learn to fully love because this is where we find our ultimate satisfaction and purpose in life. Three key words—heart, soul, and mind—provide depth in what love truly looks like. The Greek word for *heart* is *kardia*, referring to our emotions, passions, and thoughts. Our love for God demands a willingness to prioritize our moral character through the way we live our life. The Greek word *soul* is *psuchē*, referring to the part of us connected to God because he formed us. Loving with all our soul puts an emphasis on demonstrating through the totality of our being, including our emotions, desires, and inner self. Lastly, the Greek word for *mind* is *dianoia*, meaning the intellect of our mind. What we choose to believe is pivotal in our ability to love as God calls us to.

11. USAFacts, "How Does Marriage Vary," para. 6.
12. Wang and Parker, "Trends in the Share," para. 1–13.
13. Malcolm and Naufal, "Are Pornography and Marriage Substitutes," 1–40.
14. Klein, "Are Gen Z More Pragmatic," para. 3–5.

Fortunately, Jesus already demonstrated what love looks like on a grand scale when he died on the cross, carrying our punishment and curse. Jesus' willingness to offer himself up despite the overwhelmingly undeserved punishment showed love to God the Father through sacrificial obedience while also demonstrating sacrificial love for us.

We love because he first loved us.

—1 JOHN 4:19

It is God himself that enables us to love him more. Our ability to choose love amidst the battlefield of the mind is because he first loved us. When we encounter God's love for us, we respond with all our heart, our soul, and our mind. Only then can we see the bond we have made with porn and sexual addiction for what it truly is, an abomination.

It's time to stop bonding with the world and run back to our first love—God.

DAILY FIGHT PLAN

1. In what concrete ways has your love for pornography outranked your devotion to your responsibilities, relationships, and calling? Describe exactly how this has shown up in your life.
2. *But each person is tempted when they are dragged away by their own evil desire and enticed.* —JAMES 1:14

   In what ways can you see the love of sin demonstrated in this verse?
3. Enter into honest conversation with God. Write a prayer that confesses where lust has claimed your heart and ask him to tear down its grip and reclaim your love for himself.

DAY 5

THE WALKING DEAD

Angela was depressed. She could not remember what it felt like to authentically feel joy. Since the age of ten, porn had been a part of Angela's story. Her parents had gone through a difficult divorce earlier that year and Angela felt forgotten through it all. She said goodbye to her friends, moved into an apartment, and started attending a new church. When Angela discovered pornography, she initially did not like the way it made her feel, but it did serve as a distraction from circumstances and painful emotions.

The more she engaged with pornography, the less awkward the behavior felt. While Angela had found a method for dulling herself from painful childhood memories, she was dodging discomfort only to land in numbness.

The following two decades were filled with broken relationships, sexual promiscuity, and an ongoing consumption of pornography. Angela felt empty, lonely, and incapable of identifying her feelings or a source of joy. She found herself going through the motions of life, yet numb to experiences life offers. Angela felt empty, and that was worse than pain. Breathing, but barely being.

Angela was experiencing what we in Fight Club call *zombie brain*, the long term effects of porn consumption within the battlefield of the mind. It was not until she learned to trust God in the battlefield of her mind, where open wounds needed healing, that she began to find freedom from her addictive behavior.

Porn addiction rewires the brain's reward system, dulling our ability to experience real pleasure and joy. Over time, our brains become overstimulated by artificial, high-intensity sexual content, releasing floods of the feel-good chemical dopamine. Our brains are not meant to constantly handle that kind of overload. Consequently, our brains begin producing less dopamine and become less sensitive to it. Eventually, widespread porn use negatively impacts the consumer's well-being, including joy, as it diminishes our capacity for experiencing pleasure in real-life relationships and genuine connection.[15]

This makes everyday joys—like spiritual connection with God, relationships, nature, and creativity—feel flat, boring, or unfulfilling.[16] The

15. Paul, *Pornified*, 138–71.

16. Miller, "Effects of Pornography Use," no. 9.

addict becomes stuck in a cycle of chasing a high that gets weaker with each use while real life experience increasingly feels emptier. It's not just a loss of control; it's a loss of capacity to feel.

Joy won't vanish all at once—it just fades, dulled by the thing we turned to for pleasure.

So I tell you this, and insist on it in the Lord, that you must no longer live as the Gentiles do, in the futility of their thinking. They are darkened in their understanding and separated from the life of God because of the ignorance that is in them due to the hardening of their hearts. Having lost all sensitivity, they have given themselves over to sensuality so as to indulge in every kind of impurity, and they are full of greed.

—EPHESIANS 4:17–19

Paul warns in Ephesians against becoming calloused to feelings and emotions, leading to an apathy and indifference towards sin and God. This emotional detachment hinders our spiritual growth and disconnects us from God's presence. The danger with not feeling emotion is that we stop living with a purpose. We may still function—talk, eat, sleep, work—but it becomes mechanical as the zombie brain takes hold. Over time, our unprocessed pain and emotions will build up like a sealed pressure cooker. For us to move beyond the milling about of our dulled minds through addictive behavior, we must trust that God is bigger than our B.L.A.S.T.E.D. emotions.

That is called faith.

Faith and emotion were never meant to be strangers. They are interconnected, shaping the way we pursue Jesus and find healing from addiction. When we ignore our B.L.A.S.T.E.D. emotions, we are not just suppressing feelings; we are shutting down the very space where God wants to reveal himself and bring joy back into our lives as our Comforter, Redeemer, Healer, and Advocate.

God is big enough to navigate the trenches within the battlefield of our minds.

If we continue to avoid emotions, we are at risk of never reconciling the very triggers that keep us in chains—or even worse, becoming numb to emotions altogether. So, how do we live in the middle of that struggle? We must make room for God and invite him into our feelings. We stop pushing emotions aside and start asking Jesus what he wants to reveal through them, because he cares deeply about our wounds, whether they scream or whisper.

Emotions do not define our faith, and they certainly do not decide our destiny. But when we engage them with honesty and surrender, they can lead us into deeper intimacy with God—where he strengthens us, draws close, and carries us through. Over the last three weeks, we have been challenged to spend time reading the Bible daily, set up guardrails, and identify our B.L.A.S.T.E.D. emotions.

Recovery is not about perfection, it's about persistence—so keep showing up and keep on fighting.

DAILY FIGHT PLAN

1. How have you withdrawn from others or experiences due to the negative impact of porn?
2. What would it look like for you to demonstrate trusting God with your emotions?
3. What have you observed this week as you practiced identifying your B.L.A.S.T.E.D. emotions? Are you noticing any commonalities or patterns with your emotions?
4. Thank God for the promise of victory in the battlefield of the mind and ask him to extend grace as you grow, heal, and become further equipped during the remainder of your Fight Club journey.

WEEK 4—HIJACKED HARDWARE: A BODY'S BETRAYAL

WEEKLY MEMORY VERSE

Flee from sexual immorality. All other sins a person commits are outside the body, but whoever sins sexually, sins against their own body.

—1 Corinthians 6:18

WEEKLY COMBAT CHALLENGE

Is God enough?

THE BODY'S TORMENT

ADDICTION'S WEAR AND TEAR

Infidelity and the objectification of women was present in and around Michael's life from a very early age. The adults around him modeled promiscuous, sexualized behavior, making sin seem normal and fueling his curiosity. It wasn't long before every lustful question in his mind found an answer. When Michael was eight years old, riding his bike through the woods with friends, he stumbled across a dirty magazine near an old hobo camp. Despite the rough surroundings, he felt as though he had struck gold. And, of course, it wasn't just any magazine—it was *Hustler*, leaving nothing to the imagination. From that day forward, Michael was hooked. Every late night became a mission—from squinting at the scrambled adult channel and hoping for a freeze-frame to digging through his dad's drawers in search of hidden VHS tapes and magazines.

Michael's journey into porn addiction continued to grow rapidly through pubescence, fueled by the internet and mobile phones. As the content Michael viewed grew increasingly more graphic, his view of women shifted from seeing them as people to treating them as objects of desire. That mindset seeped into his relationships, creating unrealistic expectations. He believed every woman should act like a porn star or at least be as eager.

At the peak of his sexual depravity, Michael was no longer aroused by a real woman's body. Instead, he would slip into the bathroom with his phone to meet his sexual needs. His longing for genuine connection had withered into disappointment and his body no longer responded the same, leaving him to wonder if low testosterone or erectile dysfunction were to blame.

Then God intervened. A friend at the church Michael attended invited him to join Fight Club, a ministry his friend had used to find freedom. Michael's initial response was to laugh it off and hide the truth, but then he was asked a question he was unable to reconcile. If he was not addicted to pornography, why couldn't he give it up? This question troubled Michael because he had marriage on the horizon and his body still desired porn.

Longing to start his marriage in a healthy way, no longer chained to lust, Michael took a hesitant but hopeful step into Fight Club.

Fight Club helped Michael to realize just how far sexual sin had taken him. It brought not only a biblical approach, which some addiction classes relating to recovery are based on, but also a scientific approach. Michael began to correlate erectile dysfunction (ED) with porn addiction. Once he had some time in sobriety, subsequently, the ED became a nonissue in his marriage.

Michael went all in—months without a single glance at porn—convincing himself it was over. Then, out of nowhere, he was right back at it, phone in hand. It was not because he wanted to. It happened because this is what real addiction does to the body.

Michael knew the pattern well. He had wrestled with multiple addictions in his life, including nearly two decades of alcohol abuse. Today, he serves as a chairperson for a local Alcoholics Anonymous chapter, yet, in his experience, porn has been harder to escape than alcohol—because it's everywhere.

It hides in plain sight: on phones, computers, TV shows, movies, even commercials. There's no need to hunt for a dealer or drive to a store—it's thrown at us from every direction. Even now, the algorithms on his phone and computer keep trying to lure him back, tempting him through social media's endless stream of suggestive bait.

Because of your wrath there is no health in my body;
there is no soundness in my bones because of my sin.

—Psalm 38:3

This verse reveals the author's deep physical and spiritual distress, linking a lack of health and weakness in his bones to God's anger and his own sin. It underscores how sin erodes both body and soul. In the same way, addiction to porn can bring devastating effects on our physical well-being, mirroring the toll described in the passage.

Last week, we explored how porn wages war within the battlefield of our minds. This week, we turn our attention to the body and how sexual addiction takes its toll. Porn affects physical well-being in multiple ways that include disrupting sexual desire, distorting body image, and undermining overall health. Likewise, breaking free from porn, much like withdrawing from other illicit drugs, takes a physical toll on the body.

Over the last three weeks, our combat challenges have included actively spending time in God's word daily, setting up guardrails in our lives, and identifying our B.L.A.S.T.E.D. emotions. Chapter 4's weekly combat challenge is to bridge the gap between belief and trust. Finding freedom within the battlefield of the body will force us to reconcile the most important question. Is God enough? Because if he is not enough, the battle is already lost.

DAY 1

TEMPLE IN RUIN

For Christians, the temple theme is a recurring concept. The Hebrew word *temple* can literally be translated as *the holy house*. If we define a temple as a place where God's presence meets humanity, then the garden of Eden was the first true temple. The garden was where God walked in relationship with Adam and Eve; however, when they disobeyed—eating from the tree of the knowledge of good and evil—that intimate fellowship bond was broken and our direct experience with God's presence was cut off. Sin severed our relationship with God, but he still longed to walk and commune with us.

In his grace, God reestablished his presence among humanity.

Exodus 27 describes the second temple imagery, a beautifully crafted portable tent known as the *tabernacle*, which, in Hebrew, means *dwelling place*. God's presence dwelled within the tabernacle, a place divided into two sections. The Holy Place was a long front room, and the Most Holy Place was a perfect cube where God's presence uniquely dwelled.

Why did the God who spoke the universe into being choose to dwell in a tent made by human hands? The answer: love. Sin may have disrupted our ability to commune with God, but he was still offering a tangible symbol of his presence among the Israelites. His love for us and his longing for relationship exceeded the separation sin created. The tabernacle served as a holy house, a place to approach and meet with God.

When Israel finally settled in the land of Canaan, God's dwelling place took on a more permanent form in Jerusalem. Described in 1 Kgs 6–7, the temple in Jerusalem still had a Holy Place and a Most Holy Place like the tabernacle, but it was twice the size and far more elaborate. The temple served as the spiritual, social, and political heart of Israel. While the temple in Jerusalem, built by King Solomon, was destroyed by the Babylonians in 586 BC, it had been rebuilt by the time Jesus entered the scene.

The Word became flesh and made his dwelling among us. We have seen his glory, the glory of the one and only Son, who came from the Father, full of grace and truth.

—John 1:14

God's desire to dwell among Israel in both the portable tabernacle and then the temple foreshadowed the complete reunion God intended through Jesus' willingness to take on flesh and live among humanity. More literally, John 1:14 is saying Jesus "pitched his tent" or "tabernacle" among us. In other words, Jesus himself is the true temple—the very presence of God—not merely meeting humanity, but becoming human.

As Jesus was leaving the temple, one of his disciples said to him, "Look, Teacher! What massive stones! What magnificent buildings!" "Do you see all these great buildings?" replied Jesus. "Not one stone here will be left on another; every one will be thrown down."

—Mark 13:1–2

Jesus was not speaking literally about tearing down the temple. He was speaking about his own death and resurrection. He was declaring that he is the true temple. Colossians 2:9 describes Jesus as a place where God's presence dwells in fullness. While the Second Temple in Jerusalem was eventually destroyed in AD 70, it is not a tragedy to grieve. It marked the fulfillment of prophecy.

With Jesus, the focus shifted from a physical temple to a living temple. Like the temple, Jesus was destroyed. He was wrongfully condemned for a crime never committed. He faced destruction at the hand of his Father, bearing the wrath intended for us because of our sin. In our place, Jesus endured the judgment we deserve.

Death was not Jesus' finish line; it was the starting line for eternal victory.

Jesus defeated death. With Jesus' death and resurrection, the temple and the entire system was rendered obsolete. God's Spirit no longer dwelt *with* his people; it dwelt *within* his people. Through Jesus' death and resurrection, a new covenant was ushered in, tearing down the dividing curtain between God and man and expanding the temple far beyond a single building.

Don't you know that you yourselves are God's temple and that God's Spirit dwells in your midst? If anyone destroys God's temple, God will destroy that person; for God's temple is sacred, and you together are that temple.

—1 Corinthians 3:16–17

Jesus was a temple in ruin as he suffered on a cross, but after his ascension, we received the Holy Spirit to dwell not only with God's people but within God's people. God's people are now his temple, carrying his presence at all times and in every place. We will look closely this week at the impact of addictive behavior in our bodies. We will also be challenged to take inventory as we reconcile the way we have mistreated God's temple.

You may feel like a temple in ruin, but God is the Master Builder and he holds the blueprint for restoration. The reason is simple, God is enough.

DAILY FIGHT PLAN

1. What thoughts and emotions surface when you consider that God actively wants a personal relationship with you?
2. Where does God dwell now?
3. *Do you not know that your bodies are temples of the Holy Spirit, who is in you, whom you have received from God? You are not your own; you were bought at a price. Therefore honor God with your bodies.*
   —1 CORINTHIANS 6:19–20

   If you are a Christian, your body is the temple. How are your daily choices either honoring God—or dishonoring him—with your body?

DAY 2

BATTLE BENEATH THE SKIN

For the first time in his twenty-eight years, Clark woke up two weeks sober from porn and self-pleasure. What should have been a milestone quickly soured as the day unfolded. Irritability set in, and small frustrations of little significance sparked oversized reactions. By afternoon, his temper boiled over. In a surge of rage, Clark's anger led him to shout at his child, hurling a chair across the room.

The terror on his daughter's face stopped him cold. At that moment, Clark recognized this was not the man he wanted to be. Years of addiction had dulled Clark's emotions, numbing him into believing detachment was normal. But nothing about addiction is normal, and now he was colliding head-on with the raw turbulence of withdrawal.

Clark retreated to his bedroom, leaving behind his crying child at the kitchen table. Shaken and trembling, he sank to the floor, anxiety crashing over him in waves. He didn't know where the fury had come from, only that it terrified him. What Clark was experiencing was withdrawal, capable of unraveling a morning full of optimism into an afternoon of unbearable rage.

Withdrawal is proof that porn takes more than we give, dragging us places we never intended to travel.

You were taught, with regard to your former way of life, to put off your old self, which is being corrupted by its deceitful desires; to be made new in the attitude of your minds; and to put on the new self, created to be like God in true righteousness and holiness.

—Ephesians 4:22–24

Overcoming porn addiction comes with growing pains. The withdrawal symptoms we experience in the body mirror those seen in other substance addictions because the brain's reward system is involved in both. When we eliminate porn after prolonged and frequent consumption, a combination of psychological, emotional, and physical symptoms are expected.

Data from over 31,000 participants analyzed from fourteen different case studies revealed that mental, sexual, and physical withdrawal-like traits were evident in 72 percent of recovering porn addicts.[1] Today, we will unpack the most common withdrawal symptoms as we continue to reconcile if God is enough.

These are psychological and emotional symptoms we D.E.A.L. with:

- *Depression*—an emotional condition characterized by feelings ranging from discontent and unhappiness to intense sadness and hopelessness, which can disrupt everyday life.[2] In a cruel irony, using porn to cope with depression has a paradoxical effect, increasing the negative emotions users want to escape.[3]
- *Emotional Instability*—a tendency to exhibit unpredictable and rapid changes in emotions.[4] The mood swings experienced often shift from one feeling to the other without clear triggers because our brain's reward system is recalibrating. A low tolerance for stress and frustration heightens our inability to moderate mood.
- *Anxiety*—an emotion marked by feelings of apprehension and physical signs of tension.[5] Studies reveal that there is a significant relationship between porn addiction and elevated anxiety levels.[6] Likewise, social anxiety can intensify during withdrawal as we shift from consuming porn for comfort to seeking happiness and emotional fulfillment through real-life relationships.[7]
- *Loneliness*—while porn offers temporary relief from loneliness, it is quickly followed by a renewed emptiness, creating a self-perpetuating loop: the more we use porn to cope with loneliness, the lonelier we feel afterward, and the stronger the urge becomes to return to it. Studies suggest loneliness is magnified even more when porn consumers are already in a relationship.[8]

The following are physical symptoms our bodies S.H.A.R.E.:

1. Roza et al., "Withdrawal-Like Symptoms," 19–27.
2. American Psychological Association, "Depression," para. 1.
3. Ince et al., "Clarifying and Extending Our Understanding," 1–12.
4. American Psychological Association, "Emotional Instability," para. 1.
5. American Psychological Association, "Anxiety," para. 1.
6.. Karim et al., "Effects of Porn Addiction," 1–13.
7. Ince et al., "Clarifying and Extending Our Understanding," 1–12.
8. Lubag, "Loneliness Plays a Key Role," para. 8.

- *Sleep Fatigue*—difficulty falling asleep or intense sexual dreams, followed by persistent fatigue, regardless of sleep duration, are common porn withdrawal symptoms.[9] Insomnia is also linked to withdrawal from porn addiction.[10] The danger with sleep fatigue is that being well-rested is crucial for us to overcome addiction because sleep affects nearly every system involved in recovery.
- *Headaches*—porn use elevates dopamine, producing feelings of reward. When we stop, our brains experience a short-term chemical imbalance, triggering headaches.[11] Such responses are expected, mainly due to stress and hormonal shifts during your brain's neurochemical changes.
- *Appetite Changes*—during withdrawal, we might find ourselves eating more to cope—or not feeling like eating at all.[12] Either way, it can lead to weight changes and leave us feeling physically off balance..
- *Restlessness*—as our brains and body adjust to the absence of porn, it is common to experience agitation.[13] Mannerisms of restlessness may include fidgeting, pacing, muscle tension, inability to relax, or feelings of uneasiness.
- *Erectile Dysfunction*—a temporary dip in libido can impact our ability to achieve or maintain erections.[14] This will be discussed in detail on day 3 this week.

DAILY FIGHT PLAN

1. What troubled you the most about Clark's story?
2. Can you identify any psychological or emotional withdrawal symptoms that you *D.E.A.L.* with and what are they?
3. What physical withdrawal symptoms does your body *S.H.A.R.E.*?

9. Miller, "Porn Withdrawal Symptoms," bulleted list 1–8.
10. Noel, "Insomnia and Pornography Addiction."
11. McKenna, "10 Symptoms of Porn Addiction," para. 6.
12. Hoerr, "Porn Withdrawal Symptoms," fig. 1.
13. Abubakar, *How to Overcome Porn*, 34.
14. Wilson, *Your Brain on Porn*, 18–20.

DAY 3

WHEN FANTASY MAKES REALITY BORING

In one of his most famous experiments, Nobel Prize–winning scientist Nikolaas Tinbergen made cardboard butterflies with wings so bright, so extravagant, they outshone any butterfly God had ever created.[15] When he placed these artificial females beside real ones, the male butterflies ignored the living, breathing creatures entirely. They swarmed the cardboard fakes until the cutouts disappeared under the crush of attention. Only when the counterfeits were fully hidden did the males finally turn to the "plain," real females waiting nearby.

Tinbergen later surmised the behavior between animals and humans is comparable in nature.[16]

It's not hard to see the parallel. We live in a world where supernormal erotic stimuli—hyper-edited, hyper-posed, hyper-everything—are only a swipe away. Tinbergen's experiment proved something profound: our bodies can be seduced more powerfully by a counterfeit than by the real thing. Pornography is built on the same principle. Like the deluded butterflies, men and women alike flock to hyper-sexualized, digitally enhanced, endlessly available fakes. And the fake has an edge because it never says no, never grows tired, and never asks for patience or commitment. Day after day, porn will indulge whatever fantasy we desire.

But here is a brutal truth, there is nothing of lasting value that comes from pursuing an illusion. The drive God gave for connection is hijacked, drained, and wasted. While we chase the cheap counterfeit, our focus, energy, and capacity for real intimacy withers away.

Therefore do not let sin reign in your mortal body
so that you obey its evil desires.

—Romans 6:12

Paul reminds us that allowing sinful desires to dominate us enslaves the body's responses. Traditionally, erectile dysfunction (ED) has been seen as an age-dependent problem; however, a report from Yale indicates that

15. Williams, "Life in a World," para. 1–3.

16. Smith, *Animals in Dutch Travel Writing*, 200.

about one in four men under forty now experience some level of ED.[17] One large pediatric urology practice has reported a thirty-one-fold increase in adolescent and young adults aged fourteen to twenty-one presenting with ED since 2014.[18] In 2016, *TIME* magazine exposed this growing phenomenon in adolescent ED for what it is, labeling it PIED, porn-induced erectile dysfunction.[19]

PIED hijacks our brains' pleasure circuits, leaving our bodies like a phone with no signal—built to connect, but unable to respond.

Porn delivers excessive stimuli with visuals, novelty, and intensity far beyond what is possible in real life. Each click or swipe offers a new partner, new scene, and new category—constantly spiking dopamine and motivating the brain through its addictive reward chemical. Over time, our brains start expecting that level of novelty and stimulation for arousal and nothing less will satisfy the body.[20] Frequency in our exposure to porn directly correlates with likelihood of being impacted by PIED.[21]

PIED leads to unrealistic expectations. What this means for the body is that erections become more difficult to achieve or maintain without using porn. As we consume porn portraying exaggerated sexual scenarios, the natural progression is dissatisfaction with typical sexual experiences, leading to performance anxiety and lowered self-esteem.[22] Anxiety about not getting an erection only makes the problem worse.[23] PIED reinforces its addictive trap by leaving us feeling vulnerable and insecure, desiring to retreat back into isolation of sexual fantasy and porn, where we feel safe and certain of our bodies' performance.

Lusting over the *body* in pixels warps not just our bedroom performance but the very lens through which we see every*body* around us. While PIED can significantly impact the male body, its trap leaves women lamenting that their figure cannot compete with what is online. Meanwhile, the imitation keeps feeding us the lie that it is better than reality. But it's not better. It's emptier. And every moment spent with the imitation is a moment stolen from the real thing.

17. Capogrosso et al., "One Patient Out of Four," 1833–41.
18. Pantazis et al., "Erectile Dysfunction in Adolescents."
19. Luscombe, "Porn and the Threat," para. 4.
20. Wilson, *Your Brain on Porn*, 72.
21. Jacobs et al., "Associations Between Online," 16.
22. Wright, "Porn-Induced Erectile Dysfunction," para. 11.
23. Verywell Health, "Does Porn Cause Erectile Dysfunction," para. 15.

Is God enough?

Therefore, I urge you, brothers and sisters, in view of God's mercy, to offer your bodies as a living sacrifice, holy and pleasing to God—this is your true and proper worship.

—Romans 12:1

Paul is explaining that the body itself serves as an act of worship. Presenting our bodies as a living sacrifice is not just an act of obedience, but a full surrender. This level of total surrender is only possible when we believe that God is enough. It is a recognition that Jesus was the ultimate living sacrifice as he carried our punishment on a cross for us and then defeated that death three days later.

Trust in Jesus means believing he is worthy to control our lives and surrendering our actions, desires, and physical body to him.

DAILY FIGHT PLAN

1. Prior to today, had you encountered the concept of porn-induced erectile dysfunction (PIED)? After reading about it, what immediate thoughts, concerns, or emotions did you experience?
2. How has porn impacted the way you view your body and sexuality?
3. *Therefore, I urge you, brothers and sisters, in view of God's mercy, to offer your bodies as a living sacrifice, holy and pleasing to God—this is your true and proper worship.* —Romans 12:1

   This verse urges us to offer our bodies as a living sacrifice. Write out a prayer of surrender, asking God for the strength and obedience to surrender your wants for his.

DAY 4

GOD-SHAPED VACUUM

Blaise Pascal, the seventeenth-century French mathematician, physicist, and philosopher, once said, "All human evil comes from a single cause, man's inability to sit still in a room."[24] Too often, our restless emptiness drives us to porn. It whispers a cruel promise: relief from emptiness without the struggle of real connection. For a fleeting moment, the body's ache dulls, but the soul's deeper longing remains untouched, crying out for something—or someone—far greater than any screen can offer.

The brilliant scientist went on to observe that we all have a longing for something beyond the material world—a sense of emptiness that nothing in life can satisfy. Pascal described this emptiness as a *God-shaped vacuum* in our soul that only a relationship with Jesus can fill. All worldly pleasures, including pornography, may provide temporary distraction, but they can never truly satisfy the deepest desires of the human heart.

Pascal's insight on human nature points to the idea that our search for meaning ultimately finds its answer in God.

In our Fight Club journey, we have already taken some difficult next steps towards freedom. Our weekly combat challenges have seen us spend time reading the Bible daily, set up guardrails, and identify our B.L.A.S.T.E.D. emotions. However, this week's combat challenge is unique because it demands of us an answer we have repeatedly failed to demonstrate through our actions.

Is God enough?

For he chose us in him before the creation of the world to be holy and blameless in his sight. In love he predestined us for adoption to sonship through Jesus Christ, in accordance with his pleasure and will.

—Ephesians 1:4–5

The reason we must reconcile if God is enough is because of its significance. It begins with God. He created us so he could love us! The problem is that we ignore God's calling in our lives and follow our own selfish desires. The Bible calls this attitude *sin*, which we defined in week 2 as missing the mark. Sin is choosing to do the wrong thing. It is also knowing the right

24. Pascal, *Pensées*, frag. 136.

thing to do and not doing it. Whatever shape sin takes, it separates us from God, damaging our relationship with him. But sin does not keep God from loving you. He still provides a way to restore our relationship with him.

And Jesus Christ is the solution.

But God demonstrates his own love for us in this:
While we were still sinners, Christ died for us.

—Romans 5:8

Jesus is the solution to our separation from God. He took the fall for all our sins when he died on a cross. He did that willingly. He chose to take on all our sins and accept the punishment for them. Then he came back to life to prove he was God.

A life full of purpose that God wants to give each of us comes with a two-step choice.

If you declare with your mouth, "Jesus is Lord," and believe in your heart that God raised him from the dead, you will be saved.

—Romans 10:9

We must first declare that Jesus is Lord. Declaring him as Lord is an admission that comes with a recognition that we will no longer pretend that our way is best, confessing our sins for what they are. First John 1:9 promises "he will forgive us our sins and purify us from all unrighteousness." Essentially, God deletes our sins more effectively than we ever managed to delete our internet history and cookies.

We must, secondly, believe that Jesus died to pay for our sins, that he rose again on the third day, and is alive today. Paul states in Rom 10:9 a promise for those sincere in their belief that God is enough—"you will be saved." It is not a possible promise. It is not a performance-based promise contingent on our ability to avoid addiction or lustful thoughts. It is not a revocable promise. It is an unbreakable promise.

For I am convinced that neither death nor life, neither angels nor demons, neither the present nor the future, nor any powers, neither height nor depth, nor anything else in all creation, will be able to separate us from the love of God that is in Christ Jesus our Lord.

—Romans 8:38–39

Jesus came down and met us where we are—as a broken people—to do the impossible and bridge the gap. Why? Because there is nothing we could ever do to make God love us any more or less than he does right now. Whatever we have done, wherever we have been, whatever we will do, God loves us and God will always love us.

What we have discovered this week is that our pursuit for pleasure, satisfaction, and fulfillment—the thing that gives us a real sense of meaning and purpose—does not come from consumption of pornography and sexual addiction. It comes from knowing and following Jesus. We can ignore the truth but we cannot change it; God is enough.

DAILY FIGHT PLAN

1. Is God enough? What does that look like in your life at this point in your Fight Club journey?
2. *For God so loved the world that he gave his one and only Son, that whoever believes in him shall not perish but have eternal life.* —JOHN 3:16

   How does it make you feel to know that God could never love you any more or less than he does right now?

3. Have you ever declared Jesus as Lord of your life and believed that he died and rose from the dead for you? If so, when (date or season of life)? If not, what is preventing you from taking that next step?

DAY 5

BORN AGAIN OR PORN AGAIN?

At age eight, David discovered porn at a friend's home and the images became instantly etched in his memory. He began living a dual life—both a faithful pastor's son and addicted to porn. David knew the right answers but made the wrong choices. In high school, he began dating and the porn use lessened; however, he was simply transferring his demands from pixelated victims on a screen to a new casualty, his girlfriend. When the relationship failed, David found himself thrust back into the shackles of porn.

David's addiction hollowed him out—stealing his strength, killing his appetite, leaving him restless through the night, and drowning him in waves of panic.

For David, all of life's experiences had one ever-present filter distorting his perspective: porn. His depression was overwhelming one night, driving him to consume a number of Ambien with alcohol in a misguided effort to end his recurring nightmare.

When he woke the next day, David vowed to quit porn. He cleared his phone and hard drive, throwing his pornographic material in a nearby church dumpster. He felt good about himself, as if he had finally taken control of the situation . . .

. . . only to climb back in the dumpster, looking for the very material that nearly killed him.

Jesus often taught through parables. At the heart of one such parable, the prodigal son, lies a piercing question: Is life better apart from the Father's love? Similar to David's story, the prodigal son's answer was *yes*. The problem with sin is that it is not static—it is dynamic, taking us where we never dreamed possible.

Jesus continued: "There was a man who had two sons. The younger one said to his father, 'Father, give me my share of the estate.' So he divided his property between them. Not long after that, the younger son got together all he had, set off for a distant country and there squandered his wealth in wild living. After he had spent everything, there was a severe famine in that whole country, and he began to be in need. So he went and hired himself out to a citizen of that country, who sent him to his fields to feed pigs. He longed to fill his stomach with the pods that the pigs were eating, but no one gave him anything.

—LUKE 15:11–16

Yesterday, we discussed the most important decision anyone can ever make, stepping over the line of faith and placing full trust in Jesus. For some, that invitation resonated. But for others, you've been walking with Christ for years—maybe even decades. And yet, like today's story of David or the prodigal son, you have made a serious misstep.

Every addiction has a beginning.

Addiction is not one *serious* misstep but a *series* of missteps that pull us further from God's heart. Sin looks attractive, exciting, and promises satisfaction. But what looks like freedom at first always ends in chains. Sin will fool us, use us, and leave us empty. It may sparkle for a season, but it cannot satisfy, because outside the will of God, there is no joy, only deception. We don't start out desiring to wallow with the pigs or sift through the dumpster—but it is where we end up.

When he came to his senses, he said, "How many of my father's hired servants have food to spare, and here I am starving to death! I will set out and go back to my father and say to him: Father, I have sinned against heaven and against you. I am no longer worthy to be called your son; make me like one of your hired servants." So he got up and went to his father. But while he was still a long way off, his father saw him and was filled with compassion for him; he ran to his son, threw his arms around him and kissed him. The son said to him, "Father, I have sinned against heaven and against you. I am no longer worthy to be called your son." But the father said to his servants, "Quick! Bring the best robe and put it on him. Put a ring on his finger and sandals on his feet. Bring the fattened calf and kill it. Let's have a feast and celebrate. For this son of mine was dead and is alive again; he was lost and is found." So they began to celebrate.

—LUKE 15:17–24

The prodigal son *came to his senses*—that awakening moment we all face when the weight of sin finally crashes in and we see just how far down in the dumpster we have fallen. It is the turning point where regret becomes repentance, and repentance demands action. With humility, he admitted his failure, rose from his ruin, and took the first hard steps back toward the father's embrace.

One of the most powerful moments in Jesus' parable is when the father spots his son still a long way off and runs to him. It is the only time the Bible describes the God of the universe as running. No lecture. No conditions. Just eagerness to forgive. It's a breathtaking reminder that no matter how far we wander, God's unconditional love never wavers and his arms are always open wide to welcome us home.

David's addiction took him to the depths of a dumpster, but his story did not end there. He eventually climbed out, literally and figuratively, resolute never to return. David joined a local Fight Club group and learned to live in freedom—because God is enough.

DAILY FIGHT PLAN

1. Like David's story, in what ways have you been living a double life?
2. *But God demonstrated his own love for us in this: While we were still sinners, Christ died for us.* —Romans 5:8

   How does God's actions in Rom 5:8 parallel with the father in the prodigal son parable?
3. In what ways has the weekly combat challenge—Is God Enough?—stretched your faith and actions this week as you look at everything Jesus has done for you? Were any decisions or commitments made?

WEEK 5—STANDING TOGETHER IN THE BATTLE FOR THE SOUL

WEEKLY MEMORY VERSE

As iron sharpens iron, so one person sharpens another.

—Proverbs 27:17

WEEKLY COMBAT CHALLENGE

Find an accountability partner.

NO WARRIOR FIGHTS ALONE

THE SECRET THAT BINDS

Toby's war on the soul began as a child, wrestling with his dad. Though innocent fun, when his private parts unintentionally brushed against something, it felt pleasurable. Desiring to recreate the feeling alone, Toby discovered masturbation.

Growing up, Toby attended a Christian school and was deeply involved in church, often spending his free time outdoors with a natural curiosity about life and how the world works. But when his family relocated from Southeast Asia to the US at age eleven, he suddenly had access to high-speed internet—and with it, an endless stream of pornography that would soon wreck havoc on his soul.

As a Christian, Toby knew it was wrong. He knew the Bible said *do not commit adultery* or *lust after a woman*. In a misguided effort to appease his own conscience, Toby directed his sexual thoughts towards men, propagating same-sex attraction.

During high school, his family moved again and he began attending a new church. It was within this new fellowship that Toby developed an intense attraction to his new youth pastor—obsessed to the point he sought opportunities to meet one-on-one for counseling.

Eventually, his fixation on his youth pastor met with devastation. Toby had idolized his mentor, and when the relationship unraveled, the fallout was crushing. Ashamed and uncertain of next steps, Toby confessed to his family the same-sex attractions he had been wrestling with. The disclosure came on his dad's birthday, tainting what should have been a celebration and complicating an already turbulent struggle with sexuality.

An avid reader, Toby purchased a self-help book to aid in his pursuit of freedom, but its grand recommendation for freedom was to find an accountability partner. Likewise, his daily time spent reading the Bible provided an ongoing theme that we are not meant to do life alone—as though we are wired for relationship.

Nothing scared Toby more than exposing his darkest secrets—a terror that became the prison of Toby's solitude.

As he grew older, friendships became increasingly difficult. Toby kept most relationships shallow, never allowing them beyond surface level. Whenever he grew close to another man, unhealthy feelings eventually surfaced, forcing him to pull away. He remained guarded with women as well, careful not to send the wrong signals or unintentionally lead them on.

The underlying desire in Toby's same-sex attraction was a need for security, safety, and protection that he felt could be found in men. God began revealing in the time they spent together that he alone provides true security, safety, and protection. God began pushing Toby beyond his comfort zone, establishing that he is the source of everything good and that he gives courage and security.

Though Toby once felt doomed to loneliness, he began to trust God's promises and believe that the Lord was always with him. As he found a healthier identity in God, Toby's soul still longed for community. He had denied himself relationships and the opportunity to do life with other Christian men out of fear.

And then God graced him with the very thing his soul ached for—authentic friendships.

Toby joined a Fight Club group, a community of Christian believers standing alongside him in his fight against sexual sin. Within the group, Toby discovered that the focus was not on individual faults but on God himself. He began to let his guard down and grow closer to the group as they pursued Christ together. Toby began forming close friends that encouraged him towards Jesus without the temptation of same-sex attraction. Toby was no longer fighting alone.

Therefore confess your sins to each other and pray for each other so that you may be healed. The prayer of a righteous person is powerful and effective.

—JAMES 5:16

To be known fully is rarely something we embrace willingly. To be vulnerable involves risk as we unmask ourselves, exposing our faults and failures to a trusted friend. Sharing personal struggles creates opportunity for judgment and rejection. Being transparent requires us to remove our masks and stop pretending as if our lives are healthy. For most addicts, there will be no weekly combat challenge more difficult than this week because we have mastered the art of deception, living in constant fear of being fully known.

But we have to be fully known. There is no freedom apart from it. Finding a godly community and an accountability partner helped Toby experience grace and discover radical transformation—not just the removal of sexual sin.

The war for our soul is real—be bold, find an accountability partner, and stand united.

DAY 1

YOKE OF FREEDOM

While Israel was staying in Shittim, the men began to indulge in sexual immorality with Moabite women, who invited them to the sacrifices to their gods. The people ate the sacrificial meal and bowed down before these gods. So Israel yoked themselves to the Baal of Peor. And the Lord's anger burned against them.

—NUMBERS 25:1–3

Baal was a Canaanite deity most commonly known as the storm god—associated with weather, rain, and fertility. In an agrarian society, where survival depended on crop productivity, it is easy to understand why the pagan god was popular. Baal worship was deeply eroticized and rituals frequently involved sexual acts between priests or priestesses and worshipers as part of their offerings to entice the false god to make their lands fertile. During major religious festivals, entire communities participated in large-scale sexual ceremonies, believing the acts connected them to Baal, securing his favor.

Israel had yoked themselves to a false deity and the sexual behavior that aligned itself with the pagan beliefs. A yoke is a wooden frame put on the backs of livestock that joins two animals at the neck, uniting them most often to perform a common purpose.

Unfortunately, we still yoke ourselves to false gods like Baal; they just look different.

The top three adult websites—Pornhub, XVideos and XNXX—together draw over 5.8 billion visits each month.[1] That's roughly 135,000 new visits every single minute, with users spending an average of eighteen minutes per session. These numbers reveal just how pervasive and influential porn has become across the globe. If Num 25:2–3 had been written today, it would read, *The people logged in and lusted before the websites. So they yoked themselves to Pornhub, XVideos and XNXX. And the Lord's anger burned against them.*

Porn doesn't just tempt—it declares war on our soul, demanding us to choose either the fleeting pleasures of the flesh or the eternal worship

1. TrueAlly Team, "How Many People Watch Porn?," para. 4.

of God. Porn and sexual addiction serve as a form of worship by capturing our thoughts, shaping our decisions, and stirring our emotions while we sacrifice time, community, and relationships to consume it.

With that truth in mind, we should not give our bodies over and become yoked to sexual immorality—modern day Baal worship. It may carry a different name and be accessed by a different venue, but it's still the same thing. When we choose to be yoked with sexual immorality, like Israel, we will find ourselves in deep shittim.

Come to me, all you who are weary and burdened, and I will give you rest. Take my yoke upon you and learn from me, for I am gentle and humble in heart, and you will find rest for your souls. For my yoke is easy and my burden is light.

—MATTHEW 11:28–30

When we are yoked with sexual sin, we carry the heavy burden of compulsive addiction ourselves. But Jesus' yoke is easy and light because he already carried our addictive baggage on the cross. We are going to be yoked to something, so let us desire the beneficial, well-fitting, and gracious yoke God offers. When we feel weary and burdened, it is likely due in part because we have been carrying what Jesus intended to carry all along.

Life was never meant to be a constant burden as we pull ourselves along by our own strength. Instead, we must learn to trust the leadings of the Holy Spirit. The more we cease our efforts and surrender to him, the more we discover the quiet freedom he offers. It is in that place of trust that his words come alive—"my yoke is easy and my burden is light" (Matt 11:30).

It is for freedom that Christ has set us free. Stand firm, then, and do not let yourselves be burdened again by a yoke of slavery.

—GALATIANS 5:1

A slave has no freedom and is at the mercy of its master. Through the sacrifice Jesus poured out on the cross, the yoke of sin that once bound our bodies is broken. Lust, porn, and every form of sexual bondage no longer rules over us. As we learned in our weekly combat challenge last week, God is enough. When we choose to remain yoked to sin, it is as if we pick up the chains that bound us in slavery and wrap ourselves in them once more.

Choosing freedom over slavery is easier to achieve within a like-minded community. Our journey to freedom was never meant to be walked alone. We need others to walk beside us—to challenge us when we drift, to know us deeply, to love us honestly, and to encourage us faithfully. The following four days guide us in the wisdom necessary to join a community and find accountability in our lives.

DAILY FIGHT PLAN

1. In what ways have you yoked yourself to porn and sexual addiction?
2. How did sexual addiction resemble a form of worship in your life and in what ways does it war with your soul?
3. Compare and contrast the difference between Jesus' yoke and the one of sexual sin.
4. Is it possible to become a slave to something you have already been freed from? Explain your reasoning for the answer.

DAY 2

SHARED YOKE, SHARED STRENGTH

After nearly a decade of habitually consuming porn and casual sex, Todd reached a breaking point, determined to pursue freedom. He joined a Fight Club group and began taking positive next steps in his life. Progress came slowly but steadily, with longer stretches of sobriety. Yet, one thing kept pulling him backward; his closest friends did not share his resolve. The fact that his "friends" attended his church only complicated the situation. One night, after a church event, the group invited him out for drinks. When the evening's plan shifted toward a strip club, Todd recognized that his circle of influence had to change if he truly wanted freedom.

Todd spoke about his backslide with his Fight Club leader and identified that while he had embraced change, he had refused to adopt the weekly combat challenge to find an accountability partner. With some encouragement, Todd decided to move beyond his fear of being fully known. Over the next few months, Todd began volunteering in different areas of his church, creating opportunities to meet like-minded Christians. In his efforts, Todd struck up a friendship that eventually became a source of accountability in his life. Two years later, Todd recalled that finding an accountability partner was a difficult but worthwhile combat challenge. He experienced how accountability shines light on the shadows of secret sin, providing the courage and support needed to continue walking in true freedom.

Life in Christ, lived together, leads to lasting freedom.

Do not be yoked together with unbelievers. For what do righteousness and wickedness have in common? Or what fellowship can light have with darkness?

—2 Corinthians 6:14

When Paul warns against being *unequally yoked* in his letter to the Corinthians, our minds often jump straight to marriage. Yet, the passage context does not point there as its primary concern. Paul's focus was much broader—our spiritual walk as believers. Freedom is found in community, yet the companions we choose to walk beside chart the horizon we journey toward. To yoke ourselves with unbelievers, or reckless Christians, in Todd's case, invites distraction and drift from the Lord. This does not mean we excommunicate unbelievers from our lives. It simply means our inner circle of friends should share a common spiritual mindset.

Though one may be overpowered, two can defend themselves. A cord of three strands is not quickly broken.

—Ecclesiastes 4:12

King Solomon, the wisest and wealthiest man of his time, likely wrote Ecclesiastes. He had everything this world could offer—pleasure, power, possessions, and prestige. Yet, throughout Ecclesiastes, he called it all *meaningless* apart from God. His words remind us that true freedom and fulfillment are not found in chasing what the world offers but in fearing God and walking in his ways.

Ecclesiastes 4:7–12 tells us that a life lived in isolation is empty, but life shared with others brings strength and resilience. Accountability is not just helpful; it is essential in our fight against sexual sin. Alone, a person may fall, but with a companion, victory is possible. Consider the horse: one can pull as much as six thousand pounds, but when two are trained and yoked together, they can pull up to eighteen thousand pounds.[2] That is three times the original weight. In the same way, a "cord of three strands" paints the picture of even greater strength found in tightly woven relationships when God is woven into the relationship. Accountability weaves our lives together, creating the resilience needed to stand firm and walk in freedom.

If even Solomon, with all he had, found emptiness without the Lord, how much more do we need community, relationship, and accountability?

Carry each other's burdens, and in this way you will fulfill the law of Christ.

—Galatians 6:2

God calls us to "carry each other's burdens." The Greek word for *carry* is *bastázō*, meaning *to actively take up and help shoulder the weight of another's burden*. In a sense, Paul is calling us to be yoked in accountability as we embrace God's gift of fellowship for the journey. God never designed us to walk alone; he weaves our lives together so that when one grows weary, the other lends strength.

2. Wright, "How Much Weight," para. 4.

Like two oxen yoked together, we pull in rhythm, steadying one another when the path grows steep. For when one stumbles, the other lifts; when one grows faint, the other speaks courage; when one forgets, the other reminds. In this holy companionship, we taste the wisdom of Eccl 4:9: "Two are better than one."

Accountability breaks secrecy; freedom breaks through.

When it comes to matters of the soul—like accountability, discipleship, and spiritual partnership—we must guard against being unequally yoked. Just as two animals bound together by an ill-fitting yoke cannot plow straight, neither can we expect to move forward faithfully if our influence pulls us away from Christ.

DAILY FIGHT PLAN

1. Todd's story speaks to the influence of friends. How has your circle of friends influenced you positively and/or negatively?
2. In what ways is walking in freedom made easier when yoked with an accountability partner and those that share your faith and goals?
3. Identify the specific challenges you might face in finding an accountability partner and propose practical strategies to overcome each one.

DAY 3

DON'T TAP OUT, REACH OUT

During the gold rush era, R. U. Darby's uncle traveled from Williamsburg, Maryland, to Colorado in search of fortune.[3] Darby's uncle began digging and eventually found a vein of gold ore. Not having the necessary tools, he hid the gold and traveled back to Maryland to secure financing for the machinery needed to properly mine the gold. While home, he enlisted Darby's assistance and the two of them returned to Colorado once they had enough funds.

They bought the machinery and began mining, fueled by dreams of great wealth. But soon the vein of gold vanished. They dug desperately, finding nothing, until frustration drove them to quit. Selling their equipment to a junk man for a few hundred dollars, they returned home defeated. The junk man, however, wisely sought advice from another, hiring an engineer who discovered the gold vein just three feet beyond where they had stopped digging. While the junk man went on to make millions, Darby returned home with little left after paying his debts.

While Darby's difficult takeaway on giving up hurts, there is a more painful lesson at work—lack of community. Darby needed someone with experienced perspective, as the junk man did, to speak wisdom on the situation and shine light in the darkness.

Our addictive journey is one of relational isolation and it's painful. The community we invest in through addictive behavior is not real; it is pixelated. We allow porn, sexual addiction, and fantasy to shape our worldview with its influence.

Porn and sexual fantasy have evolved beyond images and videos, offering consumers the illusion of relationship. We can form a parasocial relationship—a one-sided emotional connection with a sexually desirable model, influencer, OnlyFan, or camgirl.[4] The relational facade makes us feel known and supported, though no real connection ever exists.

Platforms like OnlyFans deepen the effect as content creators share daily routines and personal stories, fostering a false sense of intimacy and closeness with subscribers.[5] The parasocial relationships are formed through deception as we enter the supposed lives of others. The illusion

3. Lechter and Reid, *Three Feet from Gold*, 21–24.
4. Wolfinger et al., "Probably in a Parasocial Relationship," para 2.
5. Villanueva, "Psychology of OnlyFans," para. 1–8.

causes us to forget the buyer/seller relationship. We begin rehearsing romantic fantasy, but we are not training for the real thing.[6]

Parasocial bonds imitate relationships; real community transforms it.

Let us hold unswervingly to the hope we profess, for he who promised is faithful. And let us consider how we may spur one another on toward love and good deeds, not giving up meeting together, as some are in the habit of doing, but encouraging one another—and all the more as you see the Day approaching.

—Hebrews 10:23–25

Sexual addiction is a relational disorder, made more complex by the fact that sexuality itself is inherently interpersonal, involving another person—whether real or imagined.[7]

We traverse our addictive journey in relational isolation expecting to find freedom, yet never making the necessary changes. We are merely doing the same thing over and over again while expecting different results.

Community is not found; it's forged.

Fostering meaningful relationships requires both intentionality and effort. Addiction often isolates us as we unknowingly dig trenches around ourselves to shield others from our behavior and attempt to avoid shame. It is only when we pause and look up from the depths of the pit we dug that we recognize how alone we have become. Without being authentically known, all our connections remain superficial.

The word *spur* comes from a Greek word meaning to *provoke, incite,* or *irritate.* While the word carries a negative connotation, the author of Hebrews uses the word in a positive way, encouraging us to live in a godly community. Authentic community will not allow us to remain stagnant, living within a state of sexual brokenness and isolation. We cannot remain stationary when community rallies behind us. Community with other Christians is not merely suggested by the Bible; it is commanded.

The passage in Hebrews highlights how godly relationships encourage us to live out our freedom through the faith we proclaim. Our faith is personal but should not be private because a healthy community positively shapes our beliefs and influences our choices.

6. Tukachinsky and Eyal, "Psychology of Marathon Television Viewing."

7. Haber, "Sex Addiction," para. 1–22.

Community can breathe courage into the discouraged, even when we find ourselves three feet from a breakthrough but ready to quit. Our weekly combat challenge is to find an accountability partner, a goal only achieved when we have a willingness to make God's people our people. Step out of isolation and step into a church community with an openness for relationships.

It is time for us to move from thinking about community to living in it.

DAILY FIGHT PLAN

1. Have you ever felt like R. U. Darby in your pursuit for freedom from sexual addiction, three feet from gold but ready to give up?
2. In what ways have you seen your addictive journey take on a parasocial relationship with the content you lust over?
3. In what ways have online parasocial relationships affected your time, finances, or emotional energy?
4. Are you currently attending a church? If no, why not and how would your journey out of addiction look different if you had a church community supporting you?

DAY 4

SPIRITUAL TAG-TEAM: AVOID WRESTLING ALONE

Freedom from sexual sin cannot be found in secrecy. We are created for relationships. When we hide our struggles and hope for healing without confession, we rob ourselves of one of God's greatest gifts—being truly known and deeply connected.

And if we are never fully known, we are never fully loved.

God's intention is for us to live in community as he strategically weaves relationships that offer real care, encouragement, and healing. These friendships become the soil in which our faithfulness to Jesus grows.

Freedom from sexual brokenness comes with us inviting another believer to walk closely with us—to ask the hard questions, to speak truth, and to remind us of God's promises. We call this special relationship an accountability partner. Finding an accountability partner is not easy and we must take initiative in the pursuit, seeking someone who can walk alongside us.

But what actually makes someone a good accountability partner? And how can we find the necessary healing to one day strengthen others in their walk with Christ?

As iron sharpens iron, so one person sharpens another.

—Proverbs 27:17

Their Faith

First and foremost, we need an accountability partner that is a Christ follower. Proverbs 27:17 identifies value in being equally yoked, a reoccurring theme this week as we explore the battle for our soul. Iron is sharpened through the friction and force of another piece of iron. Weaker materials cannot do the job effectively.

Their Commitment

The concept of iron sharpening iron provided by King Solomon in Proverbs involves a great deal of effort. It is hot, hard, and physical labor. Likewise, bearing burdens and confronting sin takes effort. It requires a trusted commitment that endures hardship and stands firm through adversity. More than just being available, it requires being involved. As a piece of hard iron sharpens another through repeated friction, the interactions between two people will refine one another over time, shaping and smoothing out imperfections through honest communication.

Their Gender

When accountability is shared with someone of the same gender, it reduces the risk of misplaced intimacy or emotional entanglement that will complicate healing. James 5:16 calls us to "confess your sins to one another and pray for one another, that you may be healed." Confession is powerful, but healing flows best in a space that is safe, appropriate, and free from additional temptation. Same-gender accountability partners create a safe space where vulnerability does not risk creating new struggles.

Our spouse or partner should not serve as our primary accountability partner. While honesty and transparency in a relationship are essential, unloading our baggage on their shoulders turns them into our emotional bellhop. Likewise, an accountability partner of the same-sex is still appropriate if the struggle is same-sex attraction or gender dysphoria. The only additional cautionary advice would be to ensure there is not a mutual sexual struggle.

Their Role

Listen. The responsibility of an accountability partner is to listen and ask questions, not fix our problems. Active listening is more than hearing words—it's an act of love that reflects the way God listens to us. When we give someone our full attention, we communicate their worth as an image-bearer of Christ. By slowing down, asking thoughtful questions, and seeking to understand their heart, we mirror the patience and compassion of Jesus, creating space where truth and healing can grow.

Avoid shaming. As we will explore later in our Fight Club journey, shame is toxic to our healing. Shame arises when we feel we have failed in the eyes of another—whether a spouse, friend, parent, or even God. Shame is relational. If our struggle with porn already carries deep shame, an accountability partner must give us the freedom to speak openly about our challenges, our progress, and our emotions without condemnation.

Self-awareness will help an accountability partner avoid communicating shame unnecessarily through words, tone, and body language.

Identify the problem. In 1990, James Reason introduced the Swiss Cheese Model to explain how accidents occur.[8] Each slice of cheese represents a layer of defense, while the holes symbolize weaknesses. A catastrophe happens when those holes align, allowing danger to slip through every layer. In the same way, when we practice our weekly combat challenges yet still fall to temptation, it reveals gaps in our defenses. One weekly combat challenge alone may not be enough to stop compulsive behavior, but true disaster comes when multiple vulnerabilities line up and leave us fully exposed. An accountability partner serves as a voice of reason, identifying an area of weakness or guardrails that need reinforcement.

DAILY FIGHT PLAN

1. *If we are never fully known, we are never fully loved.* What does that statement mean to you?
2. What are the consequences if iron is sharpened by a softer material, and how does this analogy apply to your own life? How might your accountability fall short if Jesus is not the foundation of that relationship?
3. Write out a prayer asking God for wisdom and discernment as you seek out and identify an accountability partner.

8. Wiegmann et al., "Understanding the 'Swiss Cheese Model.'"

DAY 5

THE BLUEPRINT FOR HEALTHY ACCOUNTABILITY

Brian was utterly exhausted. For as long as he could remember, he had struggled to form genuine friendships or sustain meaningful community, haunted by a fear of being truly known. Instead, he wore a carefully constructed facade, convinced that if anyone glimpsed his real self, they would reject him. His sense of unworthiness had been forged early in life—through neglect, verbal abuse, and conditional affection under the strict hand of his father. In search of connection and validation, Brian had turned to compulsive sexual behaviors, yet even then, true intimacy terrified him. He had trained himself to believe that revealing his authentic self would only invite more rejection. So when the opportunity arose to find an accountability partner, the weight of his fear and shame led him to abandon his Fight Club journey.

Brian's fear is a common experience for sex addicts, perpetuating a cycle of isolation and shame that makes it challenging to form and maintain healthy relationships. Believing we are unlovable makes us live as though grace does not apply to us. We work harder to perform, hide more of our true selves, and isolate ourselves from the people who could actually help carry us closer to God.

But God demonstrates his own love for us in this:
While we were still sinners, Christ died for us.

—Romans 5:8

Our freedom is built on the reality that God's grace covers our flaws. Thinking we must first become lovable before being acceptable turns faith into a transaction. We try to earn what God has already given freely. The truth is this: we don't have to change in order to be loved. We are loved, and because of that love, we are changed.

Love comes first; transformation follows.

This week, we have discussed the value of throwing off the yoke of sexual sin as we pursue a closer relationship with God, living out our faith equally yoked, the need for godly community, and the expectations for an accountability partner. Today, we will discuss what healthy accountability looks like.

Schedule

While accountability looks different for everyone, we must be willing to clearly communicate our expectations up front. For some, it will be regularly scheduled check-ins, either weekly or biweekly, via call, video, or in-person. For others, accountability is sending preemptive text messages asking for follow up after identifying a situation, emotion, guardrail, or trigger that could lead to relapse. Without establishing an expectation in communication, it will be easy for the addict to avoid confession.

Honesty

Communicating with an accountability partner requires sharing openly about struggles, temptations, and victories—big or small—without minimizing or sugarcoating behavior, and discussing the triggers and patterns that lead to relapse. Accountability only works when honesty leads the way. We must share our struggles, own our triggers, and celebrate our wins—trust grows when we refuse to hide.

Language

We have spent years deceiving others through vague answers, lies of omission, and gaslighting. We must avoid vague statements like "I struggled a bit" or "It was a long night, but I'm OK." Be specific about behaviors and triggers. The language we use to name our sin shapes whether we walk in the light of freedom or remain trapped in the shadows of shame.

Receptiveness

We must invite feedback with openness rather than defensiveness. Our accountability partners may challenge us, suggest boundaries we have not identified, or ask clarifying questions. All of this is reasonable and defensiveness will only undermine our progress.

Boundaries

Accountability is different from friendship or therapy. Though your partner may be a friend, the time scheduled for accountability discussion must be purposeful. Establishing boundaries fosters respect while preventing unhealthy dynamics, such as dependence or burnout. Boundaries that must be addressed include acceptable contact times, frequency and form of contact, expectations, and goals.

Prayer

Pray often together because it reminds us that ultimate help comes from God.

After a season of soul searching on his own, Brian eventually returned to Fight Club. He courageously confronted his distorted beliefs by embracing his worthiness in God's eyes and built an honest and safe relationship that fostered accountability. Being vulnerable is not easy, but if we are unwilling to risk rejection, we will never experience acceptance. Fear builds invisible chains that keep us from stepping into the very freedom our souls are desperate for. Don't live in fear anymore. Be brave and fight!

DAILY FIGHT PLAN

1. In what ways do you relate with Brian's story?
2. Why is the language you choose to use in articulating your struggle to your accountability partner so important?
3. What kind of boundaries would you like to see with your accountability partner?
4. Describe how the following verse applies to the weekly combat challenge and what accountability offers in your freedom journey.

   Therefore encourage one another and build each other up, just as in fact you are doing. —1 Thessalonians 5:11

WEEK 6—IDENTITY CRISIS

WEEKLY MEMORY VERSE

No, in all these things we are more than conquerors through him who loved us.

—Romans 8:37

WEEKLY COMBAT CHALLENGE

Memorize an identity verse.

CASUAL CONSUMER

YOU CAN'T LEAD WHERE YOU WON'T GO

Darryl grew up in a Christian home with parents who were not perfect but took seriously their role of pointing their children to Christ. Church attendance was consistent, family Bible studies happened occasionally, and faith conversations—though sometimes awkward—were sincere and meaningful. Overall, Darryl's upbringing in both church and family was a positive foundation. He stepped over the line of faith and trusted in Jesus at the age of nine and has continued in that faith ever since.

Unfortunately, one subject was never addressed in his home—pornography. Darryl cannot recall ever receiving "the talk," and his childhood circle of friends did not possess magazines or videos, the main forms of access at that time. It was not until the arrival of the computer and internet that Darryl experienced the tempting lure of porn.

His first exposure came at a friend's house the summer before fifth grade, during the dial-up days of 1995. While Darryl's family did not purchase a computer until much later in the decade, the few images he had been exposed to became etched in his memory. With the introduction of the internet in his home came the real battle for his heart. Darryl loved technology and quickly became the "computer guy" in his household. His parents lacked technical knowledge, offering little more than verbal caution. While porn was not his main intent when on the computer, he understood that the unrestricted, easily accessible content was available whenever curiosity stirred.

Darryl was caught and punished once in high school, but that only pushed him to get better at hiding it. Mostly, his viewing was sporadic, rarely producing deep conviction. In college, the only real difference was that he no longer worried about being discovered. Still, Darryl never considered himself addicted. His use was driven by curiosity more than compulsion, and he felt little urgency to stop. What kept him from going deeper was that much of the content he stumbled across disgusted him. So, for years, Darryl lived as both a Christian and a casual consumer of porn.

That began to change about five years ago. Darryl started reading about human trafficking and the adult entertainment industry. Insider accounts revealed that much of the material online is created involuntarily. As an adoptive father, learning how orphans are targeted internationally shook Darryl deeply. He could not escape the thought that viewing porn meant participating in the exploitation of children like his own. That was the first nail in the coffin.

The second came when one of Darryl's sons was caught trying to view porn. Darryl knew he could not expect more from his son than he was willing to expect from himself. The third came when his best friend confessed how addiction to pornography had devastated his life, marriage, and family. Listening to his friend's brokenness brought Darryl to the point of seeing his own need for freedom if he truly wanted to help others. The final nail was in joining Fight Club, where Darryl gained both conviction and practical tools to walk in freedom.

Over time, Darryl's battle took on a vivid mental picture, as if porn—with all its thoughts, desires, shame, and ugliness—was laid into a coffin. Each of his experiences and new pieces of knowledge drove another nail into the lid. And with every nail, the coffin was sealed tighter, making it harder for the past to claw its way back into his life. These nails have not only kept the coffin shut but buried it, allowing Darryl to live in freedom.

Today, Darryl holds a deep conviction that porn has no place in his life. God did not change him through a sudden voice or divine intervention but through circumstances that gradually reshaped his identity. It was through these experiences that the Holy Spirit brought conviction and freedom. Darryl's grateful for the transformation Jesus has worked in him, and for the knowledge and resources he can now share with others because he has seen his identity changed through Christ.

Our identity strongly influences what we believe, how we behave, and the choices we make. Porn warps that identity by placing a twisted lens over our vision—distorting our sexuality and leaving us dissatisfied, disoriented, and objectifying others. This week, we will begin reclaiming who we truly are, stripping off the glasses of addiction and lust that have clouded our sight. Like Darryl, we will learn to see who we are with clarity. When we root our identity in God, we no longer live chained to porn—we live free, with eyes restored to see ourselves, others, and the world through his holy vision.

God's truth not only reveals who we are, it anchors our identity in him. We cannot separate ourselves from the One in whom our true identity is found. Following are a series of summarized identity truths rooted in Scripture. For this week's combat challenge, identify one that resonates and memorize the identity verse. When God defines us, lust cannot blind us—and that is something worth fighting for.

IDENTITY CLAIMS

WHO WE ARE IN CHRIST

- I am created in the image of God (Gen 1:27).
- I am God's treasured possession (Exod 19:5).
- I am called to be holy (Lev 20:26).
- I am chosen (Deut 7:6).
- I am never alone (Josh 1:9).
- I am valued for my internal worth (1 Sam 16:7).
- I am the apple of God's eye (Ps 17:8).
- I am fearfully and wonderfully made (Ps 139:14).
- I belong to God (Isa 43:1).
- I am saved by Jesus' wounds (Isa 53:5).
- I am loved with a covenant love (Jer 31:3).
- I am protected and covered (Nah 1:7).
- I am God's delight (Zeph 3:17).
- I am God's treasured possession (Mal 3:17).
- I am sacrificially loved by God (John 3:16).
- I am set free in Jesus (John 8:31–32).
- I am Jesus' friend (John 15:14).
- I am dead to sin through Jesus' death and resurrection (Rom 6:2).
- I am no longer under condemnation (Rom 8:1).
- I am more than a conqueror through Jesus (Rom 8:37).
- I have the mind of Christ (1 Cor 2:16).
- I am the temple where the Holy Spirit dwells (1 Cor 6:19).
- I am a new creation in Christ (2 Cor 5:17).
- I am reconciled to God through Jesus (2 Cor 5:18).
- I am Christ's ambassador (2 Cor 5:20).
- I am crucified with Jesus and he lives in me (Gal 2:20).

- I am holy and blameless before God (Eph 1:4).
- I am adopted through Jesus (Eph 1:5–6).
- I am sealed with God's promise of the Holy Spirit (Eph 1:13).
- I am no longer dead in my transgressions (Eph 2:4–5).
- I am God's masterpiece, created in Jesus to do good works (Eph 2:10).
- I am close to God through the blood of Jesus (Eph 2:13).
- I am strong in the Lord's mighty power (Eph 6:10).
- I am confident that Jesus is changing me into his image (Phil 1:6).
- I am qualified to share in God's inheritance (Col 1:12).
- I am overflowing with thankfulness for what God has done in me (Col 2:7).
- I am completed in Jesus (Col 2:10).
- I am chosen (1 Thess 1:4).
- I am called to a holy life by God's grace (2 Tim 1:9).
- I am washed in Jesus' blood (Heb 9:14).
- I am redeemed from the curse of the law (1 Pet 1:18–19).
- I am born again by the living and imperishable word of God (1 Pet 1:23).
- I am forgiven of all my sins (1 John 1:9).
- I am victorious as a child of God (Rev 21:7).

DAY 1

THE VEIL FALLS, IDENTITY RISES

And when Jesus had cried out again in a loud voice, he gave up his spirit.

—MATTHEW 27:50

The Old Testament is more than just a book of rules—it is a story. An adventure about a Hero who left his home in a far-off country to reclaim his lost treasure. A love story of a Prince who gave up his throne to rescue the one he loves. It reads like the greatest fairy tale ever told, with one difference: it is true. For generations, Israel whispered his name—Messiah—as the world waited. Until Jesus came, our identity was bound to our fallen, sin-stained nature, marked by separation, imperfection, and loss. But with Jesus, the story turns from despair to redemption.

The Old Testament consistently exposes our inability to save ourselves and points to our ultimate need for Jesus. From the law given through Moses to the temple sacrifices, the message is unmistakable: sin creates separation from God, and no amount of human effort can close that gap. Even Israel's kings, priests, and prophets, with all their authority, proved deeply flawed—reminding us of our need for a perfect King, a flawless High Priest, and the true Prophet to reveal God fully. The prophet Jeremiah spoke of this coming anointed one who would carry the weight of sin and establish a new covenant written on our hearts, not on stone. In this way, the Old Testament acts both as a mirror, reflecting our brokenness, and as a signpost, pointing toward Jesus, the fulfillment of God's promises, and the only one who can reconcile us to the Father.

When Jesus stepped down onto earth and died, death itself died—defeated by an empty tomb three days later.

At that moment the curtain of the temple was torn in two from top to bottom. The earth shook, the rocks split.

—MATTHEW 27:51

This is the moment. The crescendo of God's masterful symphony, a story he had been orchestrating since sin entered the scene in the garden of Eden. The tearing of the temple curtain immediately after Jesus' death marked the climax of his story. The curtain tore in two, but its significance begins with why it hung there in the first place.

The curtain was sixty feet long, thirty feet wide, and as thick as the palm of a hand, roughly four inches.[1] The curtain was heavy, too. Some modern scholars estimate the weight as much as sixty thousand pounds, based on its specific dimensions.[2] This was not a typical curtain, requiring three hundred priests to move.[3] The curtain was also beautifully crafted from blue, purple, and scarlet materials, woven from fine linen, and skillfully knit together.[4]

While the dimensions and design speak to the curtain's magnificence, its true purpose reached beyond aesthetics. The temple consisted of two rooms, the Holy Place and the Most Holy Place, separated by the curtain. The Holy Place served as a space for priests' daily service, and the Most Holy Place was the sacred innermost chamber where God's presence resided. Access into the Most Holy Place was strict and exclusive. The high priest could enter the Most Holy Place only once a year on the Day of Atonement to perform a sacrifice for sin and for the people. The consequences of violating this was death because behind that curtain manifested all the power and glory of God.

When the curtain that separated the Holy Place from the Most Holy Place was ripped in half from top to bottom, it represented the open access we now have to God. Our sin no longer needs atonement because Jesus was the perfect substitute. Our identity in Christ is found in being God's chosen, beloved children—redeemed by his grace and given a new purpose to know and serve him. This identity provides hope, purpose, and freedom from compulsive behavior.

The Bible is very intentional in stating the curtain "was torn in two from top to bottom"—by God's hand, not man's—declaring that his presence is now open and available to all. Think of the significance if the curtain had only partially torn. Access would still be limited, suggesting God's work was not yet complete, contradicting the very message of the cross.

No more barriers, no more chains. We now have bold access to him.

Yet, we have chosen to resurrect our own curtains in place of the one he tore down. We intricately weave lies, crafting a veil that separates the

1. Edersheim, *Life and Times of Jesus*, 609.
2. Alexander, "Veil," para. 1.
3. Edersheim, *Life and Times of Jesus*, 609.
4. Gurtner, "Veil of the Temple."

truth of who we are from the lies we continue to believe. The Bible says we are set free, loved, and forgiven while we believe we are beyond rescue, unlovable, and too far gone. The lies we have believed must be deconstructed if we are to live freely as God's adopted children.

Our weekly combat challenge is to memorize an identity verse. Read through the list of identity truths we provided and identify one that challenges your perception of self-image. We have believed lies for far too long, lifting up curtains where God has already torn them down.

It is time to tear down the curtains we constructed against God and step into the identity only he offers.

DAILY FIGHT PLAN

1. What does the veil being torn in two mean to you personally?
2. Do you ever believe you have to still earn your way into God's presence, as if the curtain was still in place?
3. If Christ has torn the veil and granted you full access to God's presence, what veils are you deliberately rehanging in your life—and why?
4. Why is it easier to accept and believe identity lies than to see yourself the way God sees you?

DAY 2

LIAR, LIAR, SOUL ON FIRE

Pete hated his actions, yet he felt powerless to stop. Each time he viewed porn, he promised it would be the last—but inevitably, he found himself back on the same sites, feeding the very addiction he despised. He prayed earnestly for God's deliverance, clinging to the Bible's promises that "the prayer of a righteous person is powerful and effective" (Jas 5:16), and that even "faith as small as a mustard seed" can move mountains (Matt 17:20). Yet the chains of sin and compulsive behavior held him fast. Despair crept in, and he asked himself, "If I'm not walking in the freedom the Bible promises, is my faith real? Am I broken? What's wrong with me?"

While Pete had previously stepped over the line of faith, he could not shake the compulsive habit of porn, nor did God take it away. Pete felt helpless and hopeless.

There are essentially two tiers to the lies Pete believed. There are the lies he accepted in the moment that led to poor decision-making. But then, there are the lies he internalized, and they are far more destructive and controlling, serving as long-held identity lies.

One of the most frequent battlegrounds of spiritual warfare is the mind. The enemy bombards us with lies, trying to make us agree with discouraging, destructive, and deceitful thoughts. Yet, Satan is not all-powerful or endlessly creative. Only God is omnipresent. Satan is a created being with limited power and presence, lacking the boundless, universal presence of God. Too often, we give the enemy far more credit than is deserved for our struggles. We over-spiritualize our addictions and slip into a victim mentality, forgetting that while the enemy may have only tipped the first domino, we willingly allowed the rest to fall on our own.

We demolish arguments and every pretension that sets itself up against the knowledge of God, and we take captive every thought to make it obedient to Christ.

—2 Corinthians 10:5

This is not a passive command offered by the apostle Paul in 2 Corinthians. Clearly, God believes we are fully capable of taking our thoughts captive. The real question is if we believe it, too. It's our beliefs in who we are that dictate whether we are passive or active in our pursuit of holiness.

We must take ownership of our identity. And we must take ownership of how far our behavior takes us. We must "own-our-ship."

The wisdom of the prudent is to give thought to their ways,
but the folly of fools is deception.

—PROVERBS 14:8

The enemy's lies only hold power when we choose to entertain, believe, and act on them. It is in our acceptance of his lies that they become a part of our identity. At its core, this self-deception is foolishness. There are three forms of lies in which our identity is impacted: character, ability, and spiritual lies.

Character lies are deeply held distortions of identity that we accept over time.[5] They are lies that leave us bemoaning, "I'm broken," "I'm a mistake," or "I'm a pervert." Our ongoing porn use creates negative emotions as the unwanted behavior becomes automated.[6] The aftermath is an unrecognizable perception of self.

Ability lies do not just mislead us—they convince us we are incapable.[7] These lies leave us apathetic as we state, "I can't," "I'll never," and "I'm too weak." Apathy is the surrender of self and the refusal to grow and step into who we are meant to be.[8] It's the ultimate escape hatch, the claim that nothing will ever change, so why even try? We must move beyond apathy if we want to experience freedom.

We forget the truth of Phil 4:13 that "we can do all things through Christ who strengthens us." We can face challenges and suffering while finding contentment in any situation through our relationship with Jesus. We have divine empowerment in Jesus because of what he has already done for us.

Spiritual lies leave us believing that God does not love us or want to help us. These lies, over time, create doubt if the Bible is even true. The danger in spiritual lies is that they separate us from our very power source.[9] Porn eats away at our confidence until we find ourselves doubting not just our faith but questioning God himself. A recent study revealed that among

5. Preuter et al., "Cost of Lying."
6. Büsche et al., "Self-Regulatory Processes."
7. Grubbs et al., "Pornography Problems Due."
8. Lanctôt et al., "Distinguishing Apathy from Depression."
9. Hill, *Deception in Body of Christ*, 41–43.

Christian students who view porn, 43 percent of men and 20 percent of women said it damaged their relationship with Jesus. Even more alarming, 20 percent of men and 9 percent of women admitted it led them to lose interest in spiritual pursuits altogether.[10]

Like Pete, we may reach a point where we simply want God to just remove the addictive behavior. But what if he won't? What if that is not what God wants? God does not want 90 percent of our heart; he wants 100 percent of our heart. If he simply removes our addiction, he will never have 100 percent. That means we must rely on him as we reconcile these lies and pick up our cross and carry it daily.

DAILY FIGHT PLAN

1. Is there anything you relate with in Pete's story?
2. Which of the three lies—character, ability, or spiritual—have you embraced, and in what specific ways has that lie sabotaged, your pursuit of true freedom?
3. If God's answer is not immediate deliverance but a call to walk with him through the struggle, will you still trust his goodness? Why or why not?

10. Black, *Healing Church*, 8.

DAY 3

SMOKE, MIRRORS, AND MANIPULATION

Kelly longed for a marriage built on more than one-sided sex. She craved true connection—an intimacy where vulnerability and pleasure were shared, not taken. But her husband continually dismissed her needs, insisting the problem was hers alone.

Whenever Kelly suggested even the simplest changes—like the importance of foreplay—he brushed her off, declaring it wasn't his responsibility. When she brought up marriage counseling, he told her she was imagining problems, claiming their sex life was perfectly healthy. No matter how hard she tried to foster mutual intimacy, her voice was silenced, her desires minimized, and she was left believing that men have needs women are not meant to share.

And then Kelly discovered her husband's hidden porn addiction. The emotional grief was crushing. When confronted, he first denied it outright, stating it was in her head. But as the evidence became undeniable, the narrative shifted. He claimed the porn use was her fault, something he needed because she no longer met his sexual needs.

Her confidence stripped, Kelly was left feeling only confusion and shame.

Gaslighting is a form of psychological manipulation and abuse that creates doubt, making the victim question their perception, memory, or even sanity.[11] Gaslighting is used to plant seeds of doubt in the victim's memory, feelings, or reality to gain control or avoid blame.[12] While gaslighting often starts small, appearing innocent in nature, it will chip away at confidence over time.

Like a maniac shooting flaming arrows of death is one who deceives their neighbor and says, "I was only joking!"

—Proverbs 26:18–19

Gaslighting comes easily for those with compulsive sexual behavior and porn addiction. Like a maniac, we engage in gaslighting as a defense mechanism to conceal our behavior and preserve our double life. We shift blame, minimize the impact of our actions, and avoid accountability.

11. Sweet, "Sociology of Gaslighting."
12. Hailes and Goodman, "Qualitative Investigation of Gaslighting."

Research shows that denial, minimization, and blame-shifting are core components of sexual addiction, often manifesting in relational manipulation.[13] While one in three Americans regularly seek out porn,[14] those who use pornography disguise or diminish the extent of their use, including to their partners.[15]

The gaslighter's dismissive and deceptive behavior destabilizes another's trust in their own intuition and perceptions. This pattern protects the addictive cycle and leaves deep psychological scars on the betrayed partner, who may begin to doubt themselves rather than recognize the addict's deception. In this way, gaslighting is an embedded identity strategy to maintain secrecy and control as addicts look out for their best interests.

So in everything, do to others what you would have them do to you.

—Matthew 7:12

This verse is referred to as the Golden Rule. Gaslighting conflicts with its principle because it involves intentional manipulation for the addict's own self-protection or gain. Instead of treating others with honesty, dignity, and empathy, gaslighters create confusion and self-doubt, violating the very heart of Christ's command. Jesus was not the first to quote the Golden Rule. Similar quotes existed for centuries, always in the negative format, "Don't do to others what you wouldn't want done to you." The phrasing was morally passive, meaning no harm, no foul. Jesus turned it on its head, reframing morality from passive non-evil to actively seeking the good of others. In this way, gaslighting is the opposite of the Golden Rule—it is not giving others the truth and respect we desire but, rather, imposing deception and harm.

Gaslighting bears the fingerprints of the devil, not the image of Christ.

Now the serpent was more crafty than any of the wild animals the Lord God had made. He said to the woman, "Did God really say, 'You must not eat from any tree in the garden'?" The woman said to the serpent, "We may eat fruit from the trees in the garden, but God did say, 'You must not eat fruit from the tree that is in the middle of the garden, and you must not touch it, or you will die.'" "You will not certainly die," the serpent said to the woman.

—Genesis 3:1–4

13. Carnes, *Out of the Shadows*, 16–19.
14. Robb-Dover, "Revealing Statistics," para. 8.
15. Carroll et al., "Porn Gap."

Satan did two things in his dialogue with Adam and Eve. He planted seeds of doubt by first questioning, "Did God really say," and then convincingly lied by proclaiming, "You will not certainly die." Gaslighting draws straight from the enemy's playbook. First, we make our loved ones question the truth and then we double down on the lie.

Instead, speaking the truth in love, we will grow to become in every respect the mature body of him who is the head, that is, Christ.

—Ephesians 4:15

It is time for us to start speaking the truth. Freedom will never be found while we protect our compulsions and mask our behavior. Truth is the only soil where real growth can take root, both for us and for our relationships. We can no longer serve as the author for our loved ones' feelings. Our identity is not what we proclaim it to be. We are not the lies we live but the freedom we find in Jesus. Live in freedom.

DAILY FIGHT PLAN

1. In what ways have you been a gaslighter due to your addictive behavior?
2. List the ways in which you minimized your sex or porn addiction footprint (i.e., hiding apps, texts, internet history, etc.)? How do those actions contribute to gaslighting?
3. *So in everything, do to others what you would have them do to you, for this sums up the Law and the Prophets.* —Matthew 7:12

   Identify how your addictive behavior conflicts with the Golden Rule provided in Matt 7:12.

4. What scares you most if your behavior was fully known?

DAY 4

FROM SERVANT TO SPECTATOR

Deangelo had a bright future in ministry ahead of him. His International Mission Board application to serve as a missionary had been accepted. There was unfortunately one glaring concern with his heart's calling, an inability to walk away from porn. While Deangelo could see where God was guiding his life, the path seemed hopeless due to an inability to control lust. How could Deangelo take the great commission to the ends of the earth while nursing a secret porn addiction? The recurring question plagued his heart as he wrestled with if he could ever freely serve God.

Deangelo's story is not a unique one for those with a heart to serve God. Pastor Tommy Nelson, a board member at Dallas Theological Seminary, explained the reality of porn among seminary students: "We don't ask the students if they struggle with pornography anymore; we ask how bad their struggle is."[16] With one in five pastors admitting to a current struggle with porn, this reality is not exclusive to DTS.[17]

When sin chains the hands we want to use for God, our boldness to serve is silenced.

There is a direct correlation in how porn weakens every measure of faith. One survey revealed how porn use lowers church attendance, diminishes the importance of religious belief, reduces prayer frequency, and erodes a sense of closeness to God—while at the same time increasing religious doubts.[18] When we see ourselves defined by our unwanted compulsive sexual behavior first, our faith wavers and our willingness to serve God is limited.

A six-year study of more than three thousand people focused on how porn use affects service and leadership within the church.[19] Among churchgoing men who never or rarely viewed porn, one in three served or held some form of leadership role in their congregation. But when porn use increased, service dramatically declined. Monthly porn use dropped the odds of serving to one in ten, while weekly use reduced it to just one in twenty. The probability of a churchgoing man serving in his congregation that views daily is nearly zero. The conclusion was undeniable: the more

16. Shimer, *Freedom Fight*, 34.
17. Baer, "More Christians Are Watching Porn," para. 4.
18. Perry and Hayward, "Seeing Is (Not) Believing."
19. Perry, "How Pornography Use Reduces Participation."

frequently a believer consumes porn, the less likely he is to serve within the body of Christ.

Porn is quietly benching God's people from service.

Don't you know that when you offer yourselves to someone as obedient slaves, you are slaves of the one you obey—whether you are slaves to sin, which leads to death, or to obedience, which leads to righteousness?

—Romans 6:16

This verse by Paul highlights how being enslaved to sin prevents us from living in righteousness and serving God effectively. Our God has not changed—he is the same yesterday, today, and forever. We have not changed either; we are still made in his image, created to do good works. What has changed is our access to sin. Technology has brought new avenues of sin that disrupt our freedom to serve God wholeheartedly.

While 57 percent of pastors identify pornography as the most damaging issue in their congregation—and 69 percent admit it has harmed their church—only 7 percent say their church offers a program to help those struggling with it.[20] When churches lack programs or resources to address porn addiction effectively, individuals will feel unsupported in their journey toward healing.

To complicate things, porn is more common among pastors than most dare to admit. A recent Barna survey observed that 86 percent of pastors believe porn use is common among their peers.[21] The survey goes on to state two-thirds of US pastors report having struggled with porn at some point, and nearly one in five say it is a current struggle.

Shame and fear keep us living within the identity of porn use. When a Barna survey asked three thousand Christians what should happen if a pastor is caught viewing porn, over 40 percent said he should resign while only 8 percent of pastors agreed.[22] With such a gap, it's no surprise few pastors admit struggles with pornography or other sexual sins.

A culture of punishment breeds secrecy from the pulpit to the pew.

None of us finds freedom alone. True freedom comes when we are fully known—not in the image we project but in who we really are. Only there can authentic repentance take place. Yet, for pastors and church

20. Chancellor, "Ongoing Epidemic of Pornography," para. 10.

21. Barna Group, "Silent Problem of Pornography," para. 4.

22. Louie, "Pastors and Porn," para. 4.

leaders, confession often carries the fear of punishment or unemployment. And for church members, the fear of consequences makes silence feel safer than honesty.

We cannot keep hiding porn addiction in secrecy—sin won't stop until it consumes everything. Just as access to porn has evolved, churches must adapt. Two things are essential: first, create restorative policies that remove shame from the recovery process for leaders; second, stop ignoring the issue and admit the church already has a porn problem. Be proactive by offering ministries like Fight Club, so believers can step into freedom and live out their true identity in Christ.

DAILY FIGHT PLAN

1. In what ways has porn forced you on the sideline, from an identity of servant to spectator?
2. Why do you think only 7 percent of churches offer resources for recovering from porn addiction?
3. How would the church look and function if we moved away from a culture of punishment to one that fostered grace and restoration?
4. Write your identity verse out to see how well you have memorized it this week.

DAY 5

NARCISSISM: FROM SELF-GLORY TO GOD'S GLORY

When we think of narcissism, our minds often picture an arrogant, self-absorbed, and proud individual. But narcissism in its deeper sense is not simply vanity—it's the bending of the world around us to serve the self. And if there is anything in our modern age that feeds this spirit of narcissism, it is pornography. *Psychology Today* defines narcissism as an inflated sense of self-importance, lack of empathy, insatiable need for admiration, and the conviction that one is uniquely entitled to special treatment.[23] Though we may not see ourselves as narcissistic, the byproduct consistently relates to both porn use and the perceived addiction to sexualized content.[24]

> *People will be lovers of themselves, lovers of money, boastful, proud, abusive, disobedient to their parents, ungrateful, unholy, without love, unforgiving, slanderous, without self-control, brutal, not lovers of the good, treacherous, rash, conceited, lovers of pleasure rather than lovers of God—having a form of godliness but denying its power. Have nothing to do with such people.*
>
> —2 Timothy 3:2–5

Consider Paul's warning in 2 Timothy. While the apostle was not writing about porn directly, the spirit of self-love he describes is exactly what compulsive sexual behavior cultivates. It invites us to a life centered on "self"—our urges, our fantasy, our timing—without sacrifice, without relationship, and without accountability.

When we consume porn, we are inward focused, replacing self-giving with self-serving.

Pornography trains our heart to see others not as people but as products. Instead of image-bearers of God with souls, dignity, and value, they become objects for our pleasure. In a subtle but powerful way, porn whispers, "The world exists for you." That whisper is the heartbeat of narcissism.

Porn serves as an unhealthy "narcissistic retreat" for adolescents—a fantasy escape where we feel omnipotent and shield ourselves from the

23. Psychology Today, "Narcissism," para. 1.
24. Grubbs et al., "Pornography and Pride."

frustrations and humiliations of real life.[25] Over time, this retreat locks us into a persistent, immature state of selfishness. Like the lost boys of Neverland, porn keeps us stuck in our childhood mindset, never stepping into spiritual maturity. We simply don't grow up.

Instead, we can develop narcissistic behaviors through years of instant gratification, low frustration tolerance, and self-pleasure-seeking.[26] The concern is that even without a naturally narcissistic personality, our behavior can create a pseudo-narcissistic identity. Porn's influence on narcissism is also not gender specific, with one study revealing a link between women's porn use and a range of sexually coercive, narcissistic behavior.[27]

Porn creates for us a false mirror. Instead of drawing us outward into an identity of love, service, and intimacy, it turns us inward. Every click, video, and image reinforces the belief that we are the consumer and everything exists for our satisfaction. Over time, this warps how we see others and ourselves. We become the center of our story, blinded to the reality that life is meant to be lived in communion with God and others.

> *Anyone who listens to the word but does not do what it says is like someone who looks at his face in a mirror and, after looking at himself, goes away and immediately forgets what he looks like. But whoever looks intently into the perfect law that gives freedom, and continues in it—not forgetting what they have heard, but doing it—they will be blessed in what they do.*
>
> —James 1:23–25

James, the brother of Jesus, offered a better mirror. Porn tells us, "Look at yourself. Serve yourself. Indulge yourself." The Bible says, "Look at Christ. Deny yourself. Follow Him." One mirror enslaves; the other sets us free. The tragic irony is that porn fueled narcissism is not true self-love at all. Porn is self-destruction clothed as freedom. The more we indulge, the more we demand. The more we consume, the hungrier we become.

Freedom from porn is not just about behavior—it is about dethroning ourselves.

All week, we have meditated on identity truths that God sees in us while unpacking several identity lies we have clothed ourselves in due to

25. Prause and Binnie, "Iatrogenic Effects of Reboot."

26. Hughes et al., "Sexual Coercion by Women."

27. Wilson, "Porn Retreat."

our addictive behavior. It is time to confess that life is not about us; it is about Jesus. We must choose to see others not as objects but as brothers and sisters, as sons and daughters of the living God. It is a spiritual mind shift from "What can they provide us?" to "How can we love and serve them?"

If narcissism is the disease, the gospel is the cure.

Our identity in Jesus is the foundation for true freedom because he alone defines your worth and shows you the path to freedom. When we know who we are in Jesus, we no longer seek fulfillment in fleeting pleasures. Our worth, purpose, and power are not found in ourselves—but in him.

It's time to hold up a different mirror. Stop listening to the lies and look into the face of Jesus, who alone defines your worth and shows you the path to freedom.

DAILY FIGHT PLAN

1. How have you seen your addictive behavior as narcissistic?
2. How has pornography stalled your growth by training you to prioritize immediate self-gratification over maturity, responsibility, and self-giving love?
3. If porn creates a false mirror, how have you been viewing things incorrectly?
4. "If narcissism is the disease, the gospel is the cure." Reflecting on this statement, write out a prayer asking God to break the selfish claim porn has on your life.

WEEK 7—WHO WE ARE IN HIS EYES

WEEKLY MEMORY VERSE

Therefore, if anyone is in Christ, the new creation has come: The old has gone, the new is here!

—2 CORINTHIANS 5:17

WEEKLY COMBAT CHALLENGE

Practice F.I.G.H.T.

THE CAGE OF COMPULSION

A NAME BEYOND ADDICTION

Creed's first memory of sex was watching the Playboy channel as a kindergartner with two neighbors that lived on his cul-de-sac. While viewing the adult content, they began imitating the scenes together. Lack of supervision, easily accessible pornographic material, and a sexually abusive father served in a cascade of contributing factors that directed Creed's childhood. The neighborhood children regularly participated in sexual activities until Creed entered his fourth grade year, ending when the oldest of the girls participating ridiculed Creed, being the youngest, in front of the rest of the neighborhood for being small and hairless.

Unfortunately, the damage was done, etched deep into his soul as part of his identity.

Creed felt like an outsider as a child, unable to connect relationally with his peers. He began compulsively self-medicating through masturbation daily to minimize his unwanted emotions of loneliness and insecurity that his childhood created. It was not until his freshman year of high school that Creed began to regain his confidence in a negative way, fully embracing his sexual identity.

At age fifteen, Creed's appetite outgrew the fantasy that porn provided and demanded flesh, drawing him into destructive encounters. Creed began pursuing women, pushing them as far as they were willing to consent. With every flare of his sexual desire came devastation, leaving a trail of broken women behind him.

Unsurprisingly, Creed's first exclusive relationship was not healthy. He found a girl that was in love with the identity he presented to the outside world. While he knew the persona to be a well-constructed act, it allowed him to hide the insecurity forged at childhood. Creed admittedly loved how the facade made him feel—mysterious and masculine—but in actuality, he was scared, shallow, and full of rubbish.

After the relationship failed, Creed ventured deeper into anonymous sex, stripping away any remnants of connection until he was little more than an emotionally hollow shell.

When he found himself in anything that resembled a relationship, he did not even pretend to be kind. He would justify his actions by telling himself that as long as he was up-front about his intentions, it was acceptable. One such example was a relationship he had with Meredith that dragged on for several months. Creed did not mind the frequent hookups until Meredith complicated things with another girl he was pursuing. Creed ended the relationship, but a week later, Meredith showed him a positive pregnancy test. When she insisted on an abortion, Creed willingly paid for it. As they sat in the waiting room at a Planned Parenthood, watching young women cycle in and out of the clinic, Creed felt disgusted with himself—disgusted with what he had become—and swore off sex.

Later that night, Creed once again found himself entangled in sexual activity with Meredith. The encounter left her shattered. In one of their final conversations, she told him he "swung his dick around like a wrecking ball, destroying everything in its path." Her words struck with brutal force, and for the first time, he felt their crushing weight.

It was here, at the end of himself, Creed stumbled into the beginning of God.

Creed met the woman he would eventually marry a month after the abortion. While his transition into a serious relationship was challenging, with numerous ups and downs, there was one factor they welcomed in their relationship that had not been present in his life before: God. Over years of learning to see his identity in Jesus, Creed began seeing another man take shape. Though he recognized he was fully capable of falling back into the addictive patterns and behaviors that had defined him throughout his life, there was another identity present—one in which sanctification was evident.

Creed eventually joined a Fight Club group in his local community where he could share his past, apart from the shame that previously kept him bound.

Therefore, if anyone is in Christ, the new creation has come:
The old has gone, the new is here!

—2 CORINTHIANS 5:17

Scripture declares that our true identity is not found in our failures, sins, or addictions but in Christ alone. As we study God's view of our identity, we will see that freedom from pornography and sexual addiction is not merely about behavior modification but about transformation—being restored to the image of God in which we were created. Jesus said in John 8:36, "So if the Son sets you free, you will be free indeed." This freedom is not fragile or temporary; it is rooted in the unshakable truth that God calls us his beloved sons and daughters. In discovering who we are in his eyes, we find both the power and the hope to walk out of bondage and into lasting freedom.

Our weekly combat challenge will draw from all our previous weeks as we finally learn what it looks like to F.I.G.H.T. our addiction in a tangible way. Freedom, then, is not simply about stopping bad behavior. True freedom comes from living out of the identity God has already given us. It is time to stop playing the victim role and F.I.G.H.T.

DAY 1

IT'S TIME TO F.I.G.H.T.

As we pursue God, apart from sexual addiction and porn, we begin to see ourselves as we are meant to be: children redeemed, not slaves to sin. Addiction loses its grip when our identity is no longer chained to our past but anchored in Christ. Knowing who God is gives us hope, and knowing who we are in him gives us courage. From that place of truth, we will learn this week how to live out that resolve as we F.I.G.H.T.

F: Focus on Breathing

Combat tactical breathing is nothing new for the United States Navy SEALS. This powerful technique—also known as box breathing—has been adopted by the elite special forces to reduce stress, sharpen focus, and stay grounded under pressure. While combat tactical breathing has been proven invaluable during the chaos of combat, it is also helpful for reducing anxiety and managing overwhelming thoughts.[1]

When addictive compulsions attack, our sympathetic nervous system is activated, shunting blood away from our prefrontal cortex—"the mom brain"—as our limbic system initiates our survival instincts and fight or flight kicks in.[2] Unwanted sexual behavior can be interpreted as a survival instinct, automating the process over time. When the sympathetic nervous system overrides our parasympathetic nervous system, less oxygen reaches our prefrontal cortex, reducing our ability to stay calm and think clearly. Combat tactical breathing reactivates our parasympathetic nervous system, signaling the brain that we are safe. This shift allows more oxygen to flow back to your prefrontal cortex, improving mental clarity.[3] In a sense, combat tactical breathing is like hitting reset on the game console when everything starts spiraling.

To practice combat tactical breathing, we take three to five slow, intentional breaths following the steps below. Let the body relax more with each breath and allow the mind to settle into a calmer rhythm.

Inhale slowly through the nose: *1 . . . 2 . . . 3 . . . 4.*

1. Divine, "Breathing Technique a Navy SEAL," para. 1–5.
2. GateHouse Treatment, "Addiction" para. 2–5.
3. University Counseling Center, "Deep Breathing and Relaxation," para. 2.

Hold your breath: *1 . . . 2 . . . 3 . . . 4.*
Exhale gently through the mouth: *1 . . . 2 . . . 3 . . . 4.*
Hold with empty lungs: *1 . . . 2 . . . 3 . . . 4.*

I: Identify God's Truth

After three to five breaths, we must anchor our minds in God's truth. Psalm 1:3 compares the one who meditates on the Bible to "a tree planted by streams of water"—firm, nourished, and unshaken. God's truth keeps us rooted, reminding us of who he is while giving us strength, protection, and guidance in moments of temptation. Last week, we committed to memorizing an identity verse from the Bible and this is an appropriate time to reflect on the chosen weekly combat challenge verse.

G: Go to God

Do not be anxious about anything, but in every situation, by prayer and petition, with thanksgiving, present your requests to God.

—Philippians 4:7

After focusing our breathing and identifying his truth, we must go to God and present our requests with a clear mind, apart from our anxious thoughts and addictive compulsions. Psalm 62:8 reminds us that we can always trust him and pour out our hearts to him because he is our refuge. The Hebrew word for *refuge* is *machse*, signifying a *place of shelter* or *protection.* God is our place of safety and security during times of trouble. F.I.G.H.T. may have an *I*, but the victory comes from *I Am*.

H: Help

Carry each other's burdens, and in this way you will fulfill the law of Christ.

—Galatians 6:2

We need help. We need godly people in our corner that we can turn to when temptation is overwhelming. This is where community plays a key role. In chapter 5, our weekly combat challenge was to find an accountability partner. Seek help in the F.I.G.H.T. before desire becomes a decision. A simple text asking our accountability partner to follow up in twenty-four hours will typically suffice, but this is where the boundaries we established in week 5 take precedence.

T: Turn From

Avoid it, do not travel on it; turn from it and go on your way.

—Proverbs 4:15

We need to aggressively avoid temptation. We set up guardrails week 2 so we may pursue freedom safely, but temptation will still find us. We cannot entertain it because it is a compromise that will eventually lead to sin. After we have reached out to our accountability partner, we must turn from temptation and escape. This is where we must be intentional, replacing old habits with healthy ones—hitting the gym, catching a movie, grabbing coffee with a friend, going for a run, spending time at the library, etc.

This week we will practice F.I.G.H.T. by setting an alarm three times daily to train. Focus on breathing for three to five breaths, identify God's truth in a verse, and go to God in prayer. We are training for the day of battle, so we do not need to ask for help and turn away every time we practice. Put in the time and remember, our success is built in the unseen hours. It is time to get in the F.I.G.H.T.

DAILY FIGHT PLAN

1. F.I.G.H.T. gives you a concrete way to practice freedom. What hope does it give you to finally have something you can actively put into motion?
2. What part of F.I.G.H.T. will stretch you the most? Explain your reasoning.
3. Take intentional action right now—set three daily reminders on your phone so that you can begin practicing F.I.G.H.T.
4. Write out a prayer asking God to give you an unwavering commitment to following through with practicing F.I.G.H.T. this week.

DAY 2

SEXUALITY: DESIGNED, NOT REDEFINED

Phyllis had wrestled with questions of her sexuality since childhood. To outsiders, she was simply a tomboy who didn't fit the traditional mold, but beneath the surface raged a deeper war over identity. In high school, a counselor casually suggested that perhaps she was really male. Though the idea felt absurd at first, the seed was planted—and as culture increasingly blurred the lines of gender and sexuality, that seed began to take root, echoing the counselor's words with growing force.

After high school, bolstered by the encouragement of trusted friends, Phyllis began the transgender path. She clung to the promise that changing her outside appearance would bring peace and happiness to her heart. Hormones and surgeries followed—but along with them came side effects she was never warned about, some irreversible and devastating. In time, the bright hope she had embraced unraveled, leaving her wounded by a cruel deception. Broken and searching for truth, Phyllis walked through the doors of a church, desperate for answers. Her perception of church left her full of anxiety, expecting judgment, and fearing rejection. Instead, Phyllis discovered God, and with that, the truth in her sexuality. God doesn't make mistakes.

The world's truth on sexuality shifts like the tide—whatever feels right, whatever makes us happy, whatever we decide in the moment. Culture's claim is that our sexuality is free to be explored as we choose and no absolute overrides our right to express it as we want. We are the author and creator of our sexual journey. That conclusion makes sense if there is no God. If we are nothing more than animals, random accidents of evolution, then sex is just instinct and morality is meaningless. But if there is a Creator, then sex has design, purpose, and boundaries.

To deny a Creator, we must believe that atoms randomly defied thermodynamics, arranged themselves into molecules, produced amino acids, folded into proteins, and somehow gave birth to life. Those proteins then randomly received instruction from DNA—a written code more complex than any human language and infinitely more advanced than the binary code that drives all of our technology. That code, 1.5 gigabytes of information, is miraculously stored inside the nucleus of a single microscopic cell.[4] To call that *chance* takes enormous faith.

4. Dynomight, "How Much Information," para. 11.

Yet, God has not left himself hidden. He gave us his word and, ultimately, his Son, who demonstrated the fullness of God's love by dying for us and the fullness of his power by rising again. God claims authority over everything—including sex. Even in singleness, attraction and arousal are not evil because they are part of God's good design for sexuality.

Lust is desire gone rogue, where pleasure is pursued apart from God. This reality draws a dividing line: those who trust God's plan and those who insist on their own. And if we're honest, lustful desire easily sways us because we are creatures of convenience.

Deep down, we know that if God is real, his authority demands change in every area of our lives—including sexuality. If God sets the rules, then we are not animals, enslaved by instincts. God has called us higher. If God created sex, he defines its purpose. And his rules aren't restrictions; they're directions guiding us toward greater joy.

There is a way that appears to be right, but in the end it leads to death.

—Proverbs 14:12

The challenge is God's ways take effort, so we reach for porn believing the lie it will satisfy. That's why we need to F.I.G.H.T. We must push back on addiction's deceptive grip as we turn to God and yield to his authority over our sexuality.

Let the wicked forsake their ways and the unrighteous their thoughts. Let them turn to the Lord, and he will have mercy on them, and to our God, for he will freely pardon. "For my thoughts are not your thoughts, neither are your ways my ways," declares the Lord. "As the heavens are higher than the earth, so are my ways higher than your ways and my thoughts than your thoughts."

—Isaiah 55:7–9

Isaiah reminds us that faith means trusting God's wisdom even when our desires scream otherwise. Faith sounds like this:

- "Coworker hookups are easy, but God's way leads to real relationships."
- "Everyone's on hookup apps, but I trust God to bring me a spouse his way."
- "My boss invited me to a strip club, but I trust God with my career."

- "My friends cohabitate, but I won't play house, keeping the marriage bed pure."

The same faith that saves us sustains us. It starts with that simple, desperate cry: *Jesus, I don't know how to do this, but I know I need You. Forgive me. Help me.* That same faith carries us day by day, trusting that God's way, though hard, is always better.

We may suffer for standing against porn, for saying no when the world says yes, for walking with God when it would be easier to give in. But mark this down: we will never regret obeying God. His design is good. His commands are life. His promises never fail.

So today, let's lay down the lies porn has taught us, surrender the strength we've trusted in ourselves, and sit at the feet of our Father. It's time to F.I.G.H.T.

DAILY FIGHT PLAN

1. How does your sexual addiction journey relate with Phyllis's story by being encouraged along by "friends" and betrayed by the world's lies?
2. Up until now, have you, the world, or God had authority over your sexuality and how have your addictive patterns and life experiences reflected this reality?
3. Where, specifically, are you resisting God's authority over your sexuality—and why?

DAY 3

GOD'S VIEW OF SEX

From the opening chapters of the Scriptures, God shows us that sex and marriage are his idea, his creation, and a gift to humanity. Any notion that the Bible is prudish or "anti-sex" is flat-out wrong. The Bible talks about sex a lot, and quite often in a positive way. There are more than 120 direct mentions of sexual activity, intercourse, or sexual morality, making it one of the most discussed topics in all of Scripture.

In Gen 2, right after the creation of the world, we see God crafting a breathtaking design. He saw that "it is not good for the man to be alone" and fashioned a woman from Adam's side. Adam's response was one of awe and wonder: "This is now bone of my bones and flesh of my flesh" (v. 23).

> *That is why a man leaves his father and mother and is united to his wife, and they become one flesh. Adam and his wife were both naked, and they felt no shame.*
>
> —Genesis 2:24–25

Genesis then records the first marriage covenant, establishing God's design for the union between a man and a woman. In just two verses, God establishes the foundation of marriage, intimacy, and sex—and none of it carries shame.

From Gen 2, we learn several key truths about sex. First, sex is not dirty. Adam and Eve stood before one another naked and unashamed, showing us that God created intimacy to be pure, holy, and joy-filled. Shame only entered after sin entered. Second, admiration is not lust. Adam's first words about Eve revealed his admiration of God's masterpiece. To notice beauty is not sinful; it only becomes sin when admiration turns into coveting or objectification. Third, sex belongs only in marriage. The pattern was set from the beginning: one man, one woman, and one covenant for life. Finally, sex is more than a physical act—it reflects the whole of the relationship, flourishing best when spiritual, emotional, and physical intimacy are all present.

Sex is not the entirety of marriage; however, it is a God-ordained part of it.

In God's design, sex was never about manipulation or coercion; it was pure, prioritized, and overflowing with passion. Unfortunately, Eden ended, sin entered, and corruption distorted God's perfect design. By Gen

6, immorality was so widespread that God brought a flood to cleanse the earth. By Gen 19, the cities of Sodom and Gomorrah were destroyed because of pervasive wickedness, including sexual immorality. Even after God rescued Israel from slavery in Egypt, by Exod 32, the people turned to idolatry and immorality, rising up in drunken orgies around a golden calf.

In his mercy, God gave his people the law—not to punish but to protect and preserve them. Leviticus 18 lays it all bare: incest, adultery, homosexuality, bestiality, rape, even child sacrifice. The list is shocking, but it's also a mirror to the darkness of the human heart. And here's the hard truth, the very sins God condemned are not only alive today—they're celebrated, normalized, and sold to a culture eager to ignore the consequences.

> *Do not defile yourselves in any of these ways, because this is how the nations that I am going to drive out before you became defiled. Even the land was defiled; so I punished it for its sin, and the land vomited out its inhabitants.*
>
> —Leviticus 18:24–25

Your sin is never contained—it spreads, it infects, it destroys. In Lev 18:23–25, God lays it out bluntly: the sexual corruption of the nations brought them to ruin, and he even cursed the very ground they walked on. The devastation was total. What caused it? The practices he hates—twisted, perverse, and defiant. God is not casual about sexual sin. It does not just affect you; it radiates, leaving destruction in its wake, touching families, communities, and even the earth itself.

Sexual immorality is never private, and it is never harmless.

But, thankfully, the story does not end in corruption. Sin may have marred God's design, but it did not erase it. He redeems what sin twists. To remind us of this, he gave us the Song of Songs—a book entirely dedicated to celebrating love, passion, and intimacy within marriage. This book is unapologetically romantic. It contains the steamy exchanges of two lovers who delight in one another, yet it also carries a refrain that is repeated several times: "Do not awaken love until it so desires." Their passion is real, but it is also restrained by obedience to God's timing. This shows us that passion is not sinful when experienced within God's boundaries. On the contrary, God created passion and celebrates it when it flows in the right direction.

God's rules are not designed to restrict us but to bless us. When sex is experienced in the covenant of marriage, love is not weakened—it is strengthened. Sex becomes not a source of guilt or shame but a reflection of God's goodness. His design leads to joy, intimacy, and flourishing. When we trust him, we find that his boundaries are not about restriction but about protecting something precious. He does not call us away from passion but into a greater passion—one that is holy, safe, and beautiful.

DAILY FIGHT PLAN

1. How does God's vision for sex as covenantal and sacred differ from the world's view of sex as casual and consumable?
2. Share your thoughts on the following verse.

   Marriage should be honored by all, and the marriage bed kept pure, for God will judge the adulterer and all the sexually immoral.
   —Hebrews 13:4
3. Where have you felt tempted to awaken desire before its proper time, and what has that cost you emotionally or spiritually?
4. Are you still practicing F.I.G.H.T. this week? If so, how has it helped you respond to God's vision of sexuality obediently?

DAY 4

SINGLENESS AND MASTURBATION

All Scripture is God-breathed and is useful for teaching, rebuking, correcting and training in righteousness, so that the servant of God may be thoroughly equipped for every good work.

—2 TIMOTHY 3:16–17

At Fight Club, we believe the Bible is not simply an ancient book of wisdom, it's the very word of God, preserved for us as the ultimate authority on truth. Because it is God's word, it is inherently true—without error and useful for teaching, correcting, and training in righteousness. In other words, the Bible does not just offer advice for a better life; it provides everything we need to live in holiness and know God's will.

Curiously, the Bible speaks loudly on sexuality, but when it comes to masturbation, it leaves the mic on mute. For a book that tackles everything from how to properly boil a goat, to avoiding sex with animals, there is not one verse related directly to masturbation.

A survey from 13,000 respondents aged eighteen to seventy-four in eighteen different countries suggests 92 percent of men and 76 percent of women actively masturbate.[5] Likewise, recent data in the US suggests that 89.6 percent of men masturbate.[6] Studies on the emotional response to masturbation indicate that 19.1 percent of males report a very big sense of guilt, 18.6 percent report a big sense of guilt, and 38.9 percent report a little sense of guilt.[7] It is peculiar that such a prevalent behavior that evokes a great deal of negative emotion is not discussed once within the Bible. The scope of impact on society at large without clear guidance from God makes the discussion of masturbation incredibly challenging, yet necessitates a response.

Paul declared in 2 Cor 3:6 that the letter kills, but the Spirit gives life. The letter refers to the written law, which is rigid and focuses on external compliance. The Spirit emphasizes God's transforming work in the heart,

5. Robin, "Survey Reveals the Masturbation Habits," para. 1.
6. Diaz, "Masturbation Statistics in the US," para. 2.
7. Zhang and Zhang, "Prevalence of Masturbation," 1–9.

not just following rules. We must never add to God's perfect word because it risks turning obedience into legalism and conscience into bondage.

While opinions on masturbation vary widely, Fight Club's perspective is shaped by years of experience, reflection, and walking this journey alongside others. We make no claim of authority above God's word—on the contrary, it is God's word that grounds Fight Club's view on self pleasure. Our perspective is not intended as legalistic rule but as cautionary wisdom meant to help us remain faithful on the path of righteousness.

The Bible may not condemn the action explicitly, but God calls us to wisdom. Proverbs 14:18 states, "The prudent give thought to their steps and are crowned with knowledge." There are four concerns we must address and reconcile with masturbation before we J.E.R.K.—is it justifiable, edifying, a reliance, and kingdom-minded?

"I have the right to do anything," you say—but not everything is beneficial. "I have the right to do anything"—but not everything is constructive.

—1 CORINTHIANS 10:23

Justifiable: The Bible's absence in discussing masturbation does not mean it is morally neutral because not everything permissible is beneficial. God's word offers principles of wisdom, holiness, and stewardship that extend beyond specific commands. Therefore, when the Bible is silent on a matter, we are still called to test our choices against God's character, the fruit they produce, and whether they draw us closer to or further from him. Silence in Scripture is not permission but an invitation to discernment. We may not be under direct command from God regarding masturbation, but can we justify it?

Do you not know that your bodies are temples of the Holy Spirit, who is in you, whom you have received from God? You are not your own; you were bought at a price. Therefore honor God with your bodies.

—1 CORINTHIANS 6:19–20

Edifying: We discussed in week 4 how we are the temple where the Holy Spirit dwells. Edify comes from the Greek word *oikodomē*, which means (the act of) building or to build up. The word *oikodomē* is used eighteen times in the New Testament, often referring to both literal buildings or the spiritual "building up." With the concept of us being the temple in mind, it is difficult to be edifying when the very act of masturbation is sexual in nature. To complicate this, among men who masturbate frequently, 70 percent consume porn.[8] Of women, 35 percent admit that porn is included in their masturbation.[9] These statistics suggest that roughly two thirds of men and one third of women include porn in their self pleasure routine. For those masturbating without porn, the act without sexual thoughts is nearly impossible considering the sexual nature of the act. While the Bible is silent on masturbation, it speaks clearly on lust and instructs us to flee sexual immorality.

For sin shall no longer be your master, because you are not under the law, but under grace.

—ROMANS 6:14

Reliance: Our behavior mirrors our heart. If we rely on masturbation to meet our needs, manage stress, and cope with life's challenges, we are serving the wrong master. It may promise relief, but it cannot satisfy the soul. Our deepest needs are met in God alone. Jesus reminds us in Matt 4:4, "Man shall not live on bread alone, but on every word that comes from the mouth of God," and Paul teaches in Phil 4:19 that "God will meet all your needs according to the riches of his glory in Christ Jesus." When we run to self pleasure, we settle for less than the fullness of God. But when we draw near to him, we find true satisfaction. We must reconcile if we can stop the act. If the answer is no, you already have an answer to which master you serve.

So whether you eat or drink or whatever you do, do it all for the glory of God.

—1 CORINTHIANS 10:31

Kingdom-Minded: Every choice we make should reflect our calling as citizens of God's kingdom, not servants of our own desires. Our actions are not neutral; they either build up (edify) God's kingdom or distract us from it. When we live with eternity in view, even ordinary decisions become opportunities to honor Christ and advance his purposes.

8. Carvalheira et al., "Masturbation and Pornography Use."
9. Refinery29, "What Most Women Think About," para. 5.

DAILY FIGHT PLAN

1. What are your thoughts on the Bible not mentioning masturbation?
2. Is masturbation edifying if your body is God's temple? Explain your reasoning.
3. *"I have the right to do anything," you say—but not everything is beneficial. "I have the right to do anything"—but I will not be mastered by anything.* —1 Corinthians 6:12

   Reflecting on the verse above, even if you can masturbate without lusting, what dangers lie in the habits formed?
4. Explain how masturbation is or is not kingdom-minded.
5. Based on your answer to question 4, do you feel the action is justifiable? Why or why not?

DAY 5

SACRED UNION AND MASTURBATION CONFUSION

That is why a man leaves his father and mother and is united to his wife, and they become one flesh.

—Genesis 2:24

Sex within marriage was designed by God to be mutual, a union that goes beyond the physical act into spiritual, emotional, and relational intimacy. God embedded in us a longing to be joined to our spouse as a reflection of his own yearning to be united with his people. Sexual pleasure is part of that gift, but the deeper need is intimacy. When sex integrates body, heart, and soul, it reaches its fullest joy; however, when reduced only to sexual gratification and physical release, it becomes shallow and unsatisfying.

Porn and masturbation strip sex of intimacy, leaving behind an act without union, pleasure without presence, and desire without true connection.

Part of God's design is the difference between men and women. Men often seek sex to feel loved; women often need to feel loved to freely give themselves in sex. While this tension could drive couples apart, its intention is to draw us toward selflessness. For a man to find fulfillment, he must learn tenderness and connection. For a woman to find fulfillment, she must learn to give herself in sexual intimacy. Each spouse must look beyond self and meet the other's needs. When this happens, marriage grows holier and both partners reflect Jesus' self-giving love.

Porn and masturbation in marriage undermines this design. When one spouse chooses to satisfy sexual desire apart from the other, a chain reaction begins. First, sex becomes reduced to a purely physical act rather than a bond of intimacy. Second, we pursue pleasure individually, making our spouse incidental rather than central. Third, the drive that normally pushes a husband or wife to reach for their spouse is short-circuited. Lastly, the call to selflessness is muted, as couples live parallel lives rather than a shared one.

This is no small matter. God gave us sexual desire to draw us together. That longing is supposed to feel uncomfortable when intimacy is missing, because it compels us to address issues, rebuild connection, and grow closer. When porn and masturbation replace that process, the healing stops.

Unfortunately, masturbation can feel more intense in the moment because we know exactly how to please ourselves. It is also easier than meeting another's needs, bypassing the vulnerability in communicating about sex. But over time, this shortcut robs a marriage of passion. Sexual tension that could have fueled intimacy gets resolved privately. The result is not closeness but distance.

But the fruit of the Spirit is love, joy, peace, forbearance,
kindness, goodness, faithfulness, gentleness and self-control.
Against such things there is no law.

—Galatians 5:22–23

Forbearance is a temporary pause and self-control is not a punishment—it is a fruit of the Spirit. Seasons of waiting teach patience, deepen character, and create space for God to grow us. Desire, when channeled well, can actually increase longing and creativity within marriage. Planning intimacy, exchanging words of passion, and carrying anticipation can intensify both love and pleasure when the moment finally arrives. It leaves us echoing King Solomon's Proverb, "A longing fulfilled is sweet to the soul" (13:9).

But I tell you that anyone who looks at a woman lustfully has
already committed adultery with her in his heart.

—Matthew 5:28

Porn has no place in marriage because it's adultery in God's eyes. But what if a spouse is refusing sex, or chronic illness makes intimacy difficult? These are real and painful situations. But even here, masturbation should not become a substitute for pursuing connection. Spouses can still seek closeness in other ways—touch, affection, and vulnerability. Counseling can also aid in bringing closeness. To bypass the issue with private release is to avoid the hard but necessary work of healing.

None of this should be spoken with shame or condemnation. Masturbation is not the "unpardonable sin," and in rare circumstances (such as extended separation due to travel or deployment), some married couples may choose to navigate it together, with honesty and inclusion. But as a general practice, masturbation within marriage too easily fosters secrecy, selfishness, and disconnection.

The aim of marriage is oneness—in body, soul, and spirit. Anything that undermines that unity works against God's design. Masturbation may offer momentary relief, but it cannot deliver the intimacy and transformation that comes only when two people choose to reach for one another. Far better than seeking private satisfaction is to embrace the sometimes-difficult, always-rewarding journey of growing in love, holiness, and self-giving intimacy with your spouse.

Marriage is not for everyone, but in God's hands (not our own—no pun intended), it becomes a living masterpiece of his love. And that is worth the F.I.G.H.T.

DAILY FIGHT PLAN

1. Marriage is not for everyone, but God's call to holiness is. First Peter 1:16 says, "Be holy, because I am holy." Share your thoughts on porn and/or masturbation in marriage related to the verse.
2. Reread Gal 5:22–23 and identify how each of the fruits of the Spirit challenges your behavior in sexuality.
3. If the aim of marriage is oneness, how does porn divide that connection between body, soul, and spirit?
4. Reflecting on all the weekly combat challenges introduced so far, which one has been the most challenging to adopt and why?

WEEK 8—LIVE IN THE LIGHT (SUNGLASSES OPTIONAL)

WEEKLY MEMORY VERSE

If we claim to have fellowship with him and yet walk in the darkness, we lie and do not live out the truth. But if we walk in the light, as he is in the light, we have fellowship with one another, and the blood of Jesus, his Son, purifies us from all sin.

—1 John 1:6–7

WEEKLY COMBAT CHALLENGE

Serve somewhere.

FROM LABEL TO LIBERATION

WHEN SOMEBODY REALLY KNOWS YOU

Mose never imagined porn would take him there—that invisible line every addict dreads—the irreconcilable breaking point where reality hits and the truth of how far their addiction has carried them can no longer be ignored. For Mose, that moment came like a shock to the system.

On the surface, Mose had it all together. A devoted husband, a faithful church member, a man with all the right answers and a bold, confident Christian faith. To the outside world, he was the picture of obedience and blessing. But the image was a lie. Beneath the surface, darkness festered, a secret life gnawing at the man he pretended to be.

What Mose truly feared—but desperately needed—was to be fully known.

While addiction started for Mose in adolescence as he coped with sexual insecurities, he quickly found the internet as his refuge; an endless supply of material that numbed his mind through its limitless assortment of pornographic material. The need for more kept Mose returning to his dark secret and the fear of being fully known prevented him from seeking help. Both his addictive behavior and inability to own it kept him locked within an emotional and spiritual cage that he felt helpless to escape.

The progressive evolution of his addiction grew in silence while his public deception grew in theatrics. Mose eventually found himself entertaining camgirls, virtual reality porn, and seeing women less as God's creation and more as his personal commodity.

His life began to fracture. Mose pulled away from his family, emotionally absent from the wife and children he once cherished. His faith wavered and his spirit weakened as he questioned his faith. And even physical intimacy with his wife eroded, leaving him hollow and disconnected.

Then it happened, the invisible line was crossed and Mose broke.

A woman Mose knew began to openly flirt with him, and he liked it. While his marriage was deteriorating under his own selfishness, his calloused heart saw an opportunity to feel sexually affirmed and take his addiction to the next level. On one specific occasion, as Mose was travelling out of town and filled with liquid courage, he engaged in an explicit conversation with her, sending and receiving images. That night, as he lay in bed, the magnitude of his sin struck him.

Mose came back resolute, determined to abandon the sexual fantasies and lustful cravings that had chained him for years. He reached out online for godly counsel and was asked a piercing question: "Mose, have you ever truly experienced grace?" The question struck him as absurd. Of course he had—he was already a Christian. Mose brushed it off, convinced this was just another dead end in his desperate chase for freedom. Yet before signing off, the man promised, "That's what I'll be praying for you."

That night, at 2:00 a.m., Mose was jostled awake by a voice so clear it seemed audible: "Mose, you have a good marriage. But if you want a great marriage, you must be willing to take a step back." His smartwatch showed his heart pounding at nearly 200 beats per minute. As his wife slept, peacefully unaware, Mose assumed it was a bad dream and restlessly lay there the rest of the night.

But at the same time the following night, it happened again. The same voice. The same words. The same racing heart. And again the next night. And the next. For five long months, the 2:00 a.m. voice would not relent.

Running on three hours of sleep a night, Mose's body began to break down. Deep inside, he knew this was more than a guilty conscience, but his terror of being fully known outweighed even his health. If this really was God, then surely he was mistaken. Confession wouldn't lead to a great marriage—confession would destroy everything.

Night after night, the words pressed in until Mose landed in the hospital. Surrounded by the steady beeps of machines, he realized he could resist no longer. He would obey.

To avoid softening the truth of his confession, Mose wrote it down and read it to his wife. After telling her everything, he reached out to his closest friends and laid bare the truth to them as well. For a season, everything did step back—his marriage, his family, his friendships bore the weight of the fallout. Yet, in the middle of the wreckage, something extraordinary happened: freedom. Living in the light, Mose encountered God more vividly than he ever had before. It felt as if he had been running a marathon with heavy weights strapped to his back, and at last, they had fallen away. For the first time in years, he could breathe. And he never wanted to pick the weights up again.

We have to be known. Yet, for the addict, this is a terrifying reality because we've built walls of deception, convincing others that we're fine. We double down on the lie, but like cancer, it rots us from the inside. Real freedom begins as we tear down those walls and step into the light. This week, that freedom takes shape through the combat challenge to serve somewhere. It is time to step out of hiding and to live with courage.

DAY 1

FROM SELF-CENTERED TO CHRIST-CENTERED

Then Jesus said to his disciples, "Whoever wants to be my disciple must deny themselves and take up their cross and follow me."

—Matthew 16:24

Sexual addiction trains us to live for self—selfish, self-gratifying, and self-centered. But when we step out of bondage and into the freedom of following Jesus, we quickly discover his way is the exact opposite: a life of surrender, sacrifice, and selfless love. Jesus' invite in Matt 16 is not a timid suggestion. It is a challenge to go full on for God as we lay down our lustful desires and surrender our wills so that he can live and love through us.

Serving is where God's heartbeat becomes visible through us.

Tragically, rather than reflecting God's love and serving outward, porn and sexual addiction drives us inward, leading us into a cycle of self-centeredness, where our pursuit of personal gratification overshadows the needs and feelings of others. Research indicates that symptoms of porn addiction include decreased empathic tendencies, hindering our ability to form and maintain meaningful relationships.[1] Compounding this, our profound sense of shame can lead to self-stigma, leaving us reluctant to step into opportunities to serve because of our negative self-perception.[2] Studies also reveal that another excessive porn use symptom preventing us from serving is that it decreases motivation and productivity and increases procrastination.[3]

Do not quench the Spirit.

—1 Thessalonians 5:19

The Holy Spirit is often symbolized by fire in the Bible, and we are warned not to suppress its work in and through us. When we cling to addiction, it's like putting a lid over the flame God wants to ignite. The Spirit longs to set us ablaze, but sin chokes the flame before it can catch.

1. Kor et al., "Alterations in Oxytocin and Vasopressin."
2. Grubbs et al. "Transgression as Addiction."
3. Harmony United Psychiatric Care, "Dark Side of Desire," para. 1–9

Not so with you. Instead, whoever wants to become great among you must be your servant, and whoever wants to be first must be slave of all. For even the Son of Man did not come to be served, but to serve, and to give his life as a ransom for many.

—Mark 10:43–45

Addiction has a way of turning us inward. It traps us in isolation, convincing us that we are safest when we hide and that our needs come first. Pornography in particular feeds a self-centered cycle—seeking pleasure without sacrifice, intimacy without relationship, and fulfillment without responsibility.[4] But this endless inward focus only deepens our emptiness.

Jesus offers us a better way in Mark 10:43–45. He reminds us that real life, real joy, and real freedom are not found in being served but in serving. When we choose to step out of ourselves and give to others, something shifts inside us. We begin to see that we are valuable, needed, and capable of reflecting God's love.

Serving flows from our being, not just our doing.

Our willingness to serve is not just about meeting someone else's need—it is about reshaping our own hearts. Serving breaks the chains of selfishness and isolation that have kept us living in selfishness. When we are intentional in serving, it calls us into community, where our struggles lose power as they are exposed to the light through connection and purpose.

There are several benefits we gain as we obey God's call to serve others:

- *It Breaks Self-Centered Cycles*—Addiction is fueled by self-focus, isolation, and turning inward. Serving shifts attention outward, reorienting the heart toward others. Addiction recovery must be woven into spiritual formation, for lasting freedom is discovered in serving others, where spiritual health naturally transforms behavior.[5]
- *It Restores True Intimacy*—We are wired for intimacy, a longing for real oneness with people and the world around us.[6] Porn offers counterfeit connection, while serving cultivates real relationships, empathy, and shared purpose.

4. Mohler, "Seduction of Pornography," para. 13–17.
5. Bird, *Upside-Down Spirituality*, 13.
6. Shaw, "Porn-Addicted Men Can Learn," para. 3.

- *It Rebuilds Identity*—Addiction whispers "we are broken, worthless, and unlovable." Serving proves the opposite: we are needed, capable, and valuable.
- *It Strengthens Discipline*—Serving is directly counter to the pleasure-driven patterns of porn use. As we serve others consistently, God redirects our focus.[7]
- *It Provides Joy and Fulfillment*—In our radical abandonment of porn's promises, we find lasting joy, rooted in love and purpose, not fleeting desire.
- *It Imitates Jesus*—For Christians, serving others reflects the life of Jesus, a lesson we will unpack in detail tomorrow.

By serving others, we not only contribute to the kingdom of God but also reinforce our own commitment to recovery. Our weekly combat challenge is clear: serve somewhere. It may feel small—an open door, a helping hand, an intentional act of generosity—but it is powerful. Every act of service is a step out of darkness and into freedom. The fight will feel lighter when our focus is on others, not ourselves.

DAILY FIGHT PLAN

1. Reread Mark 10:43–45 and explain how you have seen porn and sexual addiction conflict with Jesus' call to serve.
2. In what ways have you seen the Spirit quenched by sexual sin?
3. What benefit of serving do you most look forward to and why?
4. Identify different areas where you can begin serving. If you are unsure where you should serve, reach out to a local church and ask for suggestions.

7. NewSpring Church, "How Serving in the Church," para. 13–14.

DAY 2

THE KING WHO SERVED

Jesus knew that the Father had put all things under his power, and that he had come from God and was returning to God; so he got up from the meal, took off his outer clothing, and wrapped a towel around his waist. After that, he poured water into a basin and began to wash his disciples' feet, drying them with the towel that was wrapped around him.

—John 13:3–5

Our God came to suffer and to save. Jesus stood in our place as our substitute, showing us how to live and serving us with his life. As Christians, we are called to trust his service to us and to exalt him by serving others. His service enables our obedience, and our service testifies to his sacrifice.

Jesus is the Servant-King, and we are his servants.

The King of kings knelt low, wrapped himself in a servant's towel, and touched what no one else wanted to touch—his disciples' dirty, smelly, well-traveled feet. He lowered himself down, took their filth into his hands, and washed them clean. It was so shocking and culturally out of place that Peter recoiled in John 13:8, stating, "You shall never wash my feet." Jesus' response was not what Peter expected: "Unless I wash you, you have no part with me." Suddenly, Peter wanted all of himself—head, hands, feet—to be made clean by Jesus.

The invitation Jesus presented Peter with is the same one he offers us. In our struggle, in our hidden shame, in the places we least want him or others to see, he kneels down. He doesn't look away. He doesn't hesitate. He takes the place of the lowest servant and says, "Let Me wash you. Let Me make you whole."

When he had finished washing their feet, he put on his clothes and returned to his place. "Do you understand what I have done for you?" he asked them. "You call me 'Teacher' and 'Lord,' and rightly so, for that is what I am. Now that I, your Lord and Teacher, have washed your feet, you also should wash one another's feet. I have set you an example that you should do as I have done for you."

—John 13:12–15

Jesus could not have been clearer in that moment: "You should do as I have done for you." That's what real love looks like. It lowers itself. It surprises us. It serves when no one else will. Jesus calls us to love like that—to carry compassion into the mess, to do the unexpected in the name of love.

God does not demand perfection from his disciples in order to serve others, but he does call us to do for others as he had done for us. For recovering porn and sex addicts, this will be uncomfortable because our struggle is an intimacy disorder, one that keeps us living on a relational island. That is why connection forged through serving is so important for the sex addict.

Jesus' call to serve may mean serving someone in a way that feels uncomfortable, humbling, or unseen. Maybe it means laying down pride, stepping into someone else's pain, or choosing to love where lust once ruled our heart.

Porn teaches us to take, to consume, and to use others for our own satisfaction. Jesus teaches us to serve, to give, and to love others sacrificially. He has washed our feet, even the dirtiest parts of our life, and now he calls us to wash the feet of others. To love as he has loved us. To lower ourselves down and serve in ways that reveal his shocking, cleansing, and freeing love.

Jesus' washing of the disciples' feet was a miracle of humility. What Jesus demonstrated in those humble actions, and then confirmed in his command, benefits the sexual addict immensely because we desperately need community. In serving, the more we pour ourselves out, the more we are filled. A breakthrough occurs when we show love to others without self-serving motives because we discover our worth in those moments when we forget ourselves. As we step out of isolation, we discover the truth: we have value and can be valuable to others.

This week will challenge us because we need to be known.

So the question is this: Who will you show love to today? Who will you serve in a way that makes Jesus visible? Because when we serve, our shame loses power, our chains begin to break, and the love of Christ flows through. God's call to serve is an active one, challenging us to step out from the shadows and lies we have hidden behind and begin to form genuine community. Our willingness to obey God's call on our heart will have a direct impact on our freedom because what porn imprisons through isolation, real relationships unlock through love. And we cannot be fully loved if we are not fully known.

The hands that kneel to wash feet are often the ones lifted highest in love. So, serve somewhere and keep on fighting.

DAILY FIGHT PLAN

1. Why would Jesus intentionally take on the posture of the lowest servant, and what does that demand of you as someone who follows him?
2. In what way did Jesus' demonstration of serving foreshadow his death on the cross and what significance does that have for you?
3. Explain what the following statement means for those that have addictive behavior: *We cannot be fully loved if we are not fully known.*
4. Is it possible to serve faithfully and participate in community while still remaining unknown—and how would that hiddenness affect your sobriety?

DAY 3

OUT OF THE CAGE, INTO THE KINGDOM

Lonny had been programmed and conditioned to appreciate pornography since an early age, merely a toddler in diapers. Due to exposure happening early in his life and lacking the necessary resources or support to find healing, his life spiraled under the weight of sexual addiction over the next thirty years. Lonny longed for normalcy—for connection, peace, and purpose—but every relationship eventually fractured under the pressure of his hidden struggle. Religion seemed a dead end, impossible to attain. Work and education offered brief distractions, but his compulsion eroded consistency, leaving him underqualified, underemployed, and inwardly exhausted. Lonny felt alone.

When Lonny finally married, he carried the secret of pornography with him. Fear kept him from revealing his true brokenness because he believed he was unlovable. Instead, he locked away the darkest parts of his past and addictive behavior. As their family grew, the foundation of their marriage weakened. The day his wife uncovered the truth, the betrayal proved too heavy to bear. Divorce followed and Lonny's isolation was magnified as his limited visitation rights minimized the amount of time he could spend with his children.

Lonny was stuck, isolated, and desperate for community.

God did not create us to live in isolation. Like Lonny, we are wired for connection. In week 3, we began identifying our B.L.A.S.T.E.D. emotions, including loneliness, which leads to unwanted sexual behavior and fantasy.[8] The problem is that porn pulls us away from true intimacy and healthy relationships, as it inevitably creates more loneliness.[9] The duality of loneliness and pornography is a cruel one: loneliness drives porn use, and porn use deepens loneliness.[10] In our loneliness, fake intimacy of porn becomes more appealing to us.[11] The end result is that porn consistently impacts the quality of our relationships.

The cruel irony of porn is that it promises connection while deepening the very void it pretends to fill. In an extensive meta-analysis of forty-one studies that included 70,541 participants, a significant negative correlation

8. Mestre-Bach et al., "Loneliness, Pornography Use."
9. Ugese et al., "Pornography Addiction in Emerging Adults."
10. Butler et al., "Pornography use and loneliness."
11. Hesse and Floyd, "Affection Substitution."

between pornography and quality of sexual intimacy was revealed.[12] The myth that porn amplifies our sex life is just that, as the truth reveals the negative impact it has on intimacy. Though fantasy may offer short-term escape in moments of crisis, it ultimately amplifies the underlying issue, ensuring the inevitable and intensified return of loneliness and isolation.

In everything I did, I showed you that by this kind of hard work we must help the weak, remembering the words the Lord Jesus himself said: "It is more blessed to give than to receive."

—Acts 20:35

It is not about us. Our sexual addiction may have conditioned our minds to selfishly take, but Jesus tells us it is more blessed to selflessly give. As we step out of isolation, we form healthy relationships where loneliness had previously been our closest companion. This is why our weekly combat challenge is to serve somewhere. Acts of service allow us to experience the power of healing through sacrificial giving. When we live with genuine humility and serve selflessly, shame loses its grip. In the presence of real acceptance, especially through serving with others, we experience a powerful breakthrough as we discover we are truly loved and accepted.

The deeper we grow in genuine intimacy with God and others, the more our sexual addiction fades into nothing.

In the late 1970s, Canadian psychologist Bruce Alexander challenged traditional views of addiction with an experiment known as Rat Park.[13] Previous studies had consistently demonstrated how rats caged in solitary confinement compulsively consume drug-laced bottles of water until they overdosed.[14] Dr. Alexander believed that isolation—not the drugs alone—played a key role in their drug use. To test his theory, he built Rat Park, a large environment offering food, toys, tunnels, and other rats for social interaction.[15] Rat Park offered two options for hydration, one water and the other drug-laced.

The results were fascinating. Rats in Rat Park chose to consume only a fraction of the drug-laced water, with no overdoses and many ignoring

12. Abdi et al., "Effect of Pornography."
13. Alexander, *Globalization of Addiction*, 195.
14. Alexander, "Rat Park," para. 1–7.
15. Alexander, *Globalization of Addiction*, 195.

the vice altogether.[16] This is a stark contrast to the rats kept in isolation. Even more remarkable, rats that had been previously addicted to drugs now chose social interaction over the retreat to their addictive behavior. Dr. Alexander's study revealed that environment, connection, and purpose play a critical role in addiction recovery.

Freedom from addiction isn't abstinence—it's belonging.

Like the rats, Lonny's breakthrough came when he joined a Fight Club group at a local church. There, he began to build real relationships and discover purpose rooted in God rather than shame. Though healing within his family is still unfolding, the friendships he has found shattered his cage of isolation that once held him in emotional, relational, and spiritual death. In this community, Lonny is fully known, fully accepted, and deeply valued as a child of God. Today, Lonny walks in freedom—and with joy, he reaches back to help others take their next steps toward it.

DAILY FIGHT PLAN

1. How have you seen the following statement as true in your life? *Loneliness drives porn use, and porn use deepens loneliness.*
2. What stands out to you most about Rat Park?
3. *Carry each other's burdens, and in this way you will fulfill the law of Christ.* —GALATIANS 6:2

   Explain how this verse applies to what Lonny experienced within a Fight Club group.

16. Alexander, *Globalization of Addiction*, 195.

DAY 4

GENERATION DISCONNECTED

No generation has felt loneliness like Gen Z, with rates of isolation surpassing that of millennials and Gen X.[17] Feelings of isolation are prevalent across all generations, impacting more than three out of five Americans, but Gen Z experiences it the most.[18] Though adolescent boys and girls both experience isolation, females report feeling lonely (44 percent) at nearly double that of boys (25 percent).[19] In a generation where connection is at the touch of our finger, loneliness is flourishing.

Gen Z experiences loneliness more when porn is involved. A recent study revealed that 20 percent of those who rarely or never view porn express feeling lonely, while that number jumps to 36 percent for those viewing porn daily.[20] Technology may bring the world to our fingertips, but it cannot create true intimacy.

Increased social media use often deepens feelings of loneliness, amplifying the natural vulnerabilities that come with adolescence. U.S. teens spend roughly five hours daily on social media.[21] Gen Z stands out as the first generation to live entirely in the digital age, with 95 percent of teens having smartphones and 45 percent online constantly.[22] Isolation created by social media does not just impact emotions—it takes a toll on physical and mental health, leading to poor sleep, depression, and suicidal thoughts.[23]

Social media can also have a negative impact on sexuality.[24] Porn is pervasive on social media, with 64 percent of teens admitting they have accidentally stumbled upon it while accessing a social media platform.[25] That same study warned that 80 percent of child sex crimes originate on social media platforms and predators commonly leverage those platforms to solicit victims.

17. Blake, "Why Gen Z is Loneliest," para. 1.
18. Demarinis, "Loneliness at Epidemic Levels."
19. Bledsoe and Smith, "Male Loneliness and Isolation," para. 4.
20. Wang and Toscano, "Frequent Porn Use Is Linked," para. 12.
21. DeAngelis, "Teens Spending Nearly 5 Hours."
22. Anderson and Jiang, "Teens, Social Media, and Technology," para. 2.
23. DeAngelis, "Teens Are Spending Nearly 5 Hours."
24. Pawlikowska-Gorzelańczyk et al., "Impact of Internet Addiction," 6407.
25. Culture Reframed, "Pornography and Predators," para. 4.

While social media is not inherently bad, like fire, it can burn if left unchecked.

Our chapter 2 weekly combat challenge was to set up guardrails in your life, and social media is an area where we will all spiritually drift if we are not careful. Social media invites temptation for the recovering fantasy, porn, and sex addict, especially when idly scrolling during our alone time. So often we play Russian "reelette" with our social media reels, spinning them until it lands on a loaded chamber. What we need is genuine community instead of the false relationships our screens offer.

In a world more connected by screens than by hearts, our society—and especially our youth—is crying out for real, authentic relationships like never before.

This is where *Fight Club: Live in Freedom* is unique. We put emphasis on who we need to be with, because if we get relationships right, freedom will follow. Relationship-based discipleship is an important part of our twelve-week journey. We cannot manufacture community through programs, but a program can open the door for genuine community to form. We will discuss further how you can create a Fight Club chapter in your community at the completion of this book. For now, let's explore the profound picture of community the New Testament provides.

They devoted themselves to the apostles' teaching and to fellowship, to the breaking of bread and to prayer.

—Acts 2:42

The Greek had a word for fellowship, *koinonia*, which describes an intimate bond in Jesus that is demonstrated through encouragement, spiritual growth, and active support for one another. *Koinonia* occurs twenty times in the New Testament, the first being in Acts 2, shortly after Jesus ascended to heaven. God did not intend for us to live in isolation. A powerful example of his desire is found in a study of the phrase "one another" (emphasis added below).

- *Be devoted to one another in love. Honor one another above yourselves.* —Rom 12:10
- *Live in harmony with one another.* Do not be proud, but be willing to associate with people of low position. Do not be conceited. —Rom 12:16

- *Accept one another*, then, just as Christ accepted you, in order to bring praise to God. —Rom 15:7
- You, my brothers and sisters, were called to be free. But do not use your freedom to indulge the flesh; rather, *serve one another* humbly in love. —Gal 5:13
- *Be kind and compassionate to one another*, forgiving each other, just as in Christ God forgave you. —Eph 4:32
- Let the message of Christ dwell among you richly as you *teach and admonish one another* with all wisdom through psalms, hymns, and songs from the Spirit, singing to God with gratitude in your hearts. —Col 3:16
- Therefore *encourage one another* and build each other up, just as in fact you are doing. —1 Thess 5:11
- And let us consider how we may *spur one another* on toward love and good deeds. —Heb 10:24
- *Offer hospitality to one another* without grumbling. —1 Pet 4:9
- For this is the message you heard from the beginning: We should *love one another.* —1 John 3:11

When community is absent, the heart withers; isolation is not solitude—it's a slow death. So, serve somewhere and serve one another.

DAILY FIGHT PLAN

1. Why do you believe Gen Z is the loneliest generation?
2. In what ways have you seen social media as challenging in your pursuit of freedom and how have their algorithms contributed?
3. We briefly discussed the power of community found in a Fight Club group. Explain how that fits with the following verse.

   For where two or three gather in my name, there am I with them. —Matthew 18:20
4. Read the following verse and write out a prayer asking God to inspire you to step up and out in service.

   The harvest is plentiful but the workers are few. —Luke 10:2

DAY 5

2° FROM CLARITY

In July 2023, NASA lost contact with Voyager 2 when a slight misalignment of just two degrees turned its antenna away from Earth.[26] At over 12 billion miles from home, that tiny shift was enough to sever communication, leaving the uncrewed robotic probe adrift in the silent darkness of space. For weeks, it seemed lost beyond recovery. Then NASA sent a powerful long-distance signal, known as a "shout," across the void to Voyager 2. Against all odds, connection was restored and life-giving communication flowed once again.

Addiction feels the same. We drift in a cold, empty void, convinced we're beyond rescue. But we are often only a small turn away from realignment—only a "two-degree shift" from living in the identity Christ has already spoken over us. His voice still calls across the distance, powerful enough to break through our silence and bring us home.

Whether you turn to the right or to the left, your ears will hear a voice behind you, saying, "This is the way; walk in it."

—Isaiah 30:21

Isaiah offers a promise that God will provide divine guidance to his people with a clear, unmistakable voice, even when our hearts have drifted toward the wrong path. But there's a condition: We must be willing to listen. When we accept the lie that we are too far gone, with nothing of value to give or receive because of the choices we have made, we have already lost. We have waved our white flag, another casualty drifting into the silence of oblivion when, all along, his voice is still speaking, ready to lead us home. This week, Jesus' command has been clear, do as he did and serve somewhere. As we will see below, the benefits of serving far outweigh the pull to remain in isolation.

Serving Impacts Our Well-Being

A generous person will prosper; whoever refreshes others will be refreshed.

—Proverbs 11:25

26. NASA Jet Propulsion Laboratory, "NASA Mission Update," para. 3.

Serving others does not just bless those we help—it also renews us. Research shows that volunteering strengthens our physical and mental health, fostering positive emotions and cultivating a deeper sense of life satisfaction.[27] God designed us to thrive when we live beyond ourselves. When we pour out in service, he pours back in, filling us with his Spirit and aligning our hearts with his definition of true well-being.

Serving Helps Us Discover and Refine Our Gifts

Each of you should use whatever gift you have received to serve others, as faithful stewards of God's grace in its various forms.

—1 Peter 4:10

Spiritual gifts are God-given abilities for service and ministry.[28] When we move beyond our relationally solitary confinement to serve in ways that stretch us, we often discover hidden or underdeveloped talents. God uses our willingness to serve as a workshop of the Spirit where our natural talents, inner longings, and spiritual gifts are revealed. What is more important than finding the "perfect" place to serve is to simply start serving somewhere.

Serving Cultivates Outward Focus Instead of Inward Fixation

Set your minds on things above, not on earthly things.

—Colossians 3:2

Perspective matters. Serving others exposes us to the needs of others and suffering beyond our self-centered perspective. Instead, we push ourselves out of self-absorption and create space for God's voice, because humility is tied to attentiveness. When sin keeps focus inward, it is hard to hear and follow divine promptings; however, serving breaks down those walls and softens hearts to better hear God's voice.

27. Kuonqui, "Measuring Volunteering," 31.
28. Rogers, "Spiritual Gifts," para. 3–4.

Service Gives Feedback and Confirmation

We discover our spiritual gifts through inner conviction and external feedback. Serving provides test cases on the difference we make. We must persevere when serving gets hard or loses its thrill because porn addiction is linked to lack of motivation and low self-determination.[29] Be open to feedback from fellow volunteers and leaders while serving because it's how we grow. Also, feel the freedom to serve in other areas because we should not hate how we are serving. God has given us all unique spiritual gifts, but it is our responsibility to use them.

Service Deepens Our Sense of Purpose and Meaning

For we are God's handiwork, created in Christ Jesus to do good works, which God prepared in advance for us to do.

—EPHESIANS 2:10

The Greek word for *handiwork* is *poiēma*, from which we get the English word *poem*, signifying how we are artfully made by God. We are his masterpiece, and like any poem, there is a story to tell. We will find purpose and meaning in his poem, or rewrite it a tragedy, as we continue our pursuit in addiction. Either way, our story is not done being written. We are neither defined by our worst moment nor our greatest triumph. So, let us rise and live out God's poem—each act of service is a divine line in the masterpiece he's writing through our lives.

DAILY FIGHT PLAN

1. Such a small shift made a huge difference for Voyager 2. What small shift do you believe would help you realign closer with God?
2. How does God speak to us through serving?
3. What reservations, fears, and excuses have been preventing you from stepping out and serving?
4. Write out a prayer asking God to embolden your heart to take a big next step and serve somewhere.

29. Sulyok et al., "Highs and Lows of Pornography."

WEEK 9—SHAME PEELED BACK

WEEKLY MEMORY VERSE

Therefore, there is now no condemnation for those who are in Christ Jesus, because through Christ Jesus the law of the Spirit who gives life has set you free from the law of sin and death.

—Romans 8:1

WEEKLY COMBAT CHALLENGE

Confess your story to somebody.

SHACKLED BY SECRETS

DYING BEHIND THE MASK

Ryan grew up in a small Texas town, within a faith-based home that was largely involved in the local church, attending multiple times a week. As a child, Ryan was exposed to adult content when he discovered some pornographic images. He initially kept the discovery a secret out of shame, only to continue returning for more due to the addictive lure and excitement he experienced.

When Ryan hit puberty, he was unprepared to manage the sexual desires years of porn exposure had conditioned in him. His addiction to self-gratification led him to begin seeking out images and masturbating whenever possible. With an overwhelming sense of shame, Ryan began overcompensating at church by serving in every ministry he could join.

His effort to outpace his conscience and good Christian appearance was exhausting. For a season, Ryan was able to keep the facade up, but like a house of cards built too high to stand, everything came crashing down.

While shame prevented Ryan from having the courage or confidence to speak to girls, the spirit of lust wanted more. Ryan found himself in a physically intimate relationship with a close relative and sexual acts were performed. The shame clung to him like a second skin he could not peel away. He confessed to his parents about his sexual addiction and the response was devastating. He felt like the lowest note in a broken song, vibrating with shame. Thoughts of suicide came often and the only thing keeping Ryan from acting on it was his belief in God.

His home life became stricter, with mandatory Bible studies, essays of wrongdoings, and TV time scrutinized. In addition, Ryan's parents sent him for counseling with church leadership. The unwanted behavior would improve temporarily, collapsing the moment any trigger brushed against old wounds. The slightest rejection sent him spiraling.

When Ryan started college, he suddenly found himself free from the strict rules of his home. He now had unlimited access to search for anything, at any time, from anywhere. With that freedom, his need for porn grew as his friendships and community vanished. He felt caught in an endless cycle—seeking God, feeling rejection, and then retreating back to the temporary comfort of porn.

When Ryan eventually met his wife, he believed marriage would end his struggles. For a time, he experienced freedom from unwanted sexual behavior, but soon, the familiar temptations and compulsive patterns returned. He was devastated to realize that the addiction had not disappeared. Burdened by his childhood trauma and a deeply negative view of himself, Ryan became convinced that if he confessed, divorce would be inevitable. Paralyzed by fear and shame, he wrestled with his emotions until it finally pushed him to confess to his wife.

To his surprise, she did not reject him. Instead, his wife embraced him with grace and stood by his side, willing to help however she could. Yet, even her unwavering support was not enough to break the chains of addiction. Ryan fell into a pattern of unloading his shame onto her, feeling temporary relief, and then repeating the cycle—sin, confession, relief, relapse.

One morning in church, a man stood up and shared his own story of porn addiction and the freedom he had since found. Ryan was transfixed. Up to that point, he had felt alone, unaware that others in his community struggled with the same thing, hidden in the silence of shame. Ryan realized his greatest fear was not just the addiction itself but the terror of being truly known. That thought stayed with him, and he began to wrestle with what it would mean to live in the light.

Ryan signed up for a Fight Club class and experienced freedom as he let go of the shame carried in silence throughout his life.

I have been crucified with Christ and I no longer live, but Christ lives in me. The life I now live in the body, I live by faith in the Son of God, who loved me and gave himself for me.

—Galatians 2:20

This week, we will learn to overcome shame—not by hiding it or pretending it's gone, but by facing it and putting it in its rightful place. Shame no longer has to imprison us. Like Ryan, we must understand that we are only as sick as the secrets we keep. True freedom begins when we realize we are not defined by our worst failures or our greatest successes but by the life of Jesus within us. His death on the cross broke the power of sin and shame forever.

Our weekly memory verse reminds us in Rom 8:1, "There is now no condemnation for those who are in Christ Jesus." The Greek meaning for condemnation carries a verdict of guilt. Our sin sentences us to a spiritual death and separation from God, but Paul's statement leaves no room for ongoing condemnation in those that trust in Jesus.

This week, we will learn to strip away the shame we have embraced, despite the fact Jesus already paid the ransom. We will also further step into the light as we confess our story to someone.

DAY 1

THE SHAME GAME: FROM GARDEN TO SCREEN

In the beginning, there was no shame. Adam and Eve walked freely in the garden, perfectly known and perfectly loved. But in a moment of rebellion, everything changed. When they chose to eat from the tree of the knowledge of good and evil, their eyes were opened—but not in the way they imagined. Suddenly, innocence was replaced with self-awareness, and self-awareness gave birth to shame.

Then the eyes of both of them were opened, and they realized they were naked; so they sewed fig leaves together and made coverings for themselves. Then the man and his wife heard the sound of the Lord God as he was walking in the garden in the cool of the day, and they hid from the Lord God among the trees of the garden.

—Genesis 3:7–8

When Adam and Eve heard God, they concealed themselves. Shame drove them to hide and for the first time, humanity covered what God created. Adam's confession in Gen 3:10, "I was afraid because I was naked; so I hid," has become the anthem of every heart affected by shame.

Porn, sexual addiction, and fantasy operate by the same method. What began in the garden as disobedience now plays out in the digital age through screens. Porn promises knowledge, excitement, and satisfaction, but what it really delivers is isolation, loneliness, and shame. Like Adam and Eve, we think our secret sin will give us something God is withholding, but once we take the bait, our eyes open and the weight of shame sets in.

Sin's fruit is shame.

The problem with shame is not just that it makes us feel bad; it makes us hide. We cover our tracks, clear our histories, and construct fig leaves of excuses to gaslight others. But the more we hide, the more disconnected we become—from God, from others, and even from ourselves. Shame whispers its lies and when we believe it, we isolate, we numb, and we repeat the cycle.

Fight Club: Live in Freedom

The Lord God made garments of skin for Adam and his wife and clothed them.

—Genesis 3:21

Before the fall, Adam and Eve's relationship was in perfect harmony with God. After the fall, that unity shattered, creating a gap that drove them away from God. Adam and Eve's first instinct was to cover themselves, but God's first act of grace was to cover them his way. He provided them with garments of skin, symbolic of the first sacrifice and foreshadowing the ultimate grace covering to come through Jesus' death.

The difference is profound: Our coverings hide us, but God's covering heals us.

Porn addiction thrives in secrecy, convincing us that our choices are harmless, manageable, and without consequences. But every time we consume porn, a piece of us dies—our relationships strain and our connection with God weakens. We start living as though we are back in Eden and afraid of being found out.

But like the garden, God still walks into our hiding places and asks the same question posed to Adam, "Where are you?" God already knows where we are. He's asking because we have lost track of ourselves and he wants to draw us out of hiding, not to humiliate us but to heal us. Godly freedom requires exposure as it brings what's been hidden into the light. When we confess, bringing our sin to God and to trusted people, shame loses its power.

Adam and Eve's story didn't end with their failure. God didn't abandon them in their shame. He clothed them, covered them, and set in motion a plan of redemption. Likewise, our story does not have to end a tragedy. Through Jesus, we are offered the same grace, an invitation out of hiding and into healing.

When we confess, we rediscover what Adam and Eve lost; the freedom to be fully known and fully loved. A study revealed how confession through support groups, such as Fight Club, are linked with a 72 percent reduction in shame, 61 percent increase in self-forgiveness, and 66 percent increase in sense of community.[1] The previous study aligns with findings from the National Center on Addiction and Substance Abuse, which reported that participants in faith-based recovery programs maintain up to 84 percent

1. Scalese et al., "Processes and Outcomes of Pornography."

sobriety after one year, compared to 54 percent in non-faith-based programs.[2] Healing begins when we stop concealing and start confessing. That is why our weekly combat challenge is for us to confess our story to somebody.

Confession creates both discernment of sin and the practice of relational repentance.

The same God who came searching for Adam in the garden is searching for us today. Not with condemnation but with compassion. Not to add to our shame but to cover us with grace. The question is, will we keep hiding or will we authentically reveal ourselves? Because on the other side of confession is freedom—and freedom is worth fighting for.

DAILY FIGHT PLAN

1. What was Adam and Eve's first response after eating the fruit, and how does that reflect your behavior after sexual sin?
2. How does confession change the shame narrative?
3. Identify someone you are considering confessing to, write down their name and a short prayer asking God to provide the courage to follow through.

2. Grim and Grim, "Belief, Behavior, and Belonging."

DAY 2

SHAME VS. GUILT

Yesterday, we discussed how shame was absent from God's original design. We were meant to live with nothing to hide and no need to feel embarrassment or inadequacy, both in our personal relationships and with God. Unfortunately, our world today is forever marred by sin and the consequences it carries.

The resulting burden that often stems from our sin is shame.

Shame is the subjective experience from our objective guilt—both from what we have done (or failed to do) and from what others have done (or failed to do) to us. Shame is a soul-crushing, identity-twisting emotion that rarely comes from God. Our shame has everything to do with our *sense of self*, differing greatly from guilt that comes as a result of our *actions*.

The challenge for the addict in avoiding shame is that our unwanted behavior often leaves us in a perpetual state of self-loathing. We may want to quit our addictive behavior, making surface-level promises never to return, but in a moment of weakness, our determination combusts. Repeatedly, we are put to the fire and feel the flame, withering under the intensity of its heat. And all we are left with is shame.

Though guilt and shame often overlap, they are not the same.

Both feelings are painful, but they affect us in very different ways. Guilt points to what we have done—it is the honest voice within us saying, "You're better than that." In this way, guilt can be redemptive, guiding us toward repentance and growth. Shame, however, attacks who we are. It desires to disqualify us. It distorts our identity, convincing us that our failures define our worth. While guilt can lead us closer to Jesus, shame often drives us further into isolation.

Guilt says we have done bad while shame says we are bad.

Shame traps us in a lie where our identity is defined by our worst moments, but God says otherwise. We are not measured by our failures or our greatest successes. We are defined by his grace and the forgiveness he generously gives—again and again. Understanding this is revolutionary for the porn and sex addict because if we are to break the shame cycle, our sense of self must be found in Jesus, not sin.

THE SHAME CYCLE

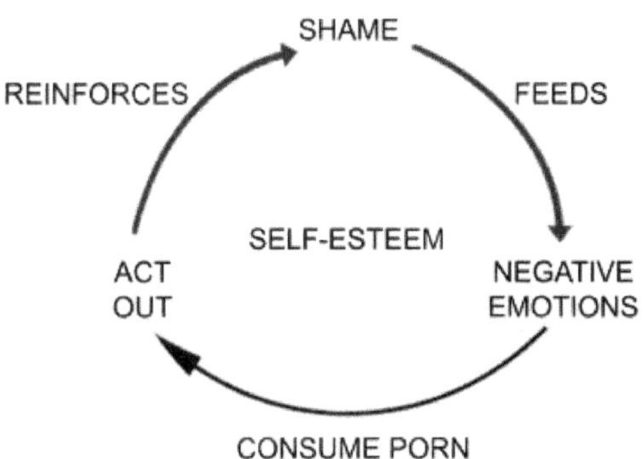

With each turn through the shame cycle, our self-esteem takes another blow. Shame makes us feel worthless, fueling our negative emotions. To escape the pain, we turn to porn, fantasy, and other forms of sexual addiction for temporary relief. But that relief quickly fades, leaving us with deeper shame than before. Once trapped in the shame cycle, breaking free becomes incredibly difficult.

In him we have redemption through his blood, the forgiveness of sins, in accordance with the riches of God's grace.

—EPHESIANS 1:7

Ephesians 1:7 offers the foundation for salvation, achieved through Jesus' life, death, and resurrection. With salvation comes the exit ramp from the shame cycle. Jesus' sacrifice provides forgiveness for our sins, and without it, we would remain trapped in shame, unable to approach a holy and perfect God. But through Jesus' sacrifice and resurrection, a way was made and all of this flows from God's grace and fulfills his promises. Throughout the Bible, God declares his intention to rescue his people from sin and restore what was broken. In Jesus, those promises are fulfilled.

Whoever conceals their sins does not prosper, but the one who confesses and renounces them finds mercy.

—PROVERBS 28:13

The Hebrew word for *renounce* is *ozev*, which means to *forsake or leave*. The charge for us in this verse is to abandon the secrecy of our sin because we are only as sick as the secrets we keep. Our shame thrives in secrecy, so we must strive to be known. Our weekly combat challenge is to confess to someone, and later this week, we will explore healthy ways to present our story safely. Remember, we cannot be unconditionally loved if we are conditionally known.

DAILY FIGHT PLAN

1. How are shame and guilt alike? How are they different?
2. How has shame been harmful to you in your pursuit of freedom?
3. Why is Jesus' sacrifice so important in combating shame?
4. What would it look like for you to renounce (forsake) your secret sins?

DAY 3

MISPLACED SHAME VS. WELL-PLACED SHAME

Yesterday, we made the distinction between guilt and shame, along with the danger of the shame cycle. But is all shame destructive to our pursuit of freedom from sexual addiction, or can it help in the healing process? Shame is generally viewed as a negative and destructive emotion that is harmful to our mental and emotional well-being, serving as a barrier to the healing process and often leading to hiding.[3]

But not all shame is equal.

Contrary to what culture, or even psychology, might suggest, there are moments when shame is exactly what we should feel—and others when it's the last thing we should carry. The difference between the two determines whether shame destroys us or drives us closer to God. The Bible makes this distinction clear. There is a *misplaced shame* we should reject and *well-placed shame* that can lead us to repentance and healing.

Misplaced Shame

Many of us carry misplaced shame—the belief that we are permanently dirty, unworthy of love, too weak, and beyond forgiveness. This is the kind of shame that Satan loves to whisper, but it is a lie. God does not shame those he has forgiven. Romans 8:1 reminds us, "There is now no condemnation for those who are in Christ Jesus." This is why our week 4 combat challenge is to reconcile if God is enough. When we step over the line of faith, our judgment is removed. To continue wearing that shame demonstrates unbelief towards his grace and mercy.

However, if you suffer as a Christian, do not be ashamed,
but praise God that you bear that name.

—1 PETER 4:16

Seeking righteousness comes at a cost, and we must unashamedly pursue freedom because we desire to honor God. If our shame is rooted in pride, not reverence, we will never confront shame at its source. Like Paul

3. Psychology Today, "Shame," para. 1.

in 2 Cor 12:10, we must "delight in our weakness" because it allows God's power to be displayed through us.

But each person is tempted when they are dragged away by their own evil desire and enticed. Then, after desire has conceived, it gives birth to sin; and sin, when it is full-grown, gives birth to death.

—James 1:14–15

We often feel misplaced shame when tempted, though we may not have done anything to dishonor God. We must recognize that temptation itself is not a sin. Our enemy is described in 1 Pet 5:8 as a "roaring lion looking for someone to devour." Temptation can be unavoidable, but entertaining temptation is always avoidable and where shame moves from misplaced to well-placed.

Well-Placed Shame

Well-placed shame is what we feel when our actions dishonor God—when we have chosen lust over love, self over surrender, and secrecy over light. This kind of shame is right, because it signals that our actions have grieved the heart of God and distorted his design for our hearts and relationships. This shame pleads with us, as it does in 1 Cor 15:34: "Come back to your senses as you ought, and stop sinning."

The woman at the well in John 4 shows how misplaced shame can become well-placed shame for the sexually and relationally broken through the grace of Jesus. During Jesus' ministry, Jews viewed Samaritans as ethnically and religiously impure, and most avoided them altogether. Yet Jesus intentionally crossed deep cultural, racial, religious, and gender divides to love a sexually broken woman others rejected.

The story describes a Samaritan woman that came to draw water from a well at noon. When Jesus asked, "Will you give me a drink?" she was stunned. Why was a Jew talking to her? Their conversation led to his offer of *living water*—eternal life. Still confused, she listened as Jesus said, "Whoever drinks the water I give him will never thirst" (John 4:14).

When Jesus suggested she bring her husband, her secret was exposed: five failed marriages and a current live-in relationship. She had chosen the hottest hour of the day to draw water to avoid public shame, as most women avoided the heat of the day. Yet, Jesus' gentle honesty confronted her sin and shame, inviting both to be redeemed.

In that moment, misplaced shame became well-placed shame, bringing her to repentance. The difference is this, misplaced shame is self-centered, but well-placed shame is God-centered. One drives us to hide, the other draws us to grace.

But in both cases of shame, the answer is the same: turn to Jesus.

When we believe the promises of God, shame no longer chains us. It becomes a teacher, not a tyrant. Sexual sin thrives in secrecy, but shame loses its power in the light. Our combat challenge this week is to confess our story to somebody. The Samaritan woman demonstrated that in John 4:42 as she left her jar with Jesus and went back to town to share her testimony. Are you willing to boldly do the same?

DAILY FIGHT PLAN

1. How do you distinguish between destructive shame and God-given conviction, and how has confusing the two affected your pursuit of freedom?
2. In what ways have you been like the Samaritan woman, going out of your way to avoid feelings of shame?
3. *No one who believes in him will be put to shame.* —Romans 10:11

   Reflecting on the verse in Romans, how does trusting that God does not shame you change the way you approach confession and accountability?

DAY 4

THREE STRIKES, BUT NOT OUT

Darryl Strawberry was an eight-time All-Star, four-time World Series champion Major League Baseball superstar.[4] Throughout his prolific sports career, Strawberry was one of the most feared sluggers in the sport, known for his remarkable home runs and intimidating presence in the batter's box. He had an illustrious career, having played for the Mets, Dodgers, Giants, and Yankees.[5] But behind the legendary swagger and accomplishments was a spiritual brokenness fueled by destructive behavior that included sexual addiction, alcohol, and drug abuse.[6]

The former National League Rookie of the Year was driven by sexually compulsive behavior that led him to sneak off into the dugout during baseball games to have sex.[7] Eventually, he was arrested and sentenced to eighteen months in jail for drug possession and soliciting an undercover cop.[8] Reflecting on his life, Darryl Strawberry stated, "I felt like such a failure. I had failed at so much. Regardless of what I had achieved in the ballpark, all the fame I had and money I made, I felt that I was a complete loser as a man and a human being."[9]

Like Darryl Strawberry, we may feel as though life has already thrown us two strikes—standing ashamedly at the plate, desperate for one clean swing to turn everything around.

Peter knew that feeling. He had walked with Jesus and witnessed miracles that were reshaping the world and touching eternity. Riding that wave of awe and conviction, he boldly proclaimed in John 13:37 at the Last Supper that he would lay down his life for Jesus. Yet, just hours later, he cowardly denied even knowing him—not once, but three times. In an instant, courage crumbled, hope vanished, and shame rushed in to replace the boldness he had carried so confidently. Regret settled like a heavy weight, pressing down on a heart that had hours earlier dared to proclaim unwavering loyalty.

4. Strawberry and Weeks, *Turn Your Season Around*, xiii.
5. ESPN, "Darryl Strawberry," fig. 1.
6. Strawberry and Weeks, *Turn Your Season Around*, 1.
7. Rapaport, "Darryl Strawberry Says," para. 2.
8. Associated Press, "Former Baseball Star Darryl Strawberry," para. 1.
9. Strawberry, "Let It All Go," para. 1.

Addicts often make bold commitments to freedom. We make these claims to self, loved ones, and God only to find ourselves, like Peter, caving hours later when the going gets tough. And the more intense the storm of negative emotions, the stronger the urge to act out sexually for relief—reinforcing the very cycle we want to escape. This very torment of shame leaves us often longing for God to simply remove the thorn from our side, a weakness we believe beyond our capability. This is an immaturity of faith we must outgrow.

God wants all of our heart because he will not reside where he does not preside.

Like Peter, we find ourselves drawn back to Jesus, the One we have denied through our addictive behavior, yet still long to know. But before sending Peter out to change the world, there was unfinished business between them. Jesus first had to heal the shame that chained his heart. On the morning of Peter's restoration, Jesus already had breakfast prepared, grilled fish and bread for the weary disciples. After they ate, Jesus turned to Peter for a private moment of restoration found in John 21:15–17. Three denials, three questions:

Do you truly love me more than these?
    Yes, Lord. You know that I love you.
Feed my lambs. . . . Do you truly love me?
    Yes, Lord, You know that I love You.
Shepherd my sheep. . . . Do you love me?
    You know all things. You know that I love you.
Feed my sheep.

Jesus did not shame Peter, he restored him. Each question was an invitation to rewrite failure instead of reliving it. In place of shame, Jesus offered grace. In place of disqualification, Jesus offered purpose.

But even in Peter's restoration, Jesus had to toss him an underhand pitch to get him moving. The first two times Jesus questioned Peter's love, he used the Greek word *agape* for *love* which means *selflessness* and *unconditional adoration*. Peter's response reflected his feelings of unworthiness and shame, as he replied with the Greek word *phileo*, meaning *warm, affectionate, brotherly love*. Jesus, always willing to patiently draw us closer to himself, handled Peter's insecurity with grace by rephrasing the question.

"Do you *phileo* me?" To which Peter comfortably responded, "Lord, you know all things; you know that I *phileo* you."

Healing takes time, but Jesus did with Peter as he desires to do in all our lives; meet us where we are and restore what is broken. Darryl Strawberry experienced that same grace as God called him into ministry to use the broken parts of his past for a new purpose—turning his pain into a platform to share the gospel and help others find hope.[10] When shame calls strike three, God's grace steps up to the plate.

DAILY FIGHT PLAN

1. What bold declarations or commitments have you made in your pursuit of freedom only to have the shame of porn and sexual addiction make you feel like a liar?
2. How does the following verse offer hope to you, despite the multiple failures you have had trying to find freedom from lust and sexual addiction?

   Being confident of this, that he who began a good work in you will carry it on to completion until the day of Christ Jesus. —Philippians 1:6
3. Write a prayer asking God to forgive you for listening to shame's lies and let him know how much you love him . . . even if that is only *phileo* at this time.

10. Strawberry and Weeks, *Turn Your Season Around*, 73–78.

DAY 5

THE LIGHT THAT DOES NOT SHAME

This is the message we have heard from him and declare to you: God is light; in him there is no darkness at all. If we claim to have fellowship with him and yet walk in the darkness, we lie and do not live out the truth. But if we walk in the light, as he is in the light, we have fellowship with one another, and the blood of Jesus, his Son, purifies us from all sin.

—John 1:5–7

Light changes everything. It exposes darkness and heals what secrecy harms.

Our enemy's domain is darkness, and his strategy is deception. Shame is one of his favorite weapons, thriving where secrets hide. As long as we remain in the shadows, we are his prisoner. That is why the Bible references light more than 250 times. Light is a recurring theme that calls us, again and again, to live in God's light and reflect it through our actions. Every time we drag our hidden sin into the light—with confession and repentance—we declare war on hell itself.

Confession is an act of war. It is our battle cry against the powers of darkness. It boldly declares, "You don't own me anymore." Breaking the chains of secrecy disrupts the shame cycle. Shame begins to die the moment we speak the truth, starving unwanted compulsive behavior that once fed off silence.

The problem is that honesty terrifies us. We want to be free without being fully known. Fear compels us to manage our sin privately, to fake healing while hiding wounds. This internal negotiation delays freedom until we run out of tomorrows. Darkness may feel safer in the moment because it's familiar, but it's holding us back. In the end, sin will always take us farther than we wanted to go, keep us longer than we wanted to stay, and cost us more than we wanted to pay.

Confession dismantles our illusion of control and lets us breathe freely again.

The silence of unconfessed sin is the static that blocks the frequency of God's rescue, but our admission of sin uproots the pride that keeps sexual sin alive and desirable. In confession, we exchange the suffocating air of secrecy for the fresh air of grace.

1. *Confess to a Small Circle of Friends*

One who has unreliable friends soon comes to ruin,
but there is a friend who sticks closer than a brother.

—Proverbs 18:24

We don't need to tell everyone, but we must tell someone. As we discussed last week, isolation is the breeding ground of relapse. We must find mature brothers or sisters who can pray with us, speak truth to us, and walk beside us. Face-to-face confession reminds us our sin isn't abstract—it wounds real people and grieves a real God.

2. *Confess Without Delay*

When I kept silent, my bones wasted away
through my groaning all day long.

—Psalm 32:3

Sin spreads like a fungus in the dark. The longer we keep it hidden, the more it grows. We must not wait until our next accountability meeting. When you stumble, delayed confession easily becomes missed confession, leaving the door open for further relapse. Like a fungus, we must quickly expose sin to the light to hinder its progress. Sin loses power when it's exposed quickly and specifically.

3. *Confess Honestly*

Have nothing to do with the fruitless deeds of darkness, but rather expose them. It is shameful even to mention what the disobedient do in secret. But everything exposed by the light becomes visible—and everything that is illuminated becomes a light.

—Ephesians 5:11–13

Vague confessions breed vague repentance. "I struggled" is not a confession; it's an omission. Speak plainly. Say 100 percent; don't leave 5 percent unconfessed. Describe your sin without dressing it up or using graphic details. Honest confession sounds like, "Last night, I chose to look at porn on my phone. I knew it was wrong, but I didn't reach out for help." That is truth spoken in humility.

The enemy wants us silent, ashamed, and isolated. But confession drags us out of darkness into the light—where grace lives, healing starts, and shame meets its end. We recognize that finding an accountability partner can be one of the most difficult combat challenges in the Fight Club journey. That is why this week offers a second chance—an invitation to step into freedom by sharing your story with someone. Yes, it's intimidating. Yes, it's uncomfortable. If you already have an accountability partner, this week is your opportunity to go deeper as you share your story: where your addiction began, where it took you, and how God is bringing you out.

If you are still searching for a trusted partner, this week's combat challenge is your launching pad. Invite someone out for coffee, a jog, or some time at the park and take your next step. Confession opens the door to authentic relationships and begins to build the kind of relationships that help you stand when the battle gets fierce.

DAILY FIGHT PLAN

1. Why does sin fester in darkness but die when exposed to the light?
2. Which of the three steps in confession do you struggle with most (to a small circle of friends, without delay, honestly)?
3. What fears surface when you consider fully sharing your story with another person?
4. Write a prayer asking the Holy Spirit to soften your heart, strengthen your resolve, and lead you to the right person to share your story with.

WEEK 10—MAKE WAR

WEEKLY MEMORY VERSE

A time to love and a time to hate, a time for war and a time for peace.

—ECCLESIASTES 3:8

WEEKLY COMBAT CHALLENGE

Identify your triggers.

TRIGGERS

FROM URGE TO ACTION

Dwight had a passion for his country and a desire to serve. After enlisting in the military, he served post-Operation Iraqi Freedom (OIF) and Operation Enduring Freedom (OEF). The tempo on base was slowing down, but the Department of Defense wanted them to remain forward-postured and prepared. Dwight found himself on perpetual alert without indication or warning if he would be needed.

To keep the alert posture, they cycled crews and equipment in and out of standby, allowing a generous amount of downtime. The living quarters had internet access with the intention to be used for mission planning; however, there was motive and opportunity for porn in abundance. Using porn became a pastime that became a habit. The entire detachment was basically on the same page, which not only normalized but encouraged porn consumption.

Wake up. Do walkthroughs. Train. Eat. Porn. Prepare. Plan. Eat. Porn. Review. Porn. Sleep.

Dwight found that the culture on base began to gamify porn consumption, turning it into a competition of sorts, where some morally unlucky soul would claim the leaderboard for cycles per day. Dwight found himself joining in on the rivalry, thinking he could do better if he just spread out his consumption throughout the day.

That's it—just more porn, more often.

Of all the issues a soldier could bring home post-deployment, porn addiction was not the one Dwight had expected or was prepared for. There was not a deployment Dwight and normal Dwight. There was just Dwight, and he had spent six months nurturing an addiction that changed his thoughts, actions, and habits.

When Dwight realized porn use was taking a toll on his marriage, he tried to quit but struggled to break free from an addiction ingrained over the last fifteen years. The same need for porn consumption and self-gratification on deployment had carried over into his civilian life. Dwight's unwanted behavior left him feeling helpless. It was not until he began to learn how to identify his triggers that he was able to take back some ground over compulsive behaviors that were sabotaging his freedom.

Dwight's story is one that Fight Club has heard numerous times, and not one that must end in defeat. Victory in war requires a good strategy and freedom from addiction will require no less. A trigger is anything—a word, action, thought, interaction, or experience—that sparks an intense emotional reaction, often disproportionate to the situation. Simply put, a trigger is something that sets you off.

In today's culture, "trigger" has become a buzzword. But the truth is, almost anything can trigger us: a song, a movie scene, a politician, a co-worker's behavior, a touch, a phrase, or even a joke.

Triggers are everywhere.

What we need to realize is that triggers point to something deeper—an area in our lives that needs healing. While human nature often drives us to avoid, suppress, or cut off triggers that plague us, this approach leads to destructive habits, such as pornography or casual sex—until we're left feeling numb, isolated, and hopeless. The world tells us to bury pain, but that merely preserves it to rear its ugly head another time because nothing has been resolved.

Porn use is not primarily a sexual trigger; it is driven by life circumstances and emotional regulations. What if we could change our perspective of triggers? What if we, like Dwight, began to view triggers as not just obstacles to avoid but invitations for healing? What if our addiction had less to do with pornography than it did with emotional triggers? What if triggers no longer reveal what's wrong with us but rather where we need God's healing?

This week, we will explore routine triggers, emotional triggers, environmental triggers, social triggers, and physical triggers. Identifying triggers will be painful at times, but it is our combat challenge to master as we continue our pursuit for freedom.

DAY 1

REIMAGINING ROUTINE

Routine can be a powerful trigger in the cycle of addiction. The predictability of daily habits—waking up, eating, turning on the computer, or winding down at night—create automatic associations with addictive behaviors. Over time, familiar patterns become linked to cravings or compulsive actions, even in the absence of conscious desire. Recognizing how routine can trigger addiction is a crucial step in making war against unwanted behavior.

While determining the triggers behind our temptation takes time to unpack, the Bible offers insight on the progression in which we are tempted.

When tempted, no one should say, "God is tempting me." For God cannot be tempted by evil, nor does he tempt anyone. But each one is tempted when, by his own evil desire, he is dragged away and enticed. Then, after desire has conceived, it gives birth to sin; and sin, when it is full-grown, gives birth to death. Don't be deceived, my dear brothers.

—JAMES 1:13–16

The passage in James reminds me of Bob, a man that previously went through Fight Club. For him, the simple act of going to the bathroom was a routine that regularly led to acting out. Bob would go in with one solitary purpose, but before he could even process his actions, the smartphone was in his hand, desire was conceived, and he was traveling a familiar descent into sin.

Bob's brain had linked certain routines with acting out, and over time, the routines became embedded in his arousal template. The very thing that was hurting Bob, routine, was what he needed to reimagine. He needed a new routine because without a consistent and healthy daily rhythm, it is easy to slip back into old patterns and unhealthy behaviors.

Reimagining routine allows us to create a battle plan that avoids negative outcomes.

After discussing his routine fallout with his Fight Club group, Bob was challenged to reimagine his routine. He stopped by a store and bought a number of wife-approved decorative baskets that he hung outside of the bathroom doors in his home. Every time Bob went to the restroom, he left his phone in the basket. That is reimagining routine!

People who are serious about recovery must understand the importance of proactively reimagining routine.[1] We cannot simply coast through recovery, hoping to handle triggers as they arise—success requires intention and preparation.

We must establish a new normal.

When we find ourselves trapped in addiction triggered by routine, the root issue is often deceptively simple: We're clinging to a false belief about what makes us truly happy. Of course, we already recognize that our sin is destructive—to ourselves and others. We might even hate it, feeling ashamed and deeply wishing to be free from it. And yet, we feel stuck, as though we're enslaved—which, in a very real sense, we are.

Jesus replied, "I tell you the truth, everyone who sins is a slave to sin.

—JOHN 8:34

At the heart of the struggle, we often believe that letting go of sin means letting go of happiness. It feels like choosing a life of less joy and more emptiness. And that is why we have not changed the routines that continually lead to pain. Our belief will not change until our understanding of happiness changes, and it requires a trust in God that exceeds our comfort of routine.

As we unpack the idea of making war against triggers that feed our addiction this week, let us leave with an illustration that further illustrates trusting God.

A squad of soldiers find themselves pinned down under enemy fire, surrounded and with no realistic escape. Every effort fails. Bullets scream overhead and they are frozen in fear, believing their safest option is to hide. Then, the commander looks into the defeated eyes of the soldiers and confidently declares, "I know what to do." Without another word, he leaps out into the enemy fire, yelling over his shoulder, "Follow me."

Nobody moves.

One proudly declares, "I'll follow him." Another hesitantly claims, "I'm about to follow him." While others quietly admit, "We are preparing to follow him."

Yet, nobody moves.

Do you trust God enough to follow him and make war with the triggers that keep you entangled? Many people, whether in recovery or not,

1. Kitzinger et al., "Habits and Routines of Adults."

recognize the difficulty in reimagining routines because building new habits takes time, effort, and trust. That's why it's important to start now and commit to the process. Christians do not fight for victory, we fight from victory. So stop playing the victim, trust God, and make war.

DAILY FIGHT PLAN

1. Is there a specific time of day, location, or activity that frequently precedes addictive behavior?
2. Where do you see opportunities to reimagine routines that are triggers?
3. Apologize to God for demonstrating a lack of trust in him through your actions.
4. Commit this week to identify triggers in your life and list them.

DAY 2

EMOTIONAL BRUISES

Injuries are a part of life. We all get them. So, picture you get a terrible bruise. Any bruise hurts, but given enough time, the pain will begin to subside. This hypothetical bruise is conveniently located in an area that is easy to cover so that no one even notices. And as the day goes, the bruise escapes your thoughts until someone unknowingly bumps into it. They did not cause the pain, but they unintentionally pushed on it, provoking a response.

Likewise, emotional bruises are often triggered unintentionally. These wounds stem from past hurts but are brought to light by present experiences. While people, relationships, or life events may not cause the original pain, they can uncover emotional bruises by stirring up responses rooted in past suffering.

Emotional bruises need our attention.

The Bible records in the book of Job a narrative that illustrates immense suffering, both physical and emotional, and the impact it unfolds in his life. Job is described as the greatest man among all the people in the East, a man blessed with wealth, family, and abundance. What Job did not know was that he was soon to suffer the loss of family, wealth, and health, leading to profound grief, despair, and even anger. When tragedy struck, Job even expressed a deep wish that he had never been born, feeling that the hardships of life had made it seem no longer worth living.

While the story of Job highlights the human struggle to reconcile faith with the reality of suffering profound emotional bruises, it also offers insight into the biblical attitude followers of Christ should have regarding freedom from emotional triggers.

Though he slay me, yet will I hope in him.

—Job 13:15

Job's prayer, amidst all the anguish and loss he had experienced, reminds us that there is always hope in God. His prayer reveals the profound depth of trusting God, even in the depths of our most painful and difficult struggles. His prayer is raw. It is uncensored. And Job was committed to waging war against the emotional hell he was experiencing.

Emotions are complex, constantly shifting in response to our experiences, and some spark the urge to medicate with sexual addiction and porn. We must stop running from our emotional bruises and commit with a mindset like Job to seeking God's healing. These emotions, known as emotional triggers, can be anything that brings on stress, anxiety, or other negative feelings.[2] The question we must ask ourselves is will we run from emotional bruises, continuing the pattern of compulsive behavior that is both destructive and eliminates margin for God to heal the pain, or will we make war?

How do we heal our emotional bruises with God's truth?

The weapons we fight with are not the weapons of the world. On the contrary, they have divine power to demolish strongholds. We demolish arguments and every pretension that sets itself up against the knowledge of God, and we take captive every thought to make it obedient to Christ.

—2 Corinthians 10:4–5

Emotional bruises can become strongholds that are recurring, compulsive thought patterns triggering a subconscious response when triggered. We must learn to recognize them, pull down their walls, and replace lies with truth. It's a discipline that must be developed over time, as it does not come naturally to us. There is nothing passive about this process.

Our thoughts shape our feelings, which, in turn, influence our behavior; at the same time, our behaviors can also reshape our thoughts and emotions.[3]

Emotional bruises are triggered when a harmful belief leads to negative feelings, medicated with negative behavior. If we fail to take our thoughts captive, pain will be triggered and the formula will play out time and time again. Instead of relying on God's truth, our belief system is rooted in past trauma. The issue in this is that our truth is distorted. We need to believe God's truth.

Then you will know the truth, and the truth will set you free.

—John 8:32

2. Silver Sands Recovery, "What Are Triggers in Addiction?," para. 8–9.
3. Beck, "Cognitive Therapy and Emotional Disorders," 3–4, 26–27.

It is time to stop viewing emotional bruises as terrible inconveniences in your life, avoiding them, and burying them in destructive behavior. These emotional bruises serve as a beautiful reminder that we need God. We need his truth. We need freedom only he provides. Though he may slay us, we must hope in him. As we lean into God we can begin to release pain that has held us captive for far too long. We will demolish strongholds, take captive every thought, and most importantly—make war.

DAILY FIGHT PLAN

1. Where has unhealed pain influenced your choices, and can you identify a moment when it clearly surfaced through your actions?
2. What would it look like for you to demolish emotional strongholds and take captive every thought to be obedient to Christ, like the apostle Paul wrote of in 2 Cor 10:4–5?
3. Write out a prayer, asking God to reveal what emotional bruises you have been avoiding.

DAY 3

SEXUALIZED SOCIETY: SEX SELLS, SOULS SLIP

And I tell you that you are Peter, and on this rock I will build my church, and the gates of Hades will not overcome it.

—MATTHEW 16:18

Matthew 16 recounts a story where Jesus stopped to talk with his disciples as they traveled through Caesarea Philippi. Hidden within this verse is a detail that's easy to overlook but holds powerful significance in finding hope in coping with triggers related to a sexualized society. Caesarea Philippi was known as the epicenter of worship for the pagan goat god, Pan. People from across the ancient world traveled there to honor this false deity. Near the base of a cliff stood a massive cavern—a deep crack in the rock that locals believed was a portal to the underworld. They called it the "gates of hell."

At this site, a temple was built for Pan, and what took place there was deeply depraved. As part of the worship rituals, people engaged in extreme sexual acts, including bestiality during the Pan festivals. It was a place of spiritual darkness, moral collapse, and public celebration of sexual perversion.

A sexualized society is nothing new. Fortunately, making war with triggers spurred by living within a sexualized society has also not changed in the last two thousand years.

Hank was overwhelmed and felt as if he was living in the "gates of hell." He was trying to avoid sexual temptation, but everywhere he turned, sexual culture was thrust upon him, whether that be entertainment, social media, advertisement, or even conversation. He tried to avoid the lure of navigating a sexualized society by keeping himself busy, but even in his greatest efforts, sexual temptation presented itself, be it the gym, grocery store, or club. It felt as if the algorithms shaping his social media had expanded to all facets of society. Hank's hopes for sobriety were continuously met with failure, despite his best efforts, and it even began to shape how he viewed his sexuality.

Hank began to take inventory of the triggers that continually fed his craving and desire to act out. He recognized one pressing issue was that he still lived in isolation, failing to seek out community. Hank was attempting, in his best efforts, to walk this journey alone. While he acknowledged a need for God, going so far as to serve within his local church, he had avoided the need for true accountability. Navigating a life that honors God is already difficult, but we must commit to bringing others alongside us as we learn to manage our triggers in healthy ways.

We are wired for community.

Let's revisit Matt 16:18 and see how that very verse offers hope within community. Jesus chose the "gates of hell," a spiritual wasteland full of sexual brokenness and selfish ambition, as the ideal location to offer Peter his new name (as he was formerly known as Simon). In Greek, Peter is translated as *petros*, meaning a detached rock or pebble. There is intentionality in Jesus' new name for Peter and the location that should not be lost on the reader. Jesus went on to say that on this *petra*, translated as *bedrock*, he (Jesus) would build his church. Christ, in a very literal sense, was stating that he is the foundation and we, his many worshippers, are the pebbles. While an unusual location to make this claim, it carries a great deal of hope for the addict struggling to navigate the sexualized society. Jesus' claim states that not even the "gates of hell" and all its deviant sexualized pagan activity can overcome the church.

Have you ever felt like an insignificant and small pebble? Have you ever felt at the mercy of the world around you? Have you felt so weak that even the thought of detoxing seems beyond your grasp because in a society where sex sells, it's impossible to avoid?

Resist him, standing firm in the faith, because you know that your brothers throughout the world are undergoing the same kind of suffering.

—1 Peter 5:9

Possibly, it was that very interaction with Jesus in Caesarea Philippi that led Peter to later speak of standing firm in the faith. Have you ever tried to stand firm on an uneven surface? Spiritually speaking, some people live their lives on shaky ground. Add to this the reality of a sexualized society—filled with sensationalized temptation and our own personal weaknesses—and it becomes clear that standing firm isn't easy.

Your plan to overcome the triggers that continually lead to relapse must include accountability. You were not designed to overcome your triggers alone. Reflecting back on Matt 16:8, we may be pebbles like Peter, but here is the amazing part—when pebbles join together, they become cemented, forming a sedimentary rock known as a conglomerate. While a pebble is easily tossed about, a sedimentary rock poses strength to withstand the chaos this world may throw at it, especially when it is firmly planted on a bedrock of faith in Christ.

Not even the gates of hell will overcome it.

DAILY FIGHT PLAN

1. What literal gates of hell have you been living through?
2. How does a firm foundation in Jesus help you survive the triggers of a sexualized society?
3. Why does an accountability partner help you in avoiding relapse?
4. As you seek out accountability, consider your friends. Are they building you up? If not, consider places—such as church small groups—where your community can begin to grow beyond accountability.

DAY 4

PHYSICAL TRIGGERS: WHEN THE BODY SPEAKS

Lonny knew it was wrong every time he viewed porn. While he committed time and time again to no longer turning to porn, nothing worked. Despite his best efforts, Lonny could not make it more than a couple of days before relapsing. To complicate things, Lonny had several physiological disorders that included autism, bipolar, and schizophrenia. It was difficult for Lonny to connect with others. Difficult to choose joy. Difficult to find a healthy balance in life.

Porn became a source of comfort for Lonny, a way to numb the pain and insecurities that he struggled with. Relationships were hard enough for Lonny, and porn began serving as a way to fill the relational void he was experiencing.

Initially, he believed he had porn, but what Lonny didn't realize is that porn had him. He was disgusted with himself because the addiction made him even more isolated than he already was. He watched his marriage fail, relationships deteriorate, and the pornographic material he viewed became more extreme and deviant.

Like Lonny, some triggers that keep bringing us back to the fountain of shame and mediocrity are more difficult to escape because they are imprinted on us like fingerprints. Physical triggers, such as illness or chronic pain, evoke strong physical sensations, often related to past trauma or negative experiences.

Healing from physical triggers cannot be accomplished apart from God.

Seeking God is a pattern that requires intentionality, as it doesn't come naturally to us—particularly when the struggles we face, like physical ailments, are deeply intertwined with our addiction. To find freedom from addiction, we will be forced to press through numerous forms of triggers, including physical triggers. The Bible offers a wonderful narrative of pressing through to God despite the physical limitations imposed within the story of the woman that had suffered with uncontrolled bleeding for twelve years.

As Jesus was on his way, the crowds almost crushed him. And a woman was there who had been subject to bleeding for twelve years, but no one could heal her. She came up behind him and touched the edge of his cloak, and immediately her bleeding stopped.

—Luke 8:42–44

This woman had endured years of continuous hemorrhaging. Despite seeking help from numerous doctors and healers, none had been able to cure her. Her actions seem desperate, as if she's making one final attempt for healing. In her culture, her condition rendered her unclean, making her presence in a crowded space socially unacceptable. People would have avoided her, careful not to brush against her or offer a friendly gesture. She lived a life of isolation, marked and remembered not for who she was but for her condition.

The unnamed woman in the Gospel story understood that pressing through every barrier, including physical, in her pursuit of wholeness was simply not enough. She was seeking Jesus and her eyes were set on entering into his presence, the only place restoration can truly manifest itself. We must be courageous like that woman in our pursuit of healing.

Lonny, much like the woman plagued with the bleeding issue, felt socially unacceptable due to factors far outside his control. He recognized that people avoided him, judged him, and left him feeling alone. The physical triggers kept him a prisoner to porn.

After a hospitalization, Lonny realized it was time for a change. He had become sick and tired of being sick and tired. He reached out to a local church and began attending. He identified an accountability partner and began redefining who he was through God's eyes. Slowly, the physical triggers that led to acting out simply held less power over him. The physical triggers weren't gone, but the need for medicating through porn had subsided. He was changing his response and finding healing through the process.

Ultimately, he was trusting God.

> *Trust in the Lord with all your heart and lean not on your own understanding; in all your ways acknowledge him, and he will make your paths straight.*
>
> —Proverbs 3:5–6

Making war is not easy to do, and we've discussed it a lot this week. But the battle becomes easier when we embrace trust. We do not simply ask God to remove your physical triggers; we believe that he will provide in spite of them. Trust is not easy because it means letting go of an addiction that you have medicated with for so long. But we cannot trust God 99 percent of the time. Compromise eventually leads to failure because it's the equivalent of almost closing the front door—the outside still creeps in, just not as swiftly. We must trust Jesus 100 percent so that our triggers no longer have influence in our lives.

DAILY FIGHT PLAN

1. What physical triggers can you identify in your life?
2. Do you see physical triggers as opportunities or adversities?
3. How does the following verse apply to triggers?

   Jesus answered them, "It is not the healthy who need a doctor, but the sick. I have not come to call the righteous, but sinners to repentance." —Luke 5:31–32

DAY 5

SONIC BOOM

Planes have come a long way over the years, and the technological advancements did not come without their challenges. Breaking the sound barrier was a groundbreaking achievement for aviation, but reaching that milestone came with much failure and cost the lives of several pilots. Early attempts ran into a number of complications. The closer planes came to reaching 767 mph, the speed of sound, the shock waves produced in front of the plane would bunch up, creating an area of higher pressure, turbulence, and drag. The sound barrier also created vibrations that caused early aircrafts to shake violently, making them difficult to control and causing structural failure.

It was not until October 14, 1947, that Chuck Yeager became the first pilot to successfully break the sound barrier, flying an experimental Bell X-1 rocket engine-powered jet over the Mojave desert. Breaking the sound barrier required a large amount of energy to overcome the violent force of resistance planes experienced as they neared the speed of sound.

We have a similar barrier to push through. We vow to quit viewing porn, but then cannot make it a day, two days, or even a couple of weeks before unwanted sexual compulsion causes us to crash and burn. The pressure of sin is overwhelmingly strong, pushing us to our limits and making us bend and break under the weight of its force. The aftermath leaves us feeling apathetic, defeated, ashamed, and isolated.

Willpower alone is not enough to bring about freedom—we must go deeper. How we respond to triggers must change. Relying on our own resolve actually hinders our recovery, especially as we develop healthier ways to manage our triggers.

What we need is our sonic boom.

Let us not become weary in doing good, for at the proper time we will reap a harvest if we do not give up.

—Galatians 6:9

Immediately following a sonic boom, the drag resistance opposing a plane's progress is reduced. We need that pivotal moment in our freedom journey where we break through barriers. We must have a mindset of unwavering commitment and not grow weary as we push past the drag and resistance set forth by our triggers. It may not be smooth sailing on the other side, but it does get easier as we create new pathways for our brain, known as neuroplasticity, to manage unwanted behaviors.[4]

In our Fight Club journey, we have learned to be in God's word, identify our B.L.A.S.T.E.D. emotions, set up guardrails, F.I.G.H.T., get an accountability partner, and start serving. This week, we have explored different triggers, but merely understanding is not enough. Our sonic boom will not come with a halfhearted effort. This is why so few seek freedom until they can count their loss and are sick and tired of being sick and tired.

To achieve our sonic boom, we must identify the triggers behind our temptations and create healthy boundaries to cope with them. The Bible offers insight on how we can identify our triggers and make war.

Watch and pray so that you will not fall into temptation.
The spirit is willing, but the body is weak.

—MATTHEW 26:41

This is not a passive verse. It encourages us to be observant, looking out for danger so we may be able to identify temptations triggering us. This Scripture also acknowledges that the reason we should be on guard is because our bodies are weak and will struggle under the pressures of temptation. If we can identify triggers before they manifest, we can work smarter, not harder, expelling less energy in our efforts for freedom.

Consider him who endured such opposition from sinful men so that you will not grow weary and lose heart. In your struggle against sin, you have not yet resisted to the point of shedding your blood.

—HEBREWS 12:3–4

Identifying your triggers is key, but then you must FIGHT. This is where we apply the practices we have already been utilizing. When triggers come upon us, we can remember: focus, identity, God, help, and thwart. The beauty in these verses is that we do not make war alone.

4. Bickel, "Neuroplasticity and Addiction," 1–3.

Week 10—make War

Submit yourselves, then, to God. Resist the devil,
and he will flee from you.

—James 4:7

We are all slaves to something. When we allow ourselves to be controlled by addictive behavior, it serves as our master and takes us places we never wanted to go. Very few people want to throw their family, career, or future away. Sexual addiction is a slow fade, desensitizing the mind to pornographic material as we allow things in through screens that we would have never let in through the front door.

There is a time to love and a time to hate, a time for war and a time for peace. This is your time to make war!

DAILY FIGHT PLAN

1. List the triggers you have identified this week.
2. What boundaries do you plan on committing to this week to better guard yourself from unwanted triggers?
3. What would it take for you to experience your sonic boom?

WEEK 11—TRAUMA DRAMA

WEEKLY MEMORY VERSE

The Lord is close to the brokenhearted and saves those who are crushed in spirit.

—Psalm 34:18

WEEKLY COMBAT CHALLENGE

Identify your trauma.

TRAUMA: THE UNINVITED NARRATOR

RESURRECTED FROM RUINS

Dan grew up in a rough household where his parents were rarely around, often coming home late, intoxicated, and frequently fighting. Responsibility fell on Dan to step up and care for his siblings, though even his best efforts failed to shield him or his three siblings from parental neglect and abuse. Dan was not traumatized in his childhood by simply being hurt; he was traumatized by being alone in the hurt. Uncertain of how to process his home life and desperate for attention, Dan began to unravel.

In elementary school, his pain erupted through aggressive behavior and frequent fights. A brief glimmer of hope appeared when a classmate invited Dan to church, and for a moment, he felt something steady and good. But when Dan's family moved, that light vanished, and Dan was dropped into a new place carrying the same old chaos and abuse.

As Dan entered middle school, he made some friends. While he recognized their behavior was destructive, it felt good to finally belong and have community. Dan was willing to try drugs, alcohol, and view pornography with his new group of friends as long as it meant he could escape the chaos of his home.

When Dan met a girl at age fourteen, he dared to believe he found what love might feel like. So, when she invited him to a party, he went eagerly. But as the night progressed, Dan's hope of finding love was shattered when the girl's father cornered him, beat him, and then raped him—turning Dan's fragile dream of love into a devastating nightmare.

Dan's following season of life was shrouded in darkness, where anger raged, depression smothered, and suicidal thoughts whispered at the edges of his mind.

Unequipped to cope with the emotional weight, Dan dropped out of school and walked away from a home life that had inflicted trauma upon him for as long as he could recall. Determined to build a different life on his own terms, he married young, and soon had three children. For a brief moment, it looked as though Dan had broken the cycle—his life appeared stable, hopeful, and everything his parents had never provided. But the trauma he never addressed waited beneath the surface, unresolved and undefeated.

When his job began requiring travel, Dan's buried wounds resurfaced and old temptations—drugs, alcohol, and porn—rushed back in with familiar force. Porn, combined with the loneliness of the road, opened the door to adultery, and Dan ultimately destroyed his marriage. Uncontrolled addiction shrank his visitation with his children and eventually cost him his job, as drugs and alcohol overtook his life.

Overwhelmed by shame, Dan ran from his failures, neglecting his children in the process. The next decade was a cycle of searching for purpose in life, and shame fueled relapses of porn addiction. During this time, Dan remarried, and though he began to rein in his porn addiction, he never fully broke free. He began experiencing moments of victory, yet binges followed whenever childhood trauma was triggered. The cycle deepened his shame and drove him into secrecy as he tried to keep his struggle hidden from his second wife, Karen.

The illusion shattered the day Karen discovered porn on his phone.

Karen was hurt by the discovery and the betrayal shattered her illusion of the man she married. As she demanded answers, the truth came out slowly—each revelation small in size but devastating in impact, like a drip that hit with the force of a fire hydrant. The most painful confession—porn had led Dan into online conversations with other women. The hurt was too much and Karen was ready for divorce.

No longer wanting addiction to control his life, Dan suggested they visit a local church because it was the only source of stability that stood out from his childhood. That Sunday, the message was about a God who never gives up on his people, and Dan saw for the first time what true love looked like. He stepped over the line of faith and began attending a Fight Club course a short time later. It was there that Dan discovered how trauma lay at the root of his self-destructive behaviors. Dan began to see the broader truth, the pain he never healed had not only wounded him but had made victims of Karen, his children, his ex-wife, and countless others who crossed his path.

Hardship and trauma can be inflicted on children, but it's often created by adults.

Like Dan, most people's pasts are a train wreck. It's just some have more cars being pulled behind it. If we do not make the decision to heal our trauma, then we may simply transfer it upon others. As we begin to uncover the truth this week, we will see how our reactions are not random—they are echoes of old trauma and unprocessed dysfunction. While we were neither ready nor capable to confront trauma early on in our Fight Club journey, we have now established healthy outlets, safeguards, and community to lean into as we find healing that only God's grace provides.

We must seek healing because unhealed trauma becomes the quiet author of every story we never wanted to live.

DAY 1

WHAT IS TRAUMA?

Martin's story began at the age of six when he suffered sexual abuse from neighborhood kids. Coupled with his discovery of sexual content on the cable channels, he was hooked. Unable to run from his trauma, Martin's sexuality became everything to him and he began medicating with porn daily. From dial-up to high-speed to smartphone, his addiction adapted and evolved with the new technology.

While Martin did get married, the trauma of his childhood and inability to cope with those wounds in a healthy manner increasingly harmed his relationship with his wife and children. His inability to find freedom pushed his family to a breaking point. When his wife confronted him on the matter, he spent thousands of dollars to attend a recovery program; however, he was not a few months into the program before he broke. Full of shame, Martin kept his relapse secret until a few years later, when during another binge, his wife confronted him and he did not have the strength to keep lying.

Quite certain this was the end, Martin was shocked when his wife encouraged him to continue seeking healing. A few short months later, he was introduced to Fight Club by a friend and they committed to the journey together. The investment was not money; it was authenticity and a willingness to fight. Martin began to live in the light where trauma and porn used to control him. Martin had experienced a lot of past trauma in his life, but until he started to address the pain, he was only treating symptoms.

Studies suggest that porn and sex addicts often struggle with their emotions when past trauma is a factor. In a landmark study, Dr. Patrick Carnes discovered staggering overlap between trauma and sex addiction: 72 percent of adults reported childhood physical abuse, 97 percent reported emotional abuse, and 81 percent had endured sexual abuse.[1] We tend to react more strongly to negative experiences and less strongly to positive ones; because of this heightened sensitivity to stress, we turn to porn as a way to cope or calm ourselves down.[2] At the same time, our reduced response to positive experiences makes it harder for us to find healthier, more fulfilling ways to replace addictive behaviors.

1. Carnes, "Making of a Sex Addict," para. 5.
2. Wang and Li, "Emotional Processing Deficits."

Disappointments, stress, failures, unmet expectations, exhaustion; it is all a part of life. When every pain or challenge we face channels our past trauma we will be incapable of handling things in appropriate ways. Turning to porn to escape that pain only makes things worse, never allowing us to grow beyond being a victim.[3] Learning to deal with trauma and understanding who we are in Jesus allows us to be vulnerable and honest.

Traumatic events in childhood whisper powerful lies that have a significant influence in our identity formation.[4] We begin perceiving ourselves as unlovable, unworthy, and deserving of our negative experiences. When we never learn healthy ways to cope with trauma, minor mistakes later in life can trigger the negative identity lies we believe about ourselves. The end result is that we turn to sexual addiction, fantasy, and porn to medicate our negative emotions to cope with the root cause—unresolved trauma.

Trauma resurfaces not as a memory we recall but as a reflex that takes over.

The lingering effects of trauma can leave us living on a relational island when our behavior is uncontrolled. Sex addiction is increasingly understood as an attachment or intimacy disorder, arising from unresolved pain that impairs our ability to form secure, enduring emotional connections.[5] The World Health Organization's ICD-11 identifies compulsive sexual behavior disorder as a pattern of overwhelming, recurring sexual impulses that a person struggles to restrain, even as these behaviors damage their well-being and relationships.[6] When trauma goes unhealed, it isolates us—making us vulnerable in the very places we most need protection.

The Lord is close to the brokenhearted and saves those
who are crushed in spirit.

—Psalm 34:18

We are never alone. It is a promise that stands against every lie we have ever believed—that we are alone, unworthy, or beyond rescue. God has never stepped back in fear or disgust. He draws near. He sits in the rubble with us. And from our brokenness comes beauty. The Hebrew meaning for brokenhearted evokes a feeling of being emotionally crushed or shattered.

3. Cardoso et al., "Difficulties in Emotion Regulation."
4. Melamed et al., "Relationship Between Negative Self-Concept."
5. Main Street Counseling, "Addiction an Attachment/Intimacy Disorder," para. 1.
6. Reed, "Emerging Experience."

Mark 14:3-9 offers a beautiful picture of how brokenness releases beauty in a story of the woman with a sealed alabaster jar containing perfume. The vessel's beautiful aroma was trapped inside unless the jar was broken. In the story, a woman came to Jesus and did not open the jar carefully; she broke it. And in that breaking, the fragrance that had been locked away flooded the room. Her shattered jar became an offering. Her brokenness became worship.

In the same way, the Bible shows that God often brings beauty out of what feels shattered. When life breaks us—through trauma, addiction, loss, or shame—God does not discard the pieces. He uses them. Our honesty, vulnerability, repentance, and surrender become a fragrance that rises to him.

The story teaches us that what is broken in God's presence is never wasted.

DAILY FIGHT PLAN

1. How were emotions handled in your family—were they allowed, dismissed, punished, or ignored?
2. How does it make you feel to know that your brokenness can bring beauty?
3. Write out a prayer, thanking God that you are never alone, even at your worst moment.

DAY 2

TRAUMA WITH A CAPITAL "T"

Nate was an energetic boy that loved Jesus, loved life, and had a compassionate heart for others. While he had a healthy upbringing, raised in a Christian family, he was unaware of the storm looming in his life. While in elementary school, Nate experienced an evil no child should endure; he was sexually abused by someone that his family considered a friend. The abuse continued throughout elementary school, shaping Nate's emotional and physical well-being well into adulthood. The impact of the sexual abuse strained his relationships, disrupted his faith, and hindered his confidence in school.

While reflecting on his past trauma, the memories from the sexual abuse feel as real and raw today as it did when initially inflicted upon him. Nate mourns the innocence, self-esteem, confidence, and joy that was stolen from him as a vulnerable adolescent. Nate still suffers from bouts of debilitating depression and anxiety that can overwhelm him at times. But what upsets Nate the most about being a victim of childhood sexual abuse is the compulsive porn addiction he acquired in an effort to medicate the shame, sexual insecurity, and depression that plagued his life.

Significant childhood traumas reshape our very foundation.

Capital "T" traumas include experiences such as abuse, severe neglect, witnessing violence, losing a parent, surviving a serious accident, or living through a natural disaster. Major childhood traumas can plant powerful messages in the hearts and minds of children and adolescents.[7] Capital "T" trauma rewires the brain's stress and reward systems, making compulsive porn use or sexual behavior a powerful, yet destructive, self-soothing mechanism for survivors.[8] A study out of the University of Georgia found a direct correlation between early childhood trauma and addictive coping later in life.[9] Often, for trauma victims, the naturally rewarding behavior of compulsive sexual addiction becomes the primary means of controlling their emotions and feelings, despite their negative consequences.

Traumatic events do more than alter the course of our lives—they are now shown to physically reshape the brain itself. A study out of the

7. Kliethermes et al., "Complex Trauma."

8. University of Rochester Medical Center, "Researchers Reveal How Trauma Changes," para. 1.

9. Giordano, "Childhood Trauma and Sex Addiction."

University of Rochester Medical Center revealed that one major complication of early childhood trauma is a disruption in stress regulation that makes it difficult to cope with normal everyday difficulties.[10] The research revealed how trauma can "rewire" parts of the brain that detect danger, making trauma survivors more sensitive to stress. A hypersensitivity to stress can create a hypersexuality to cope, perpetuating the endless cycle of addiction.

Childhood abuse can develop into post-traumatic stress disorder (PTSD) that lasts into adulthood. PTSD is a serious condition that arises after someone experiences capital "T" trauma.[11] While not everybody that endures major trauma develops PTSD, it can play a powerful role in the addiction cycle. Symptoms can surface months, or even years, after the trauma, showing up as relentless nightmares or flashbacks, intense avoidance of reminders, dark shifts in mood and thinking, and a heightened, on-edge sense of alertness that never seems to shut off.[12]

Healing from capital "T" trauma is not accidental—it requires courage, intentionality, and a willingness to fight for our future. Moving from victim to survivor and, ultimately, into a life of freedom demands practices that reshape how we think, live, and respond to the world. This is not a quick mindset shift or a comforting mantra to numb old wounds. It is the deliberate choice to rise, rebuild, and reclaim what trauma tried to steal.

Therefore everyone who hears these words of mine and puts them into practice is like a wise man who built his house on the rock. The rain came down, the streams rose, and the winds blew and beat against that house; yet it did not fall, because it had its foundation on the rock. But everyone who hears these words of mine and does not put them into practice is like a foolish man who built his house on sand. The rain came down, the streams rose, and the winds blew and beat against that house, and it fell with a great crash.

—MATTHEW 7:24–27

10. University of Rochester Medical Center, "Researchers Reveal How Trauma Changes," para. 1–8.

11. American Psychiatric Association, "What Is Posttraumatic Stress Disorder?," para. 1–2.

12. Mayo Clinic, "Post-Traumatic Stress Disorder (PTSD)," para. 3–7.

Jesus describes both of these men as builders who receive the same teaching and face the same storms of life—rain, floods, and winds. The key difference is not in what they heard or what they faced but in how they responded. One put Jesus' words into practice and built on rock, while the other ignored them and built on sand. As children, we were incapable of controlling the traumatic storms in our life, but in our healing process, we can put God's truth into practice and build on the Rock.

Healing must be built on Jesus' truth, or it will crumble, reexposing us to our trauma.

This journey is nothing less than the formation of a new way of living, a lifestyle marked by resilience, honesty, and hope. It means committing to growth even when it is uncomfortable, choosing healing over hiding, unlearning the lies we once believed true, removing unjustified blame, and embracing the disciplines that strengthen our mind and spirit. Freedom from childhood trauma is not a moment; it's a journey. And every intentional step we take on the path of healing declares that trauma may be part of our story, but it will never define your destiny.

DAILY FIGHT PLAN

1. When you think of capital "T" trauma, what comes to mind and why do you think it affects people so deeply?
2. Can you identify any capital "T" traumas from your childhood?
3. How have you seen God meet you in moments of deep pain?
4. What do you think it means in Matt 7:24–27 to "build on the rock" in the context of recovering from trauma?

DAY 3

TRAUMA WITH A LOWERCASE "T"

Capital "T" trauma refers to big, overwhelming events, like a serious accident, sexual assault, or natural disasters, that often lead to symptoms similar to PTSD.[13] We reserve the word for the shattering moments that flip life upside down in an instant. But the truth is far more complex. Trauma comes in many shapes and sizes, and while those big moments can break us in obvious ways, the overlooked, repeated, or minimized pains can cut just as deep and shape us just as powerfully.

Lowercase "t" traumas are made up by small, repeated experiences like chronic bullying, emotional neglect, or unstable living environments.[14] They may seem insignificant because they don't threaten our safety or upend our lives, yet their subtle distress can leave a deep impact on our well-being and emotional health. When we carry small, repeated wounds without healthy ways to cope, they often show up as denial, apathy, intense anger, self-destructive habits, or depression.

Avoidance does not heal trauma; it delays our ability to move beyond its hold.

These easily overlooked traumas grow quietly in the shadows of our everyday lives, yet can be just as destructive.[15] We often perceive these wounds as normal experiences in life, overlooking them instead of learning to cope in healthy ways. Dismissing lowercase "t" trauma is a form of avoidance, leading to maladaptive coping mechanisms, such as sexual fantasy, porn consumption, and sexual addiction.[16] Over time, small repeated traumas pile up, and what once felt manageable slowly becomes overwhelming.[17]

Using porn to cope with lowercase "t" trauma is destructive. It creates a cycle of treating trauma with trauma because the temporary relief it provides reinforces compulsive behavior, shame, and deeper emotional pain that ultimately compounds the original trauma. One of the significant results of this cycle is relational isolation.

13. National Institute of Mental Health, "Coping with Traumatic Events," para. 1.
14. Kliethermes et al., "Complex Trauma."
15. Cloitre et al., "Developmental Approach to Complex PTSD."
16. Butler et al., "Pornography Use and Loneliness."
17. Hamby et al., "Recognizing the Cumulative Burden."

Fight Club: Live in Freedom

Catch for us the foxes, the little foxes that ruin the vineyards, our vineyards that are in bloom.

—Song of Solomon 2:15

The Bible warns us in Song 2:15 about "little foxes that ruin the vineyards." *Little foxes* are symbolic of small problems and the *vineyard* is representative of relationships. When we neglect or fail to cope with lowercase "t" traumas in a healthy way, they can quietly erode what is growing within us and destroy healthy relationships by going unchecked.

Echezu is the Hebrew word translated *catch* in Song 2:15, meaning to grasp, seize, hold, or take possession. It implies an active and decisive effort to acknowledge and deal with threats instead of avoiding or ignoring them. Our weekly combat challenge is to identify our trauma. This is an important step in finding freedom from addictive behavior because acknowledgment allows us to integrate overwhelming memories into a coherent narrative, reconstruct our value, move beyond avoidance, and grow beyond our trauma.[18]

What if in acknowledging our lowercase "t" traumas, we move beyond avoidance or dismissal and begin seeing them as an opportunity to grow our faith?

During the early 1990s, scientists conducted an experiment known as Biosphere 2 in Arizona to see if humans could live inside a completely self-sustaining, closed ecological system on the moon or Mars. Researchers unexpectedly observed, as the artificial ecosystem developed, that many of the trees grew quickly, but their root systems remained weak and underdeveloped.[19] In the sealed environment of the biodome, there was no natural wind to push against the young trees. Without that constant pressure, the trees did not need to anchor themselves deeply into the soil. As a result, their shallow roots could not support them as they grew taller and heavier, eventually bending, cracking, or collapsing under their own weight.

This phenomenon revealed an important truth; while too much stress is harmful, some stress is beneficial. The gentle but persistent force of wind in the natural world strengthens a tree to its core and drives its roots deeper. In the same way, the winds of life—challenges, pressures, and difficulties—stretch us to grow stronger, wiser, and grounded. Without these

18. Quan et al., "Relationship Between Childhood Trauma."

19. Nelson and Dempster, "Living in Space."

experiences, we may appear to grow on the outside, but we lack the inner strength, maturity, and stability needed to withstand the weight of real life.

Not only so, but we also glory in our sufferings, because we know that suffering produces perseverance; perseverance, character; and character, hope. And hope does not put us to shame, because God's love has been poured out into our hearts through the Holy Spirit, who has been given to us.

—ROMANS 5:3–5

While God neither desires us to experience or orchestrates our trauma, we can find hope in him through it. In the very places where trauma has pressed us to the edge, Rom 5:3–5 reminds us that God can turn our suffering into perseverance, our perseverance into character, and our character into a hope that refuses to die. Our lowercase "t" traumas can become a place where God's love breaks through, transforming pain into what strengthens us.

DAILY FIGHT PLAN

1. Why do you believe it is easy to overlook lowercase "t" trauma? Why or why not?
2. Do you dismiss certain hurts because they "weren't that bad," even though they still affect you?
3. Are there any lowercase "t" trauma that you have experienced but never acknowledged before? What are they?
4. What healthy or unhealthy habits have you developed in response to repeated stresses?

DAY 4

THE TRAUMA TRANSFER

At just six years old, Helene was preparing for another ordinary day in her Cambodian village when the worst form of betrayal was thrust upon her. That morning, her aunt offered what appeared to be an unexpected gesture of love, a moped ride to spare a long walk to school. With complete trust, Helene climbed on. But the path her aunt took was not toward school, and the true destination altered the entire course of her life.

That day, Helene was sold by her aunt to Cambodian sex traffickers for one thousand dollars. The following two years of Helene's life were not her own. Recreational drugs were introduced to her and she was forced to do unthinkable things with clients or face tremendous beatings while being deprived food and drink at the hands of her captors.

Finally, at age eight, she was able to break free from her captors, finding an opportunity to flee. Helene made her way back to her home village with a sense of hope. As Helene entered her parents' small house, relief turned to dread when the only one in her home was her aunt.

Helene was sold again by her aunt back into sex trafficking, where she endured another three years of horrendous evil before she was rescued from her traffickers. Helene was welcomed by a local ministry in Phnom Penh that specializes in empowering victims of the sex industry to break free and build new lives filled with dignity, healing, and the means to thrive.

The myth that nobody is harmed by our porn consumption is a lie.

Dateline's Chris Hansen reported in 2004 how Cambodia was a popular destination for travelers seeking the sexual exploitation of children.[20] Since then, data from International Justice Mission, a global human rights agency, shows that child sex trafficking has dropped dramatically from its early-2000s' levels.[21] Yet the crisis is far from over. Child exploitation in Cambodia has not only persisted but diversified, now encompassing sexual exploitation, child labor, forced labor, and exploitation within tourism, domestic work, and illegal migration networks.[22] Together, these findings make one reality unmistakably clear—sexual exploitation remains an entrenched systemic problem in developing countries such as Cambodia.

20. Dateline NBC, "Children for Sale," para. 4.
21. International Justice Mission, "Phnom Penh," para. 2.
22. Vijghen, "Child Exploitation Situational Analysis."

More concerning, since so many cases go unreported, the true scale is almost certainly far greater than what current numbers suggest.

Globally, there are an estimated 4.8 million people being sexually exploited and 99 percent of them are women or children.[23] Tragically, one in four victims of slavery are children.[24] When we consume porn, we contribute to sex trafficking by creating and sustaining demand for paid sexual content and services.

As our past trauma plays out through addiction, it inflicts trauma upon vulnerable population groups—the foreigner, the orphan, and the widow—the very ones God calls us to care for in Deut 24:19. We may want to believe porn is consensual, but traffickers deliberately film and distribute porn using the coerced and vulnerable, effectively turning victims into products for sale.[25] Because demand drives supply in commercial sex markets, widespread porn consumption directly amplifies trafficking, making victimization profitable.

Our trauma does not simply victimize those in developing countries. The United States produces 40 percent of all adult content available online.[26] While mainstream porn companies boast that they empower women, the industry is controlled through manipulation, coercion, and violence.[27]

The majority of women have a similar start in porn, rooted in unresolved childhood trauma. Roughly 65 percent of female pornographic performers identify their past experiences of trauma as a driving force behind their career choices.[28] What makes trauma's influence on the porn industry more challenging to stop is that women are three times more likely to have been sexually abused as children.[29]

The trauma for victims lives on in infamy, and on a grand scale with access to the internet. The amount of pornographic content depicting violence, gore, children, and racist acts has consistently increased since the introduction of the smartphone.[30] Since the introduction of the smartphone,

23. International Labour Organization and Walk Free Foundation, "Global Estimates of Modern Slavery," 11.

24. International Justice Mission, "Phnom Penh," fig. 1.

25. Asservo Project, "Pornography and Human Trafficking," para. 9–11.

26. Insider Monkey, "Top 15 Countries that Supply," para. 2.

27. Hester et al., "Barriers to Sexually Exploited."

28. Molloy et al., "They Look You Up."

29. Grudzen et al., "Comparison of the Mental Health."

30. DeKeseredy, "Critical Criminological Understandings."

interest in porn featuring teens has significantly increased, regardless if they are above or below the age of consent.[31] Female performers, particularly teenagers, in pornographic videos are frequently shown expressing pleasure in response to acts of aggression, including spanking, forced penetration, and gagging.[32] Such videos perpetuate the notion that women enjoy being subject to aggressive and demeaning sexual behaviors. The degrading nature of porn is absent of joy, validated by the fact that drug abuse is prevalent among porn actors and actresses.[33] With the toxic environment that the adult entertainment industry creates, it comes as no surprise that 69 percent of porn stars have attempted suicide.[34]

Porn is not harmless, personal entertainment. The consumer's trauma is transferred to the entertainer by keeping the market thriving and the entertainer's trauma is shared with the viewer. We must no longer fuel the exploitation of others and risk trauma to be passed from one life to the next. When we choose to stop, we are choosing to break that chain.

DAILY FIGHT PLAN

1. What was the most troubling part of today's discussion?
2. Why do you believe childhood trauma directly correlates with those in the porn industry?
3. Write out a prayer for those locally and globally experiencing trauma in the adult entertainment industry and ask God for the resolve to help make a difference.

31. Walker et al., "Finding Lolita."
32. Shor, "Age, Aggression, and Pleasure."
33. Lubben, "Ex-Porn Star Tells the Truth," para. 2.
34. Donevan et al., "Experience of Individuals Filmed."

DAY 5

UNPACKING TRAUMA LIKE A STUFFED CARRY-ON

The purpose in identifying painful trauma is not to relive the wounds of the past but to process them in a healthy, Christ-centered way that leads to healing, freedom, and transformation. Scripture never minimizes suffering. From Joseph's betrayal, to David's sorrow, to Paul's hardships, the Bible is filled with stories of God meeting his people in their pain.

A recurring theme throughout our Fight Club journey is that our healing is not passive. Licensed Christian psychologist Dr. Douglas Weiss states that, "For the trauma-based sex addict . . . trauma work will need to be addressed for the addict to heal."[35] Though many sex addicts suffer from trauma in their past, these painful events must be addressed in recovery to find lasting freedom. The challenge is that compulsive porn use is how we have historically avoided negative emotions.[36] Working through trauma will heighten both our pain and desire to cope with sexually addictive behavior.

God is inviting us into the process of healing where honesty, courage, and faith become the tools that reshape our lives. Below are seven biblical principles to help us process our pain through the lens of truth and grace. While these seven principles guide us in exploring our trauma, professional counseling could further assist in processing the pain.

1. Discern the Message You Accepted from Trauma

Trauma often leaves behind a *message*—a conclusion about ourselves, others, or God. These messages play on repeat, shaping how we see the world. In Scripture, Elijah believed the message that he was alone and worthless (1 Kgs 19:4). King David believed his enemies were too strong for him (Ps 18:17). In healing from trauma, it is important to first identify the narrative our trauma has told us.

35. Weiss, "6 Types of Sex Addicts," para. 15.

36. Shirk et al., "Predicting Problematic Pornography Use."

2. *Identify the Lie Hidden Inside the Message*

Every distorted message carries a lie. *I'm not enough. I'm unwanted. I'm unlovable. I'm too weak. I'm lost.* But Jesus teaches us in John 8:44 that the enemy is the "father of lies," and many of these lies trace directly back to childhood trauma. We must first uncover the lie before we may confront it.

3. *Brace for the Hurt*

Healing requires vigilance. Scripture never asks us to pretend the process is easy. Jesus himself warned the disciples in Matt 26:41, "Watch and pray so that you will not fall into temptation." Revisiting the past can trigger deep emotions, old temptations, and familiar struggles. Our pain is not a sign of failure and does not guarantee relapse, but it can be powerful evidence that we are finally dealing with what once controlled us. Be cautious because our memories can reopen past hurt.

4. *Process the Pain With People in Your Corner*

We were not designed to heal alone. Pain grows in isolation, but healing grows in community. In week 5, our combat challenge was to find an accountability partner. We need people in our corner because processing with others brings comfort, perspective, and spiritual support.[37]

5. *Connect Your Past Trauma to Your Present Mindset*

As we connect the dots, our goal must be to search for explanations, not excuses. Learning how painful moments shaped our addictive behavior offers us perspective on patterns that once felt unbreakable. Christian therapist and author Dr. Dan B. Allender states, "The work of restoration cannot begin until a problem is fully faced."[38] As we connect our past traumas to our present mindset, pain gains clarity and loosens trauma's grip on us.

37. Simpson, "Helping the Traumatized," para. 19–25.

38. Allender, *Wounded Heart*, 14.

6. Grieve Your Losses

The psalms are full of grief. In Ps 42:3–5, David wept, questioned, lamented, and poured out his soul before God. We frequently have a poor understanding of grief because we perceive it as a negative experience, but grief is not weakness. It is worship. It is honesty before God. It does not reopen our wound—grief drains it. Jesus himself said in Matthew 5:4, "Blessed are those who mourn, for they will be comforted." We cannot heal from what we refuse to grieve.

7. Forgive and Move Forward

Forgiveness is one of the hardest steps in healing, but it is also one of the most freeing. Forgiveness is not excusing the person, denying the damage, or minimizing the offense. Instead, forgiveness is entrusting the pain to God and releasing the burden from our own heart. We will further explore this process in week 12.

We cannot embrace the Fight Club journey and avoid the pain.

We are going to experience some discomfort through the healing process, but God never wastes a wound. We can find our strength in a divine source as we courageously face our trauma through the lens of truth and apply the weekly combat challenges we have learned. Like Joseph, like David, and like Paul, we can learn to say, "God was with me," even in the places that once felt defined by suffering.

DAILY FIGHT PLAN

1. What is the purpose or benefit in identifying painful past trauma?
2. Which of the seven biblical principles will be most difficult for you and why?
3. Write out a prayer asking God for courage as you seek to identify your trauma.

WEEK 12—TIME TO FORGIVE

WEEKLY MEMORY VERSE

Bear with each other and forgive one another if any of you has a grievance against someone. Forgive as the Lord forgave you.

—Colossians 3:13

WEEKLY COMBAT CHALLENGE

Write a letter and forgive yourself.

SHACKLED BY SECRETS

DYING BEHIND THE MASK

Addiction to porn started for Hunter at a young age when he discovered a VHS tape in his parent's bedroom closet. When his curiosity led him to see what was on it, he was hooked immediately by the graphic content. Hunter continued consuming porn daily into his collegiate years. His compulsive behavior left him with little interest in pursuing a serious relationship because his porn addiction satisfied his needs enough.

Porn may not have been good sex, but it was good enough.

Self-gratification became the solution to anything affecting him. Whether it was the failure to finish college, the failure to cope with stress in a healthy way, or the failure to find a meaningful relationship with a woman—Hunter's solution was porn.

Years into Hunter's adult life, he was surprised to encounter a woman that he actually found more desirable than the attraction of porn. They eventually married and Hunter was optimistic his porn problem would go away. Unfortunately, he had never learned to cope with stress in a healthy manner, and marriage brought new stresses with kids, career, and financial strain. Instead of fighting through the fire, Hunter crawled back into a digital shadow. His porn problem grew until he began secretly reaching out to other women for hook-ups. The turning point came when his wife, Jan, pulled down the curtain and exposed his dirty secret and the double life he was living.

Jan was devastated. She felt betrayed and that she was not good enough.

Hunter realized that he was on the verge of losing everything of value in his life. His wife, his children, his community. While Hunter's family background was Catholic and Jan was Jewish, neither of them considered themselves religious. In a last ditch effort, Hunter and Jan visited a local church that offered Fight Club. Though Hunter did not understand why, he felt compelled to fill out a card at his seat requesting more information on the group.

Hunter joined a Fight Club group and began to see himself less as the addictive behavior he had been involved in and more as who God wants him to become. A few months later, Hunter stepped over the line of faith, realizing the life he had been pursuing was the very sin that was destroying everything in his life. Shortly thereafter, Jan made the same decision to trust in Jesus, becoming a Messianic Jew. Several weeks later, they were both baptized as their new church family, including the Fight Club community, celebrated their next steps in freedom.

He had thought he was surviving, but faith revealed Hunter had been drowning in sin.

Hunter now surrounded himself with Christ followers, and their shared love for Jesus gave him the strength and support he needed in his journey. As he grew in his walk with Jesus, he learned more of what it meant to be a real man, to be a father that is engaged, loving, and loyal. He began to offer his wife the faithfulness she deserved, and healing that only Jesus can offer began to unfold in their relationship.

With all the joy Hunter was experiencing in his new faith, God still had one very difficult next step ahead of him. God was calling Hunter to seek forgiveness from others. Pornography addiction is a sin with an impact that far exceeds the consumer. The negative consequences did not stay confined to his screen—spilling into every corner of his life, especially within family and marriage. Some of the damaging effects of his porn addiction are common for users: heightened aggression, warped perception about relationships and sexuality, and a neglect of the people and priorities that matter most.[1] Others were unique to his individual experience.

As we take the necessary next steps in our Fight Club journey, we start to clearly see the damage our addiction has caused, especially in the relationships that matter most. This week will call us to seek forgiveness, starting with self.

Reconciliation provides healing.

To quote the late theologian Lewis Smedes, "To forgive is to set a prisoner free and discover the prisoner was you."[2] We have experienced significant freedom in our Fight Club journey over the past three months, but we will only be as free as the level of forgiveness we are willing to seek from others and extend to ourselves. Our weekly combat challenge calls us to write a letter forgiving ourselves. Colossians 3:13 states, "Forgive as the Lord forgave you," but how can we accept God's forgiveness if we are unable to reconcile that very forgiveness in our own hearts?

One more step. One more stand. One more victory. This is where our mindset for freedom becomes forever, so embrace this week's challenge. Let's keep fighting.

1. Fight the New Drug, "10 Negative Effects of Porn," no. 1–8.

2. Smedes, *Forgive and Forget*, 170.

DAY 1

FORGIVING SELF

As Merv sat across from the counselor, reflecting on his countless years of addiction to porn and the vast number of broken relationships and lost opportunities it had cost him, the words he spoke about himself were venomous. "I'm weak, pathetic, and a failure," he indignantly spouted. Lamenting his past life of unbridled lust and affairs, Merv reasoned that the world would likely be a better place without him.

The counselor quietly listened until there was a pause in Merv's savage assessment of self, before calmly replying, "Wow, you sure can be a real jerk to yourself." The counselor's observation caught Merv off guard because up until that moment, he had been unaware how his self-hatred defined his identity.

Merv's unwillingness to forgive himself kept him in a perpetual cycle of unrest.

It has been said that unforgiveness is like drinking poison and expecting the other person to die. But what do we do when the other person is ourself? Research indicates that consuming porn is linked with more negative body image, lower self-esteem, and poorer mental health.[3]

Our inability to forgive ourselves is one of the enemy's most devastating battlegrounds. Satan is relentless—whispering our addictive past into the present, replaying our sins, our failures, and our darkest moments of depravity like a broken record. Scripture calls him a thief, a liar, a deceiver, and a murderer—and one of his favorite targets is unresolved self-hatred.

If he can keep us chained to regret . . .

If he can keep us staring backward . . .

If he can convince us our sin defines us . . .

. . . then he does not have to bind our hands—our shame will do it for him.

Forget the former things; do not dwell on the past. See, I am doing a new thing! Now it springs up; do you not perceive it? I am making a way in the wilderness and streams in the wasteland.

—Isaiah 43:19

3. SonderMind, "How Did Porn Addiction Become," para. 1–4.

How can we recognize the future God designed if we never take our eyes off the past we regret? God calls us forward toward the good works he has already prepared for us. There's a reason the rearview mirror is small and the windshield is wide. Where we have been is nothing compared to where we are going, but only if we stop believing the enemy's lies. Satan says we are damaged, but God says we are destined. Satan calls us disqualified, but God calls us chosen, and then he qualifies us with grace. If God has forgiven us, who are we to hold ourselves hostage? We must step into freedom, walk in forgiveness, and lift our eyes because the future is ahead, not behind.

All the days ordained for me were written in your book
before one of them came to be.

—Psalm 139:16

When we stay camped out in the land of regret and unforgiveness, we forfeit the ground Jesus already won for us. Shame doesn't just sting—it suffocates our God-given purpose. Self-hatred doesn't just hurt—it blinds us to hope. And while we are staring backward, time we can never regain slips through our fingers. Every person is given the same twenty-four hours in a day, yet only God knows how many days make up our lifetime. On average, a human life is roughly 29,000 days.[4] But averages don't write our stories, God does. Before our first breath, he appointed every one of our days. And not a single moment was designed to be wasted in a prison of self-loathing.

We often convince ourselves that our self-contempt and disgust for our behavior is a posture of humility. We think we are simply taking responsibility, owning our failures, and remaining grounded. However, when shame transforms into a constant expectation of punishment, it is not humility—it is self-hatred. Our inability to forgive ourselves is a destructive mindset that fuels the addictive cycle itself, reinforcing our belief that we are unworthy of good or God's blessing.

One of the most powerful steps in recovery involves exposing our inner voice of unforgiveness as we replace shame-based lies with biblical truth about our identity and value. If we truly desire self-forgiveness we must extend ourselves the same compassion and grace we would offer to someone we love unconditionally. Our weekly combat challenge is to write

4. Culurciello, "29,000 days," para. 1.

a letter and forgive yourself, but self-forgiveness requires intentionality to facilitate breakthroughs. Let these five steps guide your letter:

1. Create a peaceful environment with uninterrupted time alone with your thoughts.
2. Let prayer guide your letter as you seek God's guidance.
3. Be specific, identifying how you negatively felt about yourself as an addict (disappointed, hurt, guilty, angry, ashamed) and why you felt that way.
4. Avoid self-hatred, self-shaming, or self-condemning language.
5. Forgive your reckless behavior and perception of self and then release it.

Self-forgiveness transforms recovery from survival into restoration, freeing the heart to live in God's grace.

DAILY FIGHT PLAN

1. What negative lies have you believed about yourself?
2. How easy is it for you to no longer dwell on your past mistakes and why do you think that is so?
3. While you don't have to forgive yourself for eternal purposes since God has already forgiven you, what benefit do you find in forgiving yourself in your recovery and restoration process?
4. Write out a prayer asking God for courage this week in writing a letter of self-forgiveness.

DAY 2

SEEKING FORGIVENESS

Have mercy on me, O God, according to your unfailing love; according to your great compassion blot out my transgressions. Wash away all my iniquity and cleanse me from my sin. For I know my transgressions, and my sin is always before me. Against you, you only, have I sinned and done what is evil in your sight; so you are right in your verdict and justified when you judge. Surely I was sinful at birth, sinful from the time my mother conceived me. Yet you desired faithfulness even in the womb; you taught me wisdom in that secret place. Cleanse me with hyssop, and I will be clean; wash me, and I will be whiter than snow. Let me hear joy and gladness; let the bones you have crushed rejoice. Hide your face from my sins and blot out all my iniquity. Create in me a pure heart, O God, and renew a steadfast spirit within me. Do not cast me from your presence or take your Holy Spirit from me. Restore to me the joy of your salvation and grant me a willing spirit, to sustain me. Then I will teach transgressors your ways, so that sinners will turn back to you. Deliver me from the guilt of bloodshed, O God, you who are God my Savior, and my tongue will sing of your righteousness. Open my lips, Lord, and my mouth will declare your praise. You do not delight in sacrifice, or I would bring it; you do not take pleasure in burnt offerings. My sacrifice, O God, is a broken spirit; a broken and contrite heart you, God, will not despise. May it please you to prosper Zion, to build up the walls of Jerusalem. Then you will delight in the sacrifices of the righteous, in burnt offerings offered whole; then bulls will be offered on your altar.

—Psalm 51

King David was a strong but unassuming shepherd that went from being a boy who took down a giant to a ruler known as *a man after God's own heart*. Unfortunately, greatness is not all King David accomplished. Second Samuel 11 describes David's sexual fallout through abuse of power, adultery, and scandalous cover-up by means of murder. Psalm 51 offers a prayer by King David for mercy and forgiveness over the sins he committed.

David's prayer of forgiveness stands out because it moves in two directions, vertical and horizontal. Vertical confession is our direct admission of sin to God, restoring our relationship with him through repentance and grace. Horizontal confession, on the other hand, allows us to pursue reconciliation, healing, and unity with others as we bring our sin into the light. While Ps 51 is primarily a vertical confession before God, its reach extends horizontally, carrying implications for those David's sin wounded and opening the door for restoration with people. There are six key takeaways from Ps 51 that reveal how we, too, can seek true, biblical forgiveness.

1. *Words and feelings matter.* When it comes to forgiveness, everyone's feelings matter—including our own. Simply saying "I'm sorry" is not enough. We must move beyond what is comfortable as we truly express what is taking place in our heart. Forgiveness without authenticity is confession without conversion and empty words are just lip service without honesty.
2. *Honestly own the mess.* Partial truths cannot mend what only honest repentance can heal. Like David in Ps 51, we must move beyond the shame that has kept our sin hidden. We must honestly own and admit our behavior without excuses, manipulation, or blame. David owned his wrongdoing, tracing it all the way back to the womb. Likewise, we must comprehensively own our behavior and actions as we seek grace.
3. *Humbly ask for grace.* Sorry is easy; repentance costs something. We don't get to control whether grace is extended—that choice belongs to the one we have hurt. And even when forgiveness comes, it does not cancel the weight of the wound. Every act of grace bears a cost.
4. *Value their cost in forgiveness.* Forgiveness is not cheap. Jesus fully demonstrated on the cross the cost of forgiveness by laying down his life for his sheep. Therefore, we must understand the magnitude of unsolicited pain our apology inflicts as we seek forgiveness. Our addiction has taken years or decades to confess, yet God was always patient. We must extend that same patience to those we seek forgiveness from.
5. *Commit to patiently building trust.* Change over time rebuilds trust. We have no right to place a timeline on healing. Trust comes easy the first time—but once broken, it demands proof, not promises. What can be broken in seconds may take a lifetime to rebuild. We cannot heal relationships or place expectations on forgiveness. All we can do

is draw a circle around ourselves and work on that. Ephesians 4:2 calls us to be *humble*, *gentle*, and *patient* as we *bear with one another in love*. Forgiveness isn't a microwave moment—it's a Crock-Pot process. Real healing happens low, slow, and with a lot of prayer.

6. *Desperately pray that God restores.* David cried out in Ps 51:12, "Restore to me the joy of your salvation." As we seek forgiveness, our desire can be for restoration, but our motive must remain obedience in God. We must release control, acknowledging that the restoration we want may not be the restoration we receive. We cannot circumvent the life-changing consequences of our actions. What we can avoid is prolonged time wasted in sin and ignoring our purpose.

DAILY FIGHT PLAN

1. Why is it important for your forgiveness to be both vertical and horizontal as you extend it to others?
2. Is forgiveness more difficult for the one seeking or the one giving and why?
3. This week's combat challenge is to write a letter and forgive yourself for your past destructive actions and attitude toward self. Self-forgiveness is a powerful beginning, but why does true freedom require you to also seek forgiveness from those you've harmed?

DAY 3

PROCESSING FORGIVENESS

Before they married, Erin told Andy she was all in, completely committed, but there was one line she refused to cross: unfaithfulness. It was her unspoken limit to "for better or for worse." Seven years into their marriage, Andy confessed a long-hidden addiction to pornography, and in that moment, Erin's line was crossed. Her deepest value was dependability, doing what you say you'll do, which suddenly collided with her vow to love and honor her husband. She found herself torn between staying true to her words from seven years earlier and reevaluating the work Christ had done in her since then.

God never wastes pain. He used this crisis to teach Erin about forgiving, not only the trauma that shattered her trust, but for all the smaller fractures along the way.

Forgiveness Is Like an Onion

Andy confessed on a Tuesday, and by week's end, Erin believed she had forgiven him. And she had—at least the first layer. But healing required more. Through counseling and prayer, she began uncovering deeper layers, each demanding its own surrender.

The first layer was the direct actions of betrayal. Surprisingly, this was the easiest to forgive because it was tangible, recent, and clear. What she once believed unforgivable at the start of her marriage had become possible only because Jesus had been sanctifying her heart all along.

But then the layers got more complicated. The next layer cut deeper: forgiving the seven dishonest years of marriage where she believed she knew her husband completely and did not. Those years were lost, never to be recovered.

The hardest layer was forgiving the future. Erin had to accept that her marriage would never look like the one she imagined—sacred and holy. This story would always be a part of their past. Forgiveness here became a daily decision, a continual laying down of her right to a "perfect" marriage.

Forgetting Versus Choosing Not to Remember

Jeremiah 31:34 says, "For I will forgive their wickedness and will remember their sins no more," drawing a distinction between forgetting and choosing not to remember. Despite knowing everything we have done or will do, God chooses not to recall our sin. In the same way, Erin learned she could choose to focus on whatever is true, noble, right, pure, lovely, and admirable—instead of on things that are harmful and negative.

How to Forgive

1. *Start with prayer.* In her darkest nights, Erin found herself closer to God than ever before. His steadfast love, faithfulness, and goodness became her anchor. Even when Erin felt she could never trust another person, she could still rely on Jesus. As it turns out, being desperate in prayer is a pretty good place to start.
2. *Be honest about the pain.* Counseling helped Erin process her grief and uncover hidden layers of hurt. Growth rarely happens in comfort—it is difficult, challenging, and uncomfortable. It was in this season that Erin discovered her true shape by being stretched outside her comfort zones. In the wake of Andy's sexual betrayal, she sought for what was lost—safety—and what was hidden—the truth.
3. *Admit you feel helpless and vulnerable.* The same walls we build for protection can prevent us from experiencing hope and healing. Erin's walls were massive—and for a time, they served a necessary purpose. Trust needed to be earned before it could be given. But to rebuild trust, her walls had to come down.
4. *Release the offender from ever making it right.* Some wounds cannot be fixed. Some choices can never be reversed. This part is really hard and another example of why we need to forgive daily. Forgiveness doesn't mean pretending it never happened; it means surrendering the right to demand repayment. Healing, not fixing, must become the goal.

This does not mean the one forgiving must remain in an unsafe situation. If the person seeking forgiveness demonstrates a pattern of abuse and manipulation, the Bible is clear on how we behave in this matter. Paul warned in 2 Tim 3:1–5 that destructive, manipulative, and violent individuals should be avoided, not enabled. God hates abuse and is consistently seen as a protector of the oppressed and a champion of justice.

While forgiveness frees our hearts, boundaries protect our lives.

Forgiveness and restoration are not the same—one releases resentment, while the other rebuilds trust. In abusive situations, restoration requires far more than forgiveness; it demands genuine, sustained transformation in the abuser's behavior. While change is possible, it is rare and usually follows long periods of separation, accountability, and counseling. Ultimately, forgiveness should never mean returning to danger; safety and clear evidence of real change must guide any steps toward restoration.

God wastes nothing—not even our deepest heartbreak. Through each painful layer, God shapes us into people who reflect his grace, one act of forgiveness at a time.

DAILY FIGHT PLAN

1. How does understanding that forgiveness has layers change your perspective on the time it takes to heal from sexual betrayal?
2. What is the difference between *forgetting* and *choosing not to remember*, and how does that distinction reshape the way you understand forgiving yourself?

DAY 4

CONFESSION TO A SPOUSE AND ONGOING TRUST

AJ realized that the only path to true freedom from porn was complete honesty with his wife, Holly. Though fear had kept him silent for so long, after more than six months of sobriety, he could no longer live in deception—he was ready to confront the truth and lay it bare before her. With coaching from a mentor in Fight Club, AJ provided full disclosure to his wife. While healing eventually unfolded in their marriage, the initial pain and broken trust was complex to navigate.

In seeking forgiveness from a spouse, confession is not easy, but it is necessary.

Full disclosure is essential in confession to a loved one so that they can process the full extent of the pain all at once. When we reveal the truth over time, we inflict further trauma on our spouse. They will continually be waiting for more confessions, doubting they know the whole truth, and unable to fully heal. When we confess to the person we have wounded, honesty allows them to feel the full weight of the truth rather than being shattered by repeated revelations. Research on sexual disclosure shows that healing begins when the first confession includes the major realities of the behavior—the what, where, and why—without dragging them through the graphic details. Our spouse needs clarity, not cruelty; truth, not trauma.[5]

While full disclosure is a gift, it can be handled like a grenade.

Lysa TerKeurst, author and president of Proverbs 31 Ministries, describes trust as the oxygen of all human relationships.[6] When we deprive relationships of trust for too long, they suffocate and eventually wither. Likewise, relationships cannot move towards genuine forgiveness if the truth keeps arriving in pieces. Confession cannot come in waves, diluted by vagueness, half-truths, or lies of omission. Healing begins with a relentless commitment to full honesty—truth that starts at confession and continues without interruption.

Let's explore what a healthy confession to a spouse looks like.

5. Schneider et al., "Surviving Disclosure of Infidelity."

6. TerKeurst, *I Want To Trust You*, xv.

Before the Conversation

- *Prayerfully plan disclosure.* It is not a question of if confession is necessary, so lean into the Holy Spirit's prompting with prayer and commitment to do what is right.
- *Write it down.* Years of deceptive behavior have conditioned us to lie. Unless we clearly articulate our sin, fight-or-flight reflex will push us to minimize or omit the truth despite our best intentions.
- *Make every effort to end the behavior.* While we cannot promise a life free from every lustful thought, we must take decisive action to end the behavior. Don't place the burden on our spouse to enforce what we are capable of ending ourselves. Affairs must be cut off completely. Porn access must be eliminated. But do not wait for perfection to confess or it will never come.

During the Conversation

- *Be direct and take responsibility.* State what was done without minimizing it.
- *Avoid blaming.* Do not shift blame to your spouse or anyone else. Our actions are ours alone, and refusing to own them is emotional abuse.
- *Express remorse.* Our apology must be sincere, expressing true sorrow for the pain we have caused. This is not the time to comfort, fix, or presume we understand their feelings—doing so is dismissive and patronizing.
- *Be honest, but consider details.* Your spouse cannot forgive what they do not know. Be honest, but careful with details, avoiding graphic or unnecessary information that would deepen the wound. This will be difficult because your spouse will want to know everything, but full disclosure does not mean including specific details, such as which type of porn was abused.
- *Do not demand forgiveness.* State your desire for forgiveness and then leave the ball in their court. Understand that while freedom is unleashed on the addict in confession, your loved one is experiencing unfamiliar emotions of anger, betrayal, confusion, and hopelessness. If all you receive is silence, let it be.

- *Stay present.* Do not leave the room unless your spouse tells you to. Remain present for their reaction—even the anger— to answer any follow-up questions.

After the Confession

- *Allow time for processing.* Give your spouse the space needed to process their emotions without pressure.
- *Be accountable.* Be transparent and accept accountability for your actions. While expectations placed upon you may seem unfair, this is crucial to rebuilding trust.
- *Seek godly professional help.* Consider individual and couples counseling to heal trauma and gain valuable Christian guidance through the healing process.

If we desire genuine forgiveness, we must commit to a lifetime of building trust. This cannot be rushed. It is an honest confession without expectation. Restitution takes time because trust is earned, not assumed. In this season, your spouse has every right to ask difficult questions, to monitor access and habits, and to establish guardrails they deem necessary. These boundaries are not punishments; they are the scaffolding that supports the rebuilding of safety and trust over time. Christian author Sheri Keffer points out that sexual betrayal leaves the victim unable to trust others and ultimately themselves because they are the one that got played.[7] Time is necessary for processing.

DAILY FIGHT PLAN

1. Why is it important to clearly and concisely confess everything the first time?
2. In what ways would writing your confession help you to process it and articulate everything appropriately?
3. Are you willing to wait patiently as your spouse or loved one processes the confession? Is there a time limit to your patience and what is the justification for that, if so?

7. Keffer, *Intimate Deception*, 114.

4. If you have already shared your story to your spouse or loved one, have you given full disclosure? If not, are you willing to do so?

DAY 5

AFTER FORGIVENESS: SURRENDER WINS

As the old saying goes, *hurt people hurt people.* Forgiveness is often so difficult because pain distorts our reflexes. When we are wounded, our instinct is to strike back. But the truth cuts both ways. When our brokenness hurts others through our addictive behavior, we end up wounding ourselves as well because hurt people stay hurt until they learn to forgive.

As our negative actions cause pain, we often respond in one of two destructive ways. We either excuse ourselves or punish ourselves. Excusing ourselves means minimizing, denying, or shifting blame. It is self-deception disguised as self-protection and it keeps us from growth. Punishing ourselves means living in self-imposed prisons of shame and regret. This route keeps us locked in a prison of our own making, forgetting the worth God has already declared over us. Neither response leads to healing or brings freedom.

There is, however, a better way forward—the path of self-forgiveness.

Since, then, you have been raised with Christ, set your hearts on things above, where Christ is, seated at the right hand of God. Set your minds on things above, not on earthly things. For you died, and your life is now hidden with Christ in God. When Christ, who is your life, appears, then you also will appear with him in glory. Put to death, therefore, whatever belongs to your earthly nature: sexual immorality, impurity, lust, evil desires and greed, which is idolatry. Because of these, the wrath of God is coming. You used to walk in these ways, in the life you once lived. But now you must also rid yourselves of all such things as these: anger, rage, malice, slander, and filthy language from your lips. Do not lie to each other, since you have taken off your old self with its practices and have put on the new self, which is being renewed in knowledge in the image of its Creator. Here there is no Gentile or Jew, circumcised or uncircumcised, barbarian, Scythian, slave or free, but Christ is all, and is in all.

—Colossians 3:1–11

These verses reveal a critical truth: we are not perfect. That means our flaws, addictions, and failures do not make us uniquely broken—they make us human. When we feel unworthy, we must look to Jesus because his life, death, and resurrection reveal our worth, and his grace offers new life. However, new life does not mean we are immune to sin. While we may not be who we once were, we are still not perfect.

We need Jesus as much today as we ever did because we will never outgrow our need for his grace.

Therefore, as God's chosen people, holy and dearly loved, clothe yourselves with compassion, kindness, humility, gentleness and patience.

—Colossians 3:12

We matter deeply to God. We are *chosen* and *dearly loved*. As we clothe ourselves in compassion, kindness, humility, gentleness, and patience, we not only become better versions of ourselves. We become more like Jesus. It is here, covered in his grace, that forgiven people become forgiving people.

Addiction often makes us believe that we are beyond grace. Shame asks, "Why would God love someone like me?" The answer is simple: We don't deserve it. But grace was never about what we deserve; it is about his love. No sin disqualifies us from God's mercy, and no failure puts us beyond his reach. Grace breaks the chains of shame and opens the prison door.

Christian author and psychotherapist Alison Cook observed that false guilt is when we feel ashamed for being human—limited, imperfect, and unable to be everything or do everything—essentially holding ourselves to a God-like standard.[8] Cook concludes that the antidote is surrender, where we accept our human limitations and reframe unrealistic expectations of ourselves with humility and grace.

The answer to our unforgiveness is grace. When we surrender ourselves fully to Jesus, we courageously accept our flaws, addictive behavior, and illusion of control. In doing this, we wisely accept the truth that we are not God, but we need him.

- Our unforgiveness says, "We are a lost cause, incapable of self control," but surrender says, "We are dead to sin" (Rom 6:2).
- Our unforgiveness says, "We are failures," but surrender says, "We are completed in him" (Col 2:10).
- Our unforgiveness says, "We will never be free," but surrender says, "We are set free" (John 8:31–32).

8. Cook, "True Guilt vs. False Guilt," para. 9.

The paradox of victory is that surrender wins. As we let go, we rise free with hands raised, not fists clenched. Understanding that it is God, not us, who truly holds all things together isn't weakness—it's rebellion against the mindset that has kept us prisoner to our addiction. As we close this three-month journey, may each of us face that truth with open hands and humble hearts because we are made for freedom. The truth of Fight Club is that it was never really our battle to fight all along. Jesus is enough.

DAILY FIGHT PLAN

1. In the past, have you tended to excuse, punish, or forgive yourself for your lustful and toxic behavior? Why do you frequent that response?
2. Share your thoughts on the paradox of victory: surrender wins.
3. Evaluating the past twelve weeks, do you believe Jesus is enough and how does your behavior reflect that belief?
4. Now that you've completed *Fight Club: Live in Freedom*, what concrete next step will you take to continue walking in freedom—and how will you put it into action? We offer recommended next steps following this chapter if you are interested in creating a Fight Club community group at your local church or in your area.

FORMING A FIGHT CLUB COMMUNITY GROUP

Purpose

Fight Club: Live in Freedom is a safe, affordable, gospel-centered pathway that helps men and women find freedom from pornography and sexual addiction. Through biblical truth, community, accountability, and weekly combat challenges, participants move from shame and isolation into healing, holiness, and a renewed sense of God-given purpose.

Manageable Size

Groups should stay small—no more than twelve people—to encourage everyone to participate, feel fully known, and benefit from intentional time together.

Appropriate Makeup

All members must be of the same sex, and no one under age eighteen should join an adult Fight Club community group.

Structured Curriculum

Fight Club: Live in Freedom is a twelve-week journey offering weekly Combat challenges and Scripture, daily devotionals, journaling (five days a week), and guided discussion questions for the group meeting.

Community groups can meet in person or online through a secure videoconferencing application. Online groups are often highly successful due to minimized shame and increased anonymity during the early stages of finding freedom from addiction.

Purposeful Connection

Fight Club: Live in Freedom is intended to move those struggling with compulsive addictive behavior from isolation to deep connection—with God and with others. Group participants grow from being unknown, selfish, and hurting to becoming vulnerable, honest, and selfless. Conversation is facilitated by the questions completed throughout their weekly reading.

Equipping Fight Club Champions

Identify one or two spiritually mature, trustworthy leaders. Ensure they read the entire book before leading. While Fight Club champions should model integrity and humility, porn and/or sexual addiction in their past should not disqualify them from serving.

Fight Club champions should have a basic understanding of addiction and shame dynamics. They must also value confidentiality and group safety, recognizing when it's lawfully appropriate to breach trust or refer someone to counseling.

Transition to Ongoing Groups

The established relationships and comradery built through *Fight Club: Live in Freedom* often transitions naturally into long-term accountability and small groups, expanding the impact beyond the initial twelve weeks.

BIBLIOGRAPHY

Abdi, Fatemeh, et al. "Effect of Pornography Use on Sexual Satisfaction: A Systematic Review and Meta-Analysis." *Journal of Addictive Diseases* 43.4 (2024) 301–18. https://doi.org/10.1080/10550887.2024.2401680.

Abubakar, Munir N. *How to Overcome Porn and Masturbation Addiction: Reclaim Your Mind, Build Self-Discipline, and Live a Fulfilling Life.* N.p.: Techie, 2023.

Ahmed, Faraz, et al. "The Internet Is for Porn: Measurement and Analysis of Online Adult Traffic." IEEE 36th International Conference on Distributed Computing Systems (2016) 88–97. https://doi.org/10.1109/ICDCS.2016.81.

Alexander, Bruce K. "Addiction: The View from Rat Park (2010)." https://www.brucekalexander.com/articles-speeches/rat-park/148-addiction-the-view-from-rat-park.

———. *The Globalization of Addiction: A Study in Poverty of the Spirit.* Oxford: Oxford University Press, 2010.

———. "The Veil." St. Stephen's Episcopal Church, April 7, 2025. https://www.ssecdurham.org/lent-devotions-2025/the-veil.

Allender, Dan B. *The Wounded Heart: Hope for Adult Victims of Childhood Sexual Abuse.* Colorado Springs: NavPress, 1990.

American Psychiatric Association. "Anxiety." APA Dictionary of Psychology. https://dictionary.apa.org/anxiety.

———. "Depression." APA Dictionary of Psychology. https://dictionary.apa.org/depression.

———. "Emotional Instability." APA Dictionary of Psychology. https://dictionary.apa.org/emotional-instability.

———. "What Is Posttraumatic Stress Disorder (PTSD)?" https://www.psychiatry.org/patients-families/ptsd/what-is-ptsd.

Andamon, Lee C. J. B., et al. "Regain Consciousness: The Impact of Internet Pornography on Children and Adolescents—A Review." *International Journal of Human Research and Social Science Studies* 2.4 (2025) 160–77. https://ijhrsss.com/articles/22.

Anderson, Monica, and Jingjing Jiang. "Teens, Social Media, and Technology 2018." Pew Research Center, May 31, 2018. https://www.pewinternet.org/2018/05/31/teens-social-media-technology-2018/.

The Asservo Project. "Pornography and Human Trafficking." Sep. 27, 2022. https://www.theasservoproject.org/pornography-and-human-trafficking/.

Associated Press. "Former Baseball Star Darryl Strawberry Gets 18-Month Sentence for Probation Violation." NewsOn6, Apr. 29, 2002. https://www.newson6.com/

story/5e3682cf2f69d76f620977c8/former-baseball-star-darryl-strawberry-gets-18-months-in-prison-for-probation-violation.

Austin, Ashley, et al. "Suicidality Among Transgender Youth: Elucidating the Role of Interpersonal Risk Factors." *Journal of Interpersonal Violence* 37.5–6 (2020) NP2696–NP2718. https://doi.org/10.1177/0886260520915554.

Baer, Maria. "More Christians Are Watching Porn, But Fewer Think It's a Problem." *Christianity Today*, Sep. 26, 2024. https://www.christianitytoday.com/2024/09/pornography-use-christians-study-barna-research-pure-desire-ministries/.

Barna Group. "Beyond the Porn Phenomenon: Equipping the Church for a New Conversation About Pornography, Betrayal Trauma, and Healing." Barna Group and Pure Desire Ministries, 2024. https://static1.squarespace.com/static/60246cd30685761e93a015ed/t/67b0d36d29ab1059a067f402/1739641722100/Barna+-+Beyond+the+Porn+Phenomenon.pdf.

———. "Porn in the Digital Age: New Research Reveals 10 Trends." Barna Group, Apr. 6, 2016. https://www.barna.com/research/porn-in-the-digital-age-new-research-reveals-10-trends/.

———. "The Porn Phenomenon: The Impact of Pornography in the Digital Age." Barna Group and Josh McDowell Ministries, 2016. https://access.barna.com/wp-content/uploads/2019/07/The-Porn-Phenomenon_Access.pdf.

———. "The Silent Problem of Pornography Use Among Pastors." Nov. 22, 2024. https://www.barna.com/research/pastors-pornography-use/.

Beck, Aaron T. *Cognitive Therapy and the Emotional Disorders*. New York: International Universities, 1976.

Bickel, M. Andrew. "Neuroplasticity and Addiction: Understanding Brain Rewiring During Substance Use and Recovery." *Journal of Addiction Research & Therapy* 15.12 (2024) 1–3. https://www.omicsonline.org/open-access/neuroplasticity-and-addiction-understanding-brain-rewiring-during-substance-use-and-recovery-134423.html.

Birches Health. "Porn Addiction by the Numbers: Demographics, Stats, and Trends." Birches Health, Sep. 8, 2024. https://bircheshealth.com/resources/porn-addiction-stats.

Bird, Chad. *Upside-Down Spirituality: The 9 Essential Failures of a Faithful Life*. Grand Rapids: Baker, 2019.

Black, Sam. *The Healing Church: What Churches Get Wrong about Pornography and How to Fix It*. New York: Morgan James, 2023.

Blaise, Pascal. *Pensées*. Translated by A. J. Krailsheimer. London: Penguin, 1995.

Blake, Suzanne. "Why Gen Z Is the Loneliest Generation." Newsweek, Dec. 6, 2024. https://www.newsweek.com/gen-z-loneliest-generation-1996926.

Blakeman, Katherine. "Your Brain on Porn." National Center on Sexual Exploitation, Dec. 19, 2017. https://endsexualexploitation.org/articles/your-brain-on-porn/.

Bledsoe, Isaac, and Ben Smith. "Male Loneliness and Isolation: What the Data Shows." American Institute for Boys and Men, Aug. 20, 2025. https://aibm.org/research/male-loneliness-and-isolation-what-the-data-shows/.

Bőthe, Beáta, et al. "Problematic and Non-Problematic Pornography Use Among LGBTQ Adolescents: A Systematic Literature Review." *Current Addiction Reports* 6.4 (2019) 478–94. https://doi.org/10.1007/s40429-019-00289-5.

Buchwald, Natalie. "The Hidden Cost of Pornography: How It Shapes Your Brain and Behavior." Manhattan Mental Health Counseling, Mar. 11, 2025. https://

manhattanmentalhealthcounseling.com/the-hidden-cost-of-pornography-how-it-shapes-your-brain-and-behavior/.

Büsche, Kjell, et al. "Self-Regulatory Processes in Problematic Pornography Use." *Current Addiction Reports* 9.4 (2022) 344–52. https://doi.org/10.1007/s40429-022-00447-2.

Butler, Mark H., et al. "Pornography Use and Loneliness: A Bidirectional Recursive Model and Pilot Investigation." *Journal of Sex & Marital Therapy* 44.2 (2018) 127–37. https://doi.org/10.1080/0092623X.2017.1321601.

Capogrosso, Paolo, et al. "One Patient Out of Four with Newly Diagnosed Erectile Dysfunction Is a Young Man—Worrisome Picture from the Everyday Clinical Practice." *Journal of Sexual Medicine* 10.7 (2013) 1833–41. https://doi.org/10.1111/jsm.12179.

Cardoso, Jorge, et al. "Difficulties in Emotion Regulation and Problematic Pornography Use: The Mediating Role of Loneliness." *International Journal of Sexual Health* 35.3 (2023) 481–93. https://doi.org/10.1080/19317611.2023.2224807.

Carnes, Patrick. "The Making of a Sex Addict." Adapted from "The Obsessive Shadow," 1998. https://cdn.ymaws.com/iitap.com/resource/resmgr/arie_files/m1_article_the-making-of-a-s.pdf.

———. *Out of the Shadows: Understanding Sexual Addiction*. Center City, MN: Hazelden, 2001.

Carroll, Jason S., et al. "The Porn Gap: Differences in Men's and Women's Pornography Patterns in Couple Relationships." *Journal of Couple & Relationship Therapy* 16.2 (2017) 146–63. https://doi.org/10.1080/15332691.2016.1238796.

Carvalheira, Ana, et al. "Masturbation and Pornography Use among Coupled Heterosexual Men with Decreased Sexual Desire: How Many Roles of Masturbation?" *Journal of Sex & Marital Therapy* 41.6 (2015) 626–35. https://doi.org/10.1080/0092623X.2014.958790.

Castillo, Maci. "Porn Addiction Tops List of Google Searches Seeking Help for Addictions." Local 10 News, Jun. 17, 2024. https://www.local10.com/health/2024/06/17/porn-addiction-tops-list-of-google-searches-seeking-help-for-addictions/.

Chancellor, Michael. "The Ongoing Epidemic of Pornography in the Church." Baptist News Global, Jan. 27, 2021. https://baptistnews.com/article/the-ongoing-epidemic-of-pornography-in-the-church/.

Cloitre, Marylene, et al. "A Developmental Approach to Complex PTSD: Childhood and Adult Cumulative Trauma as Predictors of Symptom Complexity." *Journal of Traumatic Stress* 22.5 (2009) 399–408. https://doi.org/10.1002/jts.20444.

Cook, Alison. "True Guilt vs. False Guilt." Dr. Alison Cook. https://www.dralisoncook.com/blog/true-guilt-vs-false-guilt.

Culina, Steliana A. "A Socio-Economic Portrait of Child Pornography Offenders." *Revista Universitară de Sociologie* 3 (2024) 155–63. https://sociologiecraiova.ro/revista/wp-content/uploads/2024/12/FULL-VERSION-155-163.pdf.

Culture Reframed. "Pornography and Predators: Understanding the Dangers of Social Media and Video Games." Culture Reframed, Jul. 28, 2023. https://culturereframed.org/pornography-and-predators-understanding-the-dangers-of-social-media-and-video-games/.

Culurciello, Eugenio. "29,000 Days." Medium (blog), Oct. 21, 2018. https://culurciello.medium.com/29-000-days-97a403b2f72.

Daneback, Kristian, et al. "An Internet Study of Cybersex Participants." *Archives of Sexual Behavior* 34.3 (2005) 321–28. https://link.springer.com/article/10.1007/s10508-005-3120-z.

Dateline NBC. "Children for Sale." *MSNBC*, Jan. 30, 2004. https://www.justice.gov/file/290371/dl?inline.

DeAngelis, Tori. "Teens Are Spending Nearly 5 Hours Daily on Social Media." *Monitor on Psychology* 55.3 (2024) 80. https://www.apa.org/monitor/2024/04/teen-social-use-mental-health.

DeKeseredy, Walter S. "Critical Criminological Understandings of Adult Pornography and Woman Abuse: New Progressive Directions in Research and Theory." *International Journal for Crime, Justice, and Social Democracy* 4.4 (2015) 4–21. https://www.crimejusticejournal.com/article/view/776.

Demarinis, Susie. "Loneliness at Epidemic Levels in America." *Explore* 16.5 (2020) 278–79. https://doi.org/10.1016/j.explore.2020.06.008.

Diaz, Nelsi. "Masturbation Statistics in the US (2025)." HeraHaven, Apr. 22, 2025. https://herahaven.com/blog/masturbation-statistics-us/.

Divine, Mark. "The Breathing Technique a Navy SEAL Uses to Stay Calm and Focused." *TIME*, May 4, 2016. https://time.com/4316151/breathing-technique-navy-seal-calm-focused/.

Donevan, Meghan, et al. "The Experience of Individuals Filmed for Pornography Production: A History of Continuous Polyvictimization and Ongoing Mental Health Challenges." *Nordic Journal of Psychiatry* 79.2 (2025) 156–65. https://doi.org/10.1080/08039488.2025.2464634.

Douthat, Ross. "Is Pornography Adultery?" *Atlantic* 302.3 (2008) 80–86. https://www.theatlantic.com/magazine/archive/2008/10/is-pornography-adultery/306989/.

Drah, Hermina. "30 Surprising Cell Phone Addiction Statistics for 2022." Disturbmenot!, Jan. 15, 2022. https://disturbmenot.co/cell-phone-addiction-statistics/.

Dwulit, Aleksandra D., and Piotr Rzymski. "Prevalence, Patterns, and Self-Perceived Effects of Pornography Consumption in Polish University Students: A Cross-Sectional Study." *International Journal of Environmental Research and Public Health* 16.10 (2019) 1–15. https://doi.org/10.3390/ijerph16101861.

Dynomight. "How Much Information Is in DNA?" Asimov Press, 2025. https://press.asimov.com/articles/dna-information.

Edersheim, Alfred. *The Life and Times of Jesus the Messiah*. Vol. 2. Peabody, MA: Hendrickson, 1993.

Enough Is Enough. "Statistics: Youth and Porn." https://enough.org/stats-youth-and-porn.

ESPN. "Darryl Strawberry—Career Stats." 2025. https://www.espn.com/mlb/player/stats/_/id/1350/darryl-strawberry.

European Commission. "Communication from the Commission to the European Parliament, the Council, the European Economic and Social Committee and the Committee of the Regions: EU Strategy for a More Effective Fight Against Child Sexual Abuse." Publications Office of the European Union, Jul. 24, 2020. https://eur-lex.europa.eu/legal-content/EN/TXT/?uri=celex:52020DC0607.

Feehs, Kyleigh, and Alyssa Currier. "2020 Federal Human Trafficking Report." Human Trafficking Institute, 2021. https://traffickinginstitute.org/wp-content/uploads/2022/01/2020-Federal-Human-Trafficking-Report-Low-Res.pdf.

Fight the New Drug. "10 Negative Effects of Porn on Your Brain, Body, Relationships, and Society." Sep. 10, 2025. https://fightthenewdrug.org/10-reasons-why-porn-is-unhealthy-for-consumers-and-society/.

———. "'Teen': Why Has This Porn Category Topped the Charts for 6+ Years?" https://fightthenewdrug.org/this-years-most-popular-genre-of-porn-is-pretty-messed-up/.

———. "What the 'Fight the New Drug' Billboards Mean." Jul. 12, 2023. https://fightthenewdrug.org/what-the-fight-the-new-drug-billboards-mean/.

———. "Why Do Some People Fight Against Sex Trafficking and Also Support Porn?" https://fightthenewdrug.org/why-do-some-people-fight-against-sex-trafficking-but-unconditionally-support-porn/.

The Freedom Fight. "Porn Addiction Research and Data." https://thefreedomfight.org/research-data/.

GateHouse Treatment. "Addiction: The Brain Hijacker." https://www.gatehousetreatment.com/blog/addiction-the-brain-hijacker/.

Gilkerson, Luke. "Your Brain on Porn." Covenant Eyes. https://renewalcs.org/wp-content/uploads/2016/09/covenant_eyes_your_brain_on_porn.pdf.

Giordano, Amanda L., et al. "Childhood Trauma and Sex Addiction Among Adult Men." *Journal of Addictions & Offender Counseling* 45.1 (2024) 221–33. https://doi.org/10.1002/jaoc.12134.

Grim, Brian J., and Melissa E. Grim. "Belief, Behavior, and Belonging: How Faith Is Indispensable in Preventing and Recovering from Substance Abuse." *Journal of Religion and Health* 58.5 (2019) 1713–50. https://doi.org/10.1007/s10943-019-00876-w.

Grubbs, Joshua B., et al. "Pornography and Pride: Antagonism Drives Links Between Narcissism and Perceived Addiction to Pornography." *Journal of Research in Personality* 107 (2023) 104419. https://doi.org/10.1016/j.jrp.2023.104419.

Grubbs, Joshua B., et al. "Pornography Problems Due to Moral Incongruence: An Integrative Model with a Systematic Review and Meta-Analysis." *Archives of Sexual Behavior* 48.2 (2019) 397–415. https://pubmed.ncbi.nlm.nih.gov/30076491/.

Grubbs, Joshua B., et al. "Self-Reported Addiction to Pornography in a Nationally Representative Sample: The Roles of Use Habits, Religiousness, and Moral Incongruence." *Journal of Behavioral Addictions* 8.1 (2019) 88–93. https://doi.org/10.1556/2006.7.2018.134.

Grubbs, Joshua B., et al. "Transgression as Addiction: Religiosity and Moral Disapproval as Predictors of Perceived Addiction to Pornography." *Archives of Sexual Behavior* 44.1 (2015) 125–36. https://doi.org/10.1007/s10508-013-0257-z.

Grudzen, Corita R., et al. "Comparison of the Mental Health of Female Adult Film Performers and Other Young Women in California." *Psychiatric Services* 62.6 (2011) 639–45. https://doi.org/10.1176/ps.62.6.pss6206_0639.

Gurtner, Daniel M. "The Veil of the Temple in History and Legend." *Journal of the Evangelical Theological Society* 49.1 (2006) 97–114. https://etsjets.org/wp-content/uploads/2010/06/files_JETS-PDFs_49_49-1_JETS_49-1_97-114_Gurtner.pdf.

Haber, Darren. "Sex Addiction Is a Relational Disorder." GoodTherapy, Nov. 21, 2011. https://www.goodtherapy.org/blog/sex-addiction-as-relational-disorder-1121115/.

Hailes, Helen P., and Lisa A. Goodman. "'They're Out to Take Away Your Sanity': A Qualitative Investigation of Gaslighting in Intimate Partner Violence." *Journal of Family Violence* 40.3 (2025) 269–82. https://doi.org/10.1007/s10896-023-00652-1.

Hamby, Sherry, et al. "Recognizing the Cumulative Burden of Childhood Adversities Transforms Science and Practice for Trauma and Resilience." *American Psychologist* 76.2 (2021) 230–42. https://doi.org/10.1037/amp0000763.

Harmony United Psychiatric Care. "The Dark Side of Desire: The Emotional and Mental Health Costs of Porn Addiction." HUPCFL, Jul. 7, 2025. https://hupcfl.com/the-emotional-and-mental-health-costs-of-porn-addiction/.

Hesse, Colin, and Kory Floyd. "Affection Substitution: The Effect of Pornography Consumption on Close Relationships." *Journal of Social and Personal Relationships* 36.11–12 (2019) 3887–907. https://doi.org/10.1177/0265407519841719.

Hester, Tricia J., et al. "Barriers to Sexually Exploited Cambodian Women Integrating into Churches: Perspectives of Sexually Exploited Women and the Christian Community." *Dignity: A Journal on Sexual Exploitation and Violence* 5.1 (2020) 1–20. https://doi.org/10.23860/dignity.2020.05.01.04.

Hill, Robert E. *Deception in the Body of Christ: Unveiled Mysteries and Neurolinguistic Dialectics*. Eugene, OR: Wipf & Stock, 2010.

Hoerr, Alexandra Joy. "Porn Withdrawal Symptoms: 8 Signs and How to Cope." Optimum Joy, Jul. 9, 2025. https://optimumjoy.com/blog/recognizing-porn-withdrawal-symptoms/.

HostingAdvice. "33 Most Visited Websites in the World." Jun. 2025. https://www.hostingadvice.com/how-to/most-visited-websites-in-the-world/.

Hughes, Abigail, et al. "Sexual Coercion by Women: The Influence of Pornography and Narcissistic and Histrionic Personality Disorder Traits." *Archives of Sexual Behavior* 49.3 (2020) 885–94. https://doi.org/10.1007/s10508-019-01538-4.

Human Trafficking Institute. "Federal Human Trafficking Report: Executive Summary 2023." https://traffickinginstitute.org/wp-content/uploads/2024/06/2023-Federal-Human-Trafficking-Report-Executive-Summary.pdf.

Ince, Campbell, et al. "Clarifying and Extending Our Understanding of Problematic Pornography Use Through Descriptions of the Lived Experience." *Scientific Reports* 13.1 (2023) 1–12. https://doi.org/10.1038/s41598-023-45459-8.

Insider Monkey. "Top 15 Countries that Supply the Most Pornography Online: Understanding Global Trends and the Role of Ethical Content Creation." Feb. 3, 2025. https://www.insidermonkey.com/blog/top-15-countries-that-supply-the-most-pornography-online-understanding-global-trends-and-the-role-of-ethical-content-creation-1441936/.

International Justice Mission. "Phnom Penh, Cambodia." 2019. https://assets-na.ijm.org/documents/2019_IJM_FactSheets_SA_Cambodia-UPDATED.pdf.

International Labour Organization and Walk Free Foundation. "Global Estimates of Modern Slavery: Forced Labour and Forced Marriage." Geneva: International Labour Office, 2017. https://www.ilo.org/sites/default/files/wcmsp5/groups/public/@dgreports/@dcomm/documents/publication/wcms_575479.pdf.

Irizarry, Ricardo, et al. "How the Rise of Problematic Pornography Consumption and the COVID-19 Pandemic Has Led to a Decrease in Physical Sexual Interactions and Relationships and an Increase in Addictive Behaviors and Cluster B Personality Traits: A Meta-Analysis." *Cureus* 15.6 (2023) 1–11. https://doi.org/10.7759/cureus.40539.

Jacobs, Tim, et al. "Associations Between Online Pornography Consumption and Sexual Dysfunction in Young Men: Multivariate Analysis Based on an International Web-Based Survey." *JMIR Public Health and Surveillance* 7.10 (2021) 1–20. https://doi.org/10.2196/32542.

Jahnen, Matthias, et al. "The Role of Pornography in the Sex Life of Young Adults—a Cross-Sectional Cohort Study on Female and Male German Medical Students." *BMC Public Health* 22.1287 (2022) 1–12. https://doi.org/10.1186/s12889-022-13699-4.

Kaplan, Michael. "The More Porn You Watch, the More Likely You Are to Be Bisexual." *New York Post*, Feb. 26, 2019. https://nypost.com/2019/02/26/people-who-watch-porn-are-more-likely-to-be-bisexual-study/.

Karim, Nashwa Ahmed Hussein Abdel, et al. "Effects of Porn Addiction on Mental Health and Personality of Nursing Students: A Cross-Sectional Study in Egypt." *BMC Nursing* 24.1 (2025) 414. https://doi.org/10.1186/s12912-025-02918-z.

Keffer, Sheri. *Intimate Deception: Healing the Wounds of Sexual Betrayal.* Colorado Springs: WaterBrook, 2015.

Kitzinger, Robert H. Jr., et al. "Habits and Routines of Adults in Early Recovery from Substance Use Disorder: Clinical and Research Implications from a Mixed Methodology Exploratory Study." *Sage* 17 (2023) 1–12. https://doi.org/10.1177/11782218231153843.

Klein, Jessica. "Are Gen Z More Pragmatic About Love and Sex?" BBC Worklife, Jan. 7, 2022. https://www.bbc.co.uk/worklife/article/20220104-are-gen-z-more-pragmatic-about-love-and-sex.

Kliethermes, Matthew, et al. "Complex Trauma." *Child and Adolescent Psychiatric Clinics of North America* 23.2 (2014) 339–61. https://doi.org/10.1016/j.chc.2013.12.009.

Kor, Ariel, et al. "Alterations in Oxytocin and Vasopressin in Men With Problematic Pornography Use: The Role of Empathy," *Journal of Behavioral Addictions* 11, no. 1 (2022) 116–27. https://doi.org/10.1556/2006.2021.00089.

Kruger, Ann Cale, et al. "Facilitating a School-Based Prevention of Commercial Sexual Exploitation of Children." *Health Promotion Practice* 17.4 (2016) 530–36. https://doi.org/10.1177/1524839916628863.

Kuonqui, Christopher. "Measuring Volunteering for the 2030 Agenda: Toolbox of Principles, Tools and Practices." Plan of Action on Integrating Volunteering in the 2030 Agenda, Jul. 2020. https://knowledge.unv.org/system/files/2022-03/Measuring%20Volunteering%20for%20the%202030%20Agenda-21032022.pdf.

Lanctôt, Krista L., et al. "Distinguishing Apathy from Depression: A Review Differentiating the Behavioral, Neuroanatomic, and Treatment-Related Aspects of Apathy from Depression in Neurocognitive Disorders." *International Journal of Geriatric Psychiatry* 38.2 (2023) 1–14. https://doi.org/10.1002/gps.5882.

Lechter, Sharon L., and Greg S. Reid. *Three Feet from Gold: Turn Your Obstacles into Opportunities!* Updated anniversary ed. Shippensburg, PA: Sound Wisdom, 2020.

Ley, David J. "Do Accessibility and Anonymity Lead to Problematic Porn Use?" *Psychology Today*, Nov. 26, 2023. https://www.psychologytoday.com/us/blog/women-who-stray/202311/do-accessibility-and-anonymity-lead-to-problematic-porn-use.

Lo, Ven-hwei, and Ran Wei. "Exposure to Internet Pornography and Taiwanese Adolescents' Sexual Attitudes and Behavior." *Journal of Broadcasting & Electronic Media* 49.2 (2005) 221–37. doi:10.1207/s15506878jobem4902_5.

Logue, Jeff. "Pornography Statistics: Who Uses Porn?" Nelson University ThoughtHub, Oct. 22, 2015. https://www.nelson.edu/thoughthub/pornography-statistics-who-uses-pornography/.

Louie, Sam. "Pastors and Porn: Why Many Pastors Suffer in Silence and Secrecy." *Psychology Today*, Jan. 30, 2020. https://www.psychologytoday.com/us/blog/minority-report/202001/pastors-and-porn.

Lubag, Stacey Coleen. "Loneliness Plays a Key Role in Problematic Porn Use, Study Shows." PsyPost, Oct. 22, 2023. https://www.psypost.org/loneliness-plays-a-key-role-in-problematic-porn-use-study-shows/.

Lubben, Shelley. "Ex-Porn Star Tells the Truth About the Porn Industry." Covenant Eyes, Sep. 5, 2024. https://www.covenanteyes.com/blog/ex-porn-star-tells-the-truth-about-the-porn-industry/.

Luscombe, Belinda. "Porn and the Threat to Virility." *Time* 187.13 (2016). https://time.com/4277510/porn-and-the-threat-to-virility/.

Main Street Counseling. "Is Sex Addiction an Attachment/Intimacy Disorder?" Main Street Counseling, 2024. https://mainstreetcounselor.com/sex-addiction-is-an-intimacy-disorder/.

Malcolm, Michael, and George Naufal. "Are Pornography and Marriage Substitutes for Young Men?" IZA discussion paper no. 8679 (2014) 1–40. https://ssrn.com/abstract=2534707.

Mayo Clinic. "Post-Traumatic Stress Disorder (PTSD): Symptoms and Causes." Mayo Clinic, Aug. 16, 2024. https://www.mayoclinic.org/diseases-conditions/post-traumatic-stress-disorder/symptoms-causes/syc-20355967.

McKenna, Chris. "10 Symptoms of Porn Addiction Withdrawal (and How to Manage Them)." Covenant Eyes, May 23, 2025. https://www.covenanteyes.com/blog/10-symptoms-of-porn-addiction-withdrawal-and-how-to-manage-them/.

McKinley Irvin Family Law. "32 Shocking Divorce Statistics." Oct. 30, 2012. https://www.mckinleyirvin.com/family-law-blog/2012/october/32-shocking-divorce-statistics/.

Melamed, Daniela M., et al. "The Relationship Between Negative Self-Concept, Trauma, and Maltreatment in Children and Adolescents: A Meta-Analysis." *Clinical Child and Family Psychology Review* 27.1 (2024) 220–34. https://pubmed.ncbi.nlm.nih.gov/38386241/.

Mengzhen, Lim, et al. "The Decline in Intentions to Stop Watching Pornography Among Young Adults." *Sexual and Relationship Therapy* 40.1 (2024) 89–106. https://doi.org/10.1080/14681994.2024.2304673.

Mestre-Bach, Gemma, and Marc N. Potenza. "Loneliness, Pornography Use, Problematic Pornography Use, and Compulsive Sexual Behavior." *Current Addiction Reports* 10 (2023) 664–76. https://doi.org/10.1007/s40429-023-00516-0.

Miller, Jessica. "Effects of Pornography Use." AddictionHelp.com, Jul. 28, 2025. https://www.addictionhelp.com/porn/effects/.

———. "Porn Withdrawal Symptoms." AddictionHelp.com. https://www.addictionhelp.com/porn/withdrawal-symptoms/.

Mohler, R. Albert Jr. "The Seduction of Pornography and the Integrity of Christian Marriage, Part Two." Albert Mohler, Jun. 1, 2012. https://albertmohler.com/2012/06/01/the-seduction-of-pornography-and-the-integrity-of-christian-marriage-part-two-2/.

Molloy, E., et al. "'They Look You Up and Down Like You Are Nothing': A Qualitative Exploration of Sex Workers' Health Needs and Interactions with UK Healthcare Services." *International Journal of Nursing Studies Advances* 9 (2025) 1–16. https://doi.org/10.1016/j.ijnsa.2025.100392.

NASA Jet Propulsion Laboratory. "NASA Mission Update: Voyager 2 Communications Pause." Jul. 28, 2023. https://www.jpl.nasa.gov/news/nasa-mission-update-voyager-2-communications-pause/.

National Institute of Mental Health. "Coping with Traumatic Events." May 2024. https://www.nimh.nih.gov/health/topics/coping-with-traumatic-events.

Nelson, Michael, and W. F. Dempster. "Living in Space: Results from Biosphere 2's Initial Closure—an Early Testbed for Closed Ecological Systems on Mars." In *Strategies for Mars: A Guide to Human Exploration*, edited by C. R. Stoker and C. Emmart, 363–90. Science and Technology Series 86. Springfield, VA: American Astronautical Society, 1996.

NewSpring Church. "How Serving in the Church Grows Your Faith." https://newspring.cc/articles/how-serving-in-the-church-grows-your-faith.

Noel, Jonathan K., et al. "Insomnia and Pornography Addiction in Rhode Island Young Adults." *Rhode Island Medical Journal* 108.6 (2025) 16–21. https://www.rimed.org/rimedicaljournal/2025/06/2025-06-16-riyas-noel.pdf.

Omega Recovery Treatment Center. "Has the Internet Led to an Increase in Porn Addiction?" Aug. 9, 2021. https://omegarecovery.org/has-the-internet-led-to-an-increase-in-porn-addiction/.

Pantazis, Amelia, et al. "Erectile Dysfunction in Adolescents and Young Adults." *Current Urology Reports* 25.9 (2024) 225–32. https://doi.org/10.1007/s11934-024-01213-9.

Parents Television and Media Council. "Families Need Not Subscribe: An Analysis of the Scarcity of Family Content on Streaming Platforms." Oct. 2023. https://www.parentstv.org/resources/Families-Need-Not-Subcribe-2023-OTT-Report-Final.pdf.

Paul, Pamela. *Pornified: How Pornography Is Transforming Our Lives, Our Relationships, and Our Families.* New York: Times, 2005.

Pawlikowska-Gorzelańczyk, Anna, et al. "Impact of Internet Addiction, Social Media Use and Online Pornography on the Male Sexual Function in Times of the COVID-19 Pandemic." *Journal of Clinical Medicine* 12.19 (2023) 6407. https://doi.org/10.3390/jcm12196407.

Perry, Samuel L. "How Pornography Use Reduces Participation in Congregational Leadership: A Research Note." *Review of Religious Research* 61.1 (2019) 57–74. https://link.springer.com/article/10.1007/s13644-018-0355-4.

Perry, Samuel L., and Cyrus Schleifer. "Till Porn Do Us Part? A Longitudinal Examination of Pornography Use and Divorce." *Journal of Sex Research* 55.3 (2017) 284–96. https://doi.org/10.1080/00224499.2017.1317709.

Perry, Samuel L., and George M. Hayward. "Seeing Is (Not) Believing: How Viewing Pornography Shapes the Religious Lives of Young Americans." *Social Forces* 95.4 (2017) 1757–88. https://doi.org/10.1093/sf/sow106.

Pew Research Center. "Mobile Fact Sheet." Nov. 20, 2025. https://www.pewresearch.org/internet/fact-sheet/mobile/.

Polluck, Logan. "The Veil." St. Stephen's Episcopal Church, Apr. 7, 2025. https://www.ssecdurham.org/lent-devotions-2025/the-veil.

Prause, Nicole, and James Binnie. "Iatrogenic Effects of Reboot/NoFap on Public Health: A Preregistered Survey Study." *Sexualities* 27.8 (2023) 1608–40. https://doi.org/10.1177/13634607231157070.

Preuter, Sanne, et al. "The Costs of Lying: Consequences of Telling Lies on Liar's Self-Esteem and Affect." *British Journal of Social Psychology* 63.2 (2024) 894–908. https://doi.org/10.1111/bjso.12711.

Prison Legal News. "FBI Claims 2,500 Percent Increase in Child Porn Arrests." Oct. 15, 2011. https://www.prisonlegalnews.org/news/2011/oct/15/fbi-claims-2500-percent-increase-in-child-porn-arrests/.

Psychology Today. "Narcissism." https://www.psychologytoday.com/us/basics/narcissism.

———. "Shame." https://www.psychologytoday.com/us/basics/shame.

Quan, Lijuan, et al. "The Relationship Between Childhood Trauma and Post-Traumatic Growth Among College Students: The Role of Acceptance and Positive Reappraisal." *Frontiers in Psychology* 13 (2022) 1–9. https://doi.org/10.3389/fpsyg.2022.921362.

Rapaport, Daniel. "Darryl Strawberry Says He Used to Have Sex Between Innings." Sports Illustrated, Dec. 21, 2017. https://www.si.com/mlb/2017/12/21/darryl-strawberry-sex-addiction-dr-oz-between-innings-during-games.

Reed, Geoffrey M., et al. "Emerging Experience with Selected New Categories in the ICD-11: Complex PTSD, Prolonged Grief Disorder, Gaming Disorder, and Compulsive Sexual Behaviour Disorder." *World Psychiatry* 21.2 (2022) 189–213. https://doi.org/10.1002/wps.20960.

Refinery29. "This Is What Most Women Think About When They Masturbate." May 3, 2018. https://www.refinery29.com/en-gb/2018/05/197918/women-masturbation.

Regnerus, Mark, et al. "Documenting Pornography Use in America: A Comparative Analysis of Methodological Approaches." *Journal of Sex Research* 53.7 (2016) 873–81. https://doi.org/10.1080/00224499.2015.1096886.

Robb, Michael B., and Supreet Mann. "Teens and Pornography." Common Sense Media, 2023. https://www.commonsensemedia.org/sites/default/files/research/report/2022-teens-and-pornography-final-web.pdf.

Robb-Dover, Kristina. "Revealing Statistics Re:Pornography Addiction." FHE Health, Dec. 1, 2025. https://fherehab.com/learning/pornography-addiction-stats.

Robin, Marci. "Survey Reveals the Masturbation Habits of American Men and Women." Allure, May 17, 2018. https://www.allure.com/story/masturbation-survey-statistics-american-men-women.

Rogers, Adrian. "Spiritual Gifts: How to Be Faithful in Serving the Body of Christ." Love Worth Finding Ministries. https://www.lwf.org/articles/spiritual-gifts-how-to-be-faithful-in-serving-the-body-of-christ.

Rosen, David. "Pornography and the Erotic Phantasmagoria." *Sexuality & Culture* 27.1 (2023) 242–65. https://doi.org/10.1007/s12119-022-10011-9.

Rostad, Whitney L., et al. "The Association Between Exposure to Violent Pornography and Teen Dating Violence in Grade 10 High School Students." *Archives of Sexual Behavior* 48.7 (2019) 2137–47. https://doi.org/10.1007/s10508-019-1435-4.

Roza, Thiago Henrique, et al. "Withdrawal-Like Symptoms in Problematic Pornography Use: A Scoping Review." *Journal of Addiction Medicine* 18.1 (2024) 19–27. https://doi.org/10.1097/ADM.0000000000001227.

Rutt, Samantha. "Kaylee Goncalves' Dad: Bryan Kohberger Motive in Idaho Murders." *Daily Mail*, Jul. 19, 2025. https://www.dailymail.co.uk/news/article-14920517/kaylee-goncalves-dad-bryan-kohberger-motive-idaho-murders.html.

Santos-Longhurst, Adrienne. "Why Is Oxytocin Known as the 'Love Hormone?' And 11 Other FAQs." Healthline, Jul. 12, 2023. https://www.healthline.com/health/love-hormone#TOC_TITLE_HDR_1.

Scalese, Adam M., et al. "Processes and Outcomes of Pornography Addiction Support Groups." *Sexual Health & Compulsivity* 30.1 (2023) 81–99. https://doi.org/10.1080/26929953.2022.2161027.

Scatliffe, Naomi, et al. "Oxytocin and Early Parent-Infant Interactions: A Systematic Review." *International Journal of Nursing Sciences* 6.4 (2019) 445–53. https://doi.org/10.1016/j.ijnss.2019.09.009.

Schneider, Jennifer P., et al. "Surviving Disclosure of Infidelity: Results of an International Survey of 164 Recovering Sex Addicts and Partners." *Sexual Addiction & Compulsivity* 5.3 (1998) 189–217. https://doi.org/10.1080/10720169808400162.

Sekulić, Ana. "Neuroendocrinology of Romantic Love." Master's thesis, University of Rijeka, 2024. https://repository.medri.uniri.hr/object/medri:8757.

Semrush. "Most Visited Websites in the World." https://www.semrush.com/trending-websites/global/all/.

———. "Top 100: The Most Visited Websites in the US [2022 Top Websites Edition]." https://www.semrush.com/blog/most-visited-websites/.

Shaw, Ed. "How Porn-Addicted Men Can Learn True Intimacy." *Times*, Jul. 19, 2025. https://www.thetimes.com/comment/register/article/how-porn-addicted-men-can-learn-true-intimacy-s57qjpz32#:~:text=He%20is%20the%20greatest%20example,in%20the%20God%2Dman%20Jesus.

Shimer, Ted. *The Freedom Fight: The New Drug and the Truths That Set Us Free*. Houston: High Bridge, 2021.

Shirk, Steven D., et al. "Predicting Problematic Pornography Use Among Male Returning U.S. Veterans." *Addictive Behaviors* 112 (2021) 106647. https://doi.org/10.1016/j.addbeh.2020.106647.

Shor, Eran. "Age, Aggression, and Pleasure in Popular Online Pornographic Videos." *Violence Against Women* 25.8 (2019) 1018–36. https://doi.org/10.1177/1077801218804101.

Silver Sands Recovery. "What Are Triggers in Addiction?" Sep. 3, 2025. https://silversandsrecovery.com/uncategorized/what-are-triggers-in-addiction/.

Simpson, Kelly. "Helping the Traumatized." Gospel Coalition. https://www.thegospelcoalition.org/article/helping-traumatized/.

Smedes, Lewis B. *Forgive and Forget: Healing the Hurts We Don't Deserve*. New York: Harper & Row, 1984.

Smith, Paul J. *Animals in Dutch Travel Writing: 1800 to Present*. Leiden: Leiden University Press, 2023.

Smith, Travis. "Recovery and Treatment of Sexual Addiction: An Interview with Dr. Patrick Carnes." *Open Access Journal of Addiction and Psychology* 2.5 (2019) 1–9. https://doi.org/10.33552/OAJAP.2019.02.000549.

SonderMind. "How Did Porn Addiction Become So Common—and So Quiet?" Jul. 24, 2024. https://www.sondermind.com/resources/articles-and-content/porn-addiction/.

Stack, Steven, et al. "Adult Social Bonds and Use of Internet Pornography." *Social Science Quarterly* 85.1 (2004) 75–88. https://doi.org/10.1111/j.0038-4941.2004.08501006.x.

Strawberry, Darryl. "Let It All Go." LIFE Today, Sep. 15, 2019. https://lifetoday.org/words-of-life/let-it-all-go/.

Strawberry, Darryl, and Lee Weeks. *Turn Your Season Around: How God Transforms Your Life*. Grand Rapids: Zondervan, 2021.

Substance Abuse and Mental Health Services Administration. "2020 National Survey on Drug Use and Health: Lesbian, Gay, or Bisexual (LGB) Adults." Jul. 2022. https://www.samhsa.gov/data/sites/default/files/reports/slides-2020-nsduh/2020NSDUHLGBSlides072522.pdf.

Sulyok, Kármen, et al. "The Highs and Lows of Pornography Use: Does Motivation Affect Users' Life Satisfaction?" *Studia Universitatis Babeș-Bolyai Psychologia-Paedagogia* 69.1 (2024) 183–200. https://doi.org/10.24193/subbpsyped.2024.1.10.

Sweet, Paige L. "The Sociology of Gaslighting." *American Sociological Review* 84.5 (2019) 851–75. https://doi.org/10.1177/0003122419874843.

TerKeurst, Lysa. *I Want to Trust You, but I Don't: Moving Forward When You're Skeptical of Others, Afraid of What God Will Allow, and Doubtful of Your Own Discernment.* Nashville: Thomas Nelson, 2024.

Thorn, Caroline N., et al. "Youth Perspectives on Online Safety, 2023." Thorn, 2024. https://www.thorn.org/research/library/2023-youth-perspectives-on-online-safety.

TrueAlly. "How Many People Watch Porn?" May 29, 2024. https://trueally.app/blog/how-many-people-watch-porn-2024-stats-trends/.

Tukachinsky, Riva, and Keren Eyal. "The Psychology of Marathon Television Viewing: Antecedents and Viewer Involvement." *Mass Communication and Society* 21.3 (2018) 275–95. https://doi.org/10.1080/15205436.2017.1422765.

Ugese, Iornenge J., et al. "Pornography Addiction in the Emerging Adults: The Role of Social Isolation, Self-Control and Stress Coping." *British Journal of Psychology Research* 12.1 (2024) 26–36. https://doi.org/10.37745/bjpr.2013/vol12n12636.

University Counseling Center. "Deep Breathing and Relaxation." University of Toledo, Jul. 15, 2024. https://www.utoledo.edu/studentaffairs/counseling/anxietytoolbox/breathingandrelaxation.html.

University of Rochester Medical Center. "Researchers Reveal How Trauma Changes the Brain." ScienceDaily, Dec. 7, 2022. https://www.sciencedaily.com/releases/2022/12/221207142255.htm.

USAFacts. "How Does Marriage Vary by State?" https://usafacts.org/articles/how-does-marriage-vary-by-state/.

Verywell Health. "Does Porn Cause Erectile Dysfunction (ED)?" Sep. 2, 2021. https://www.verywellhealth.com/can-porn-cause-erectile-dysfunction-5196444.

Vijghen, John L. "Child Exploitation Situational Analysis in Cambodia 2023." Terre des Hommes Netherlands, 2023. https://int.terredeshommes.nl/uploads/5d3bd302-1691408301-cambodia-situational-analysis-report-final.pdf.

Villanueva, Marco. "The Psychology of OnlyFans Explained in Less Than 11 Minutes." Virtual Staffer Philippines, Apr. 11, 2025. https://www.virtualstaffer.ph/blogs/psychology-of-onlyfans-explained.

Vincos. "Sex and the Searches." https://vincos.it/sex-the-searches/.

Walker, Andrea, et al. "Finding Lolita: A Comparative Analysis of Interest in Youth-Oriented Pornography." *Sexuality & Culture*, 20.3 (2016) 657–83. https://doi.org/10.1007/s12119-016-9355-0.

Wang, Jianfeng, and Hong Li. "Emotional Processing Deficits in Individuals with Problematic Pornography Use: Unpleasant Bias and Pleasant Blunting." *Journal of Behavioral Addictions* 12.4 (2023) 1046–60. https://doi.org/10.1556/2006.2023.00058.

Wang, Wendy, and Kim Parker. "Trends in the Share of Never-Married Americans and a Look Forward." Pew Research Center, Sep. 24, 2014. https://www.pewresearch.org/social-trends/2014/09/24/chapter-2-trends-in-the-share-of-never-married-americans-and-a-look-forward/.

Wang, Wendy, and Michael Toscano. "Frequent Porn Use Is Linked to Negative Mental Health Among Gen-Z and Millennials." Institute for Family Studies, Sep. 12, 2024. https://ifstudies.org/blog/frequent-porn-use-is-linked-to-negative-mental-health-among-gen-z-and-millennials.

Weiss, Douglas. "6 Types of Sex Addicts." Heart to Heart Counseling Center, May 11, 2015. https://www.drdougweiss.com/6-types-of-sex-addicts.

Wiegmann, Douglas A., et al. "Understanding the 'Swiss Cheese Model' and Its Application to Patient Safety." *Journal of Patient Safety* 18.2 (2022) 119–23. https://doi.org/10.1097/PTS.0000000000000810.

Wilkinson and Finkbeiner. "Divorce Statistics: Over 115 Studies, Facts and Rates for 2024." https://www.wf-lawyers.com/divorce-statistics-and-facts/.

Williams, Michael. "Life in a World of Super-Normal Stimulation." *Standard Journal*, Oct. 5, 2015. https://www.rexburgstandardjournal.com/opinion/columns/life-in-a-world-of-super-normal-stimulation/article_9e33b682-6ba2-11e5-a66e-4b355aacaeef.html.

Wilson, Gary. *Your Brain on Porn: Internet Pornography and the Emerging Science of Addiction*. N.p.: Commonwealth, 2015.

Wilson, Peter J. B. "The Porn Retreat: Narcissism and Adolescence." *Psychodynamic Practice* 27.3 (2018) 235–48. https://doi.org/10.1080/14753634.2018.1494621.

Wolfinger, Matt, et al. "You're Probably in a Parasocial Relationship—Whether You Know It or Not." Northeastern University School of Journalism, 2021. https://mediainnovation.camd.northeastern.edu/2021/loveinthetimeofcovid/love-during-the-loneliness-virus/.

Wright, Sarah. E. "Porn-Induced Erectile Dysfunction: Why It Happens and How to Stop It." ChoosingTherapy.com, Dec. 6, 2024. https://www.choosingtherapy.com/porn-induced-erectile-dysfunction/.

Wright, Susanna. "How Much Weight Can a Horse Pull? (You'll Be Surprised!)" Horse Rookie, 2023. https://horserookie.com/how-much-weight-can-a-horse-pull/.

Your Brain On Porn. "Unwiring and Rewiring Your Brain: Sensitization and Hypofrontality." https://www.yourbrainonporn.com/tools-for-change-recovery-from-porn-addiction/rebooting-basics-start-here/unwiring-rewiring-your-brain-sensitization-and-hypofrontality/.

Zhang, Zheng, and Nan Zhang. "Prevalence of Masturbation and Masturbation Guilt and Associations with Partnered Sex Among Married Heterosexual Chinese Males in an Outpatient Clinical Setting: A Retrospective Single Center Study." *Basic and Clinical Andrology* 35.15 (2025) 15. https://doi.org/10.1186/s12610-025-00261-6.

www.ingramcontent.com/pod-product-compliance
Lightning Source LLC
LaVergne TN
LVHW050621100826
845148LV00011B/1685
9798385272822